DEADOLOGY
Volume II

THE EVOLUTION OF 33
GRATEFUL DEAD JAM
ANTHEMS

By

HOWARD F. WEINER

Table of Contents

PRELUDE

THE ART OF SELECTION

The Grateful Dead songbook is a vast American treasure that validates them as one of the most important musical acts of the twentieth century thanks to the sublime work of their lyricists, Robert Hunter and John Perry Barlow, and the band's knack for breathing new life into carefully selected cover songs. However, their music still thrives in a timeless manner that separates them from any other band. The Grateful Dead's performance archive, consisting of more than 2,000 shows, is the most explored, revered, and scrutinized collection of live music. Twenty-five years after the death of Jerry Garcia, Deadheads still fervently buzz around the archive as the music grows in stature and is more relevant than ever. The band's jams are the honey that draws Deadheads to the archive. And since the Dead relished the opportunity to improvise anew every time they took the stage, their devotees have an endless amount of music to obsess over. *Deadology Volume 2* will examine the Dead's iconic jam anthems and trace their evolutions through the years.

You might be wondering why I chose to go with thirty-three jam anthems. This number seemed to work well in the first volume of this series, *Deadology: The 33 Essential Dates of Grateful Dead History*. I like continuity, flow, and selectivity—not every jamming song is worthy of anthem status. The thirty-three entries actually consist of forty-seven songs. Combinations like Scarlet Begonias > Fire on the

Mountain, and Help on the Way > Slipknot! > Franklin's Tower, each count as one anthem. And I took the liberty of pairing off some numbers like "Spanish Jam" and "Caution (Do Not Stop on the Tracks)." It was hard for me to leave one of these essential early jam tunes out of the book. The Dead once combined these tunes together as a fifteen-minute instrumental in the Nassau Coliseum on May 6, 1981.

I established some loose guidelines for the selection process. As it applies to popular music, I think of an anthem as an uplifting and important musical piece that stands the test of time and best represents the essence of that group to their fanbase. Unfortunately, outstanding Dead jam tunes like "Alligator," "New Potato Caboose," "Born Cross Eyed," and "Here Comes Sunshine" were eliminated because their playing days were numbered too soon. "Here Comes Sunshine" had a spectacular run in 1973. When it was reintroduced into the lineup in 1993, it had lost some of its luster. It was only played sixty-six times in total. If it had been played ten or fifteen times more in '74, it would have been a tough number to omit.

My favorite Pigpen jam tune, "Hard to Handle," was played 104 times between 1969 and 1971. There were two additional performances of "Hard to Handle" featuring Etta James and the Tower of Power horn section during the Dead's New Year's Eve 1982 run. The reason I couldn't elevate "Handle" to jam anthem status was that it didn't reach its full potential until its final year. Between April and August 1971, "Hard to Handle" peaked. The jam developed into a showstopper that became too hot to handle. If the Dead continued to play "Hard to Handle" through Pigpen's final days, there would have been more blockbuster renditions, and it surely would have cracked this list. "Here Comes Sunshine" and "Hard to Handle" were my toughest cuts. They simply failed the test of time.

One of the most beloved Dead anthems, "Ripple," has no jam. A batch of excellent Hunter tunes with tight, thrilling solos were eliminated because the totality of the song was bigger than the instrumentals within. It was easy, and it made sense, to eliminate songs like "Brown-Eyed Women," "Candyman,"

"Ramble on Rose," and "To Lay Me Down." The elimination process for some second set songs was tougher. Tunes like "Crazy Fingers," "Wharf Rat," "Black Peter," and "China Doll" had multiple jams, but not on a grand enough scale to consider them for the elite thirty-three. But the omission of one epic Hunter anthem had me waking up in a cold sweat in the middle of the night.

You will love the thirty-three entries selected here, but "Terrapin Station" will not be one of them because the enormity of the lyrical masterpiece precludes me from labeling this as a jam anthem. The song contains skillful instrumental passages, but these segments set up and glorify the brilliant prose of Robert Hunter. The mighty instrumental refrain frames the magnificence of the composition. Jerry's performance as a vocalist is paramount here. He was usually on his game because if he screwed up the words, the structured instrumental passages of "Terrapin" didn't present an opportunity for redemption. If Jerry flubbed a verse or two in "Morning Dew," he could still turn it into an all-time great version. The solos in "Morning Dew" are that intense and explosive.

Another example of a lyrical masterpiece that could never become a jam anthem is Dylan's "Desolation Row," whether performed by Dylan or the Dead. It doesn't matter how many instrumental breaks are inserted, the majesty of the lyrics are too much to overcome. "Terrapin Station" isn't a jam anthem, but it is the national anthem of Deadhead Nation. *Attention. Ladies and gentlemen. Please rise for the singing of Terrapin Station. Feel free to swing and sway along in reverence.*

One of the jam anthems that made the cut, "Viola Lee Blues," didn't stand the test of time, but I made an exception to include it. "Viola Lee" was played fifty-four times over the course of four years. But since it was the Dead's first jam anthem, and its abundant power can't be denied, it demanded representation here. Several of the tunes from *Anthem in the Sun* and *Aoxomoxoa* owe a huge debt of gratitude to "Viola Lee Blues."

Since there are many fine books and sources that dig into the wonders of Grateful Dead lyrics, my primary focus here is the ever-shifting improvisation within these thirty-three jam anthems. After introducing the compositions and tracing their development, I'll continue the conversation by examining the best versions of these jam anthems. In most cases, the first two versions I write about are the ones I consider the best. But these are opinions, and therefore, they are not absolute. For decades you may fall under the spell of the 9-2-80 "Morning Dew" from Rochester, and then you hear the 9-10-74 "Dew" from Alexandria Palace, London, and you suddenly think that version reigns supreme. I avoided the trap of ranking renditions. After this book is published, Deadheads will be turning me on to spectacular versions that I didn't list here, and I'll be kicking myself for missing them. Internet debates over best-ever versions are never a waste of time if you keep an open mind. Discovering an inspirational piece of music is priceless.

Great versions often happened in bunches during certain years. I decided to limit the amount of noteworthy performances of any song from any one given year to four. If I picked out ten noteworthy "Sugarees" and eight of them were from 1977, it would be hard to argue with that logic. Although, describing eight "Sugarees" from the same year might become a redundant task, and it would take away from the discussion of how the jams evolved over time. With songs like "Playin' in the Band" and "The Other One," I tried to stay true to discussing the best versions without overdosing on the landmark year of 1972.

As I edited my "Dark Star" chapter, I realized that I had selected six 1972 versions. I made an exception and let that stand because each one of these performances was unique. "Dark Star" is a timeless improvisational piece. The year of liftoff is irrelevant. This was my trickiest and most rewarding research. To listen to every "Dark Star" and comprehend it all would be a never-ending project. I took my existing knowledge of the Dead's celestial anthem and spent five days in Montego Bay, Jamaica, over Thanksgiving weekend 2019, soaking in "Dark Star" after "Dark Star." I jotted down notes on the beach, on the balcony of my hotel as twilight faded to night, and blurry-eyed in airport bars. I tried to put it all in perspective when I returned to New York City.

In a fortuitous twist of fate, I was invited to join the 213 Dark Star Project group on Facebook the day I got home from Jamaica—a sign I was aligned with the universal mind. This group was created to celebrate the impending 50th anniversary of the beloved 2-13-70 Fillmore East "Dark Star." The administrator, Ric Rabinowitz, asked me if I would take part in the group and compare random "Dark Stars" that he would assign. The group had around 100 members who accepted these challenges and shared their listening experiences. *Your homework tonight is to decide which "Dark Star" will move on, 11-8-69 Fillmore West, or 7-18-72 Roosevelt Stadium.* The data was collected, and I can't recall what the results were, but it was a mind-expanding exercise for all involved, and I discovered a '69 "Dark Star" that made the cut for this endeavor.

The thirty-three jam anthems are not ranked in any particular order. I started with the songs where I felt I had a solid grasp on the best renditions. I opened with "Jack Straw" and "Sugaree," a powerful one-two punch to kick off for any show. As I moved forward, I trusted the process. A flow emerged, as if I was creating my own show, so I didn't tamper with the way things lined up. One song led to the next. *Blues for Allah* numbers stepped back towards *Wake of Flood*. "Shakedown Street" latched onto "Feel Like a Stranger," and "Dark Star" reunited with its former running partners, St. Stephen > The Eleven.

I saved "The Other One" for last. Since this meaty jam anthem continually mutated through the years, and it was played about 350 times more than "Dark Star," my research would be time-consuming. As I was finishing my "Turn on Your Love Light" entry and preparing for "The Other One," the coronavirus hit New York City. My focus shifted to stockpiling essentials: food, beer, wine, and coffee. And of course, a few rolls of toilet paper. As soon as NYC was put on pause, I was infected with COVID-19. Outside of two weeks of fever, a slight cough, and body aches, I was fortunate to recover without a visit to a hospital. I watched two seasons of *Narcos Mexico* and the Ken Burns series, *New York*. I lose the will to write when I'm ill. *Deadology Volume 2* was put on pause for three weeks.

Even though I was temporarily unemployed, and isolated from friends and family, my heart was filled with gratitude as I swiftly recovered. I had good health, and I had a mission. Every day I walked for miles and miles up and down the pathways of Pelham Parkway listening to epic "Other Ones" on my headphones. I finished the first draft of this book and relished the editing process. I wasn't exactly sheltering in place as I continued my marathon marches through my bucolic Bronx neighborhood lost in a world of Grateful Dead jam anthems. My two passions are writing and listening to music, and in April of 2020, I had an abundance of time. In the thick of a national nightmare, I had no choice but to embrace this gift.

This is my fifth critical study involving the live music of the Grateful Dead and/or the Jerry Garcia Band. On this go-round, I reached out to some allies for help. I knew I could count on my long-time friend Doug Schmell, who turned me on to the Grateful Dead forty years ago. I'd send him emails asking for recommendations on hot "Other Ones" or "Playin' in the Bands," and he'd return animated replies that often pointed me in the direction of smoking versions I didn't know existed. I also reached out to Deadheads on the many Grateful Dead Internet groups I take part in. Ask, and you shall receive!

However, when it comes to critiquing the Dead, I was never swayed by popularity. It's either a transcendent version that demands to be heard time and time again or it's just another pleasurable listening experience courtesy of the good ol' Grateful Dead.

It was an uncanny thirty-year run for these lads from San Francisco. Thanks to cosmic serendipity, the Grateful Dead's ascent as a band was aligned with the Acid Tests and the Merry Pranksters. They fine-tuned their craft in a psychedelic laboratory that gave them a unique sound and a boundless vision for what was possible within their music. Although they flew under the commercial radar, the Dead were at all the major festivals—Monterey Pop, Woodstock, and Altamont—but they wisely passed on playing Altamont due to the mayhem and violence that unfolded on that day. The Dead stayed true to their calling as they developed a mind-boggling archive of live music that nurtured a massive underground following. With minimal commercial output in the first half of the '80s, the Dead sold out the largest arenas tour after tour.

Destiny pulled commercial success to the Grateful Dead universe in 1987, a year after Jerry Garcia's coma. The release of *In the Dark* featured their first and only top-ten hit, "Touch of Grey." The band's immense popularity brought another generation of Deadheads into the fold and ensured the incredible legacy of their archive, even if the years to follow weren't artistically on the level of the Dead's first twenty years. If Jerry had died in 1986, a generation of newbies would have missed out on the last great American adventure, touring and tripping with the Grateful Dead.

This mega popularity connected fans to the computer age. It was the perfect storm that kept the Dead relevant after Garcia's death. I don't think there would be any Dead & Company tours, a Grateful Dead Channel on Sirius Radio, and I'm sure I wouldn't be obsessively involved in critiquing Garcia's oeuvre if the Long Strange Trip had ended in 1986.

During the '80s I was fortunate, focused, and crazy. I saw the Grateful Dead 148 times, and the Jerry Garcia Band 52 times. That equals a neat 200 shows. I only saw four Dead shows during their last five years. There was a sliding decline in Jerry's virtuosity, and I hit a point in my life where I didn't have the resources or desire to continue. The overcrowded stadium show scene didn't help either.

My love of Bob Dylan's music and jazz pulled me through the '90s. Garcia helped connect me to Dylan. By the time Dylan and the Dead toured together in 1987, I was a budding Dylan aficionado. And even though I wasn't there, the stunning Branford Marsalis guest appearance with the Dead on March 29, 1990, in the Nassau Coliseum, turned me on to the world of jazz. Within a year, I had an impressive jazz collection with at least fifty Miles Davis CDs.

Grateful Dead archivist Dick Latvala released *Dick's Picks Vol. 1* on Halloween of 1993. At last, I had a *bootleg* in my CD collection. My passion for the Dead's music never dimmed, but I became a CD guy. A large part of my Dead bootleg collection had suffered irreparable damage: too much rewinding of hot jams, cracked cassette covers, coffee spillage, and too much direct sunlight on the loose tapes in my car. Maxell Holdings, LTD never imagined that someone who revered music could ever abuse tapes as I did. I was a sloppy obsessive. As a youth, I beat the crap out of my albums, scratching vinyl before it became fashionable. Even the album covers were torn, tattered, and shredded.

In the year 2000 I met a Deadhead, Jim Kerr Jr., son of the famous classic rock DJ in New York. Jim informed me that there were Dead sites where you could download shows. I immediately purchased my first PC and my Dead obsession was rekindled. Depending on the site, in those days, downloading a show could take anywhere from an hour to three days. After downloading, I burned the files to disc. It was a miracle! My only cost was about ten cents for the blank CD.

I connected with Deadheads on various sites and established a huge CD trading operation. My curious mailman was obliged to ask me what was in these bubble mailers he was delivering daily. Within a few years, I had almost the entire live archive downloaded onto 5,000 CDs, which I neatly filed in plastic bins. I was a kid in a toy factory and every day was Christmas.

Little did I know that those CDs would soon become obsolete. Another decade brought about a technological revolution that changed the way people listened to music. Just about all the music I ever collected on albums, 8-track tapes, cassette tapes, and CDs could be downloaded or streamed on a device that I could operate in the palm of my hand. Smartphones? These things should be called Einsteins. Hell, I didn't even need a sophisticated stereo system anymore. A high-quality Bose speaker and killer headphones did the trick.

I'm guessing most people are familiar with the Relisten app, but in case there are any Deadheads behind the technology curve like I used to be, let me explain. Downloading this app changes your life. Multiple versions of just about every Grateful Dead show are available with a simple tap of a finger. There's a smorgasbord of recording options: Soundboards, audience tapes, matrix mixes, pre this, post that…But when in doubt, look for one name: Charlie Miller. This sound maven has apparently dedicated his life to remastering the best available recordings of a healthy percentage of Dead shows. In Charlie Miller I trust. And so should you.

Do I regret spending the money and time downloading those CDs, and of course, purchasing numerous official releases? Absolutely not. Those of us who went through the process of collecting boots on both tape and CD will appreciate the Relisten app more than someone coming to it without having gone through the thrilling yet cumbersome process of collecting boots. This music is intimate to old-school Deadheads. We've romanced these shows in several stages. I'll never forget how exciting it was to get a new tape and write the set list on the cover. I had terrible penmanship, but when it was time to create an attractive tape cover, suddenly I was Michelangelo. The disadvantage of downloading music is that there is no tangible product to romance, and on some level, I believe album and CD covers enhance our enjoyment of the music; but that's an essay for another day.

"The world of research has gone berserk, too much paperwork," sings Bob Dylan in the song "Nettie Moore," from the album *Modern Times*. The Internet bombards us with research, paperwork, and information on Grateful Dead set lists and song stats. *Deadbase XI* (1999) was the gold standard for Grateful Dead stats, as well as stats for the Jerry Garcia Band and other touring projects involving the other members of the Dead. To honor the 50th anniversary of the Grateful Dead, *Deadbase 50* was released. There were updates to what was already published, as well as updated set lists from all the offshoot bands featuring members of the Grateful Dead. That means in *Deadbase 50*, 400 pages were added to the existing 575 pages of *Deadbase XI* in one volume. If you choose not to lug this bulky but wonderful hardcover beast around with you,

I'd suggest *Listen to the Music Play, A Comprehensive and Interactive Guidebook to the Set Lists and Available Recordings of the Grateful Dead* by Justin Mason. This a thoroughly researched digital guide that has been updated in 2020. Apparently, we're still receiving new info on mysterious set lists from the early years. I tried to use this as the main source of fact-checking for my book, but I bear full responsibility for any factual mistakes in *Deadology Vol. 2.*

In the year 2020, I've been sucked deeper into the rabbit hole—*Julie catch a rabbit by his hair.* The music never stops. Each ensuing endeavor studying Garcia and the Dead is more satisfying than the last. This is my fountain of youth. I never could have imagined when I was on tour in 1985 that I would still be obsessed with what I was experiencing thirty-five years down the road. Back in the day, I was the town crier, extoling the virtues of the hottest Dead jams by word of mouth, usually in one-on-one situations. Now I have multiple pulpits to preach from.

There's nothing like the pleasure of transcendent music. The Grateful Dead archive is stocked with treasures that will swamp your mind with feel-good dopamine every time you hit play. Listen closely to all the "Mississippi Half Steps" I've listed in chapter five. You will discover the purpose of life, lose twenty pounds in three weeks, and become impossibly attractive to members of the opposite sex. I'm only half kidding. Never underestimate the infinite power of this music launched from the heart and soul of the finest band in the land. For thirty years, they gave us everything they had. And almost forty years after my first Grateful Dead show, I'm staying true to my calling.

JACK STRAW

I 'll launch this endeavor with "Jack Straw" because it's one of my favorite songs and it opened many Grateful Dead shows, although many of the greatest "Straws" emerged towards the end of the opening set. With Robert Hunter's lyrics and Bob Weir's arrangement, "Jack Straw" was born on October 19, 1971, in Northrop Auditorium, Minneapolis. On this evening, the Dead also debuted five other originals that would become prominent songs in their live repertoire: "Tennessee Jed," "Comes a Time," "Mexicali Blues," "Ramble on Rose," and "One More Saturday Night." "Jack Straw" was played 473 times, more than any of these other first-time tunes. Amidst all that was new, Keith Godchaux made his debut as the Dead's piano player in Minneapolis. Pigpen was recovering from illness. The legendary harp-blowing singer and organist would return for a few more tours, but the band had to move on without him. Songs like "Jack Straw" would help the Dead thrive and elevate their music to a level beyond anyone's comprehension.

Of the three new Weir numbers performed on 10-19-71, "One More Saturday Night" was the most explosive. "Jack Straw" quietly emerged as a fan favorite and one of the most beloved tunes off the triple live album *Europe '72*. "Straw" starts off deceptively sentimental as the band harmonizes the opening lines, "We can share the women, we can share the wine. We can share what we got of yours because we done share all of mine." The tenderness dissipates into a folk tale of revenge, murder, and survival on the run—classic Americana.

A rumbling force propels the music as the band sings together, and then Garcia and Weir trade lines. Jerry sets the stage, Weir vents, and the music explodes in two short (by Grateful Dead standards) instrumental bursts. Night by night, these instrumental bursts became edgier as the length of the second solo gradually extends. Following the fury, the tune returns to its serene beginning. *We can share the women, we can share the wine.* The herky-jerky flow of "Straw" is balanced by the gorgeous start and finish. The album version from 5-3-72 Paris is a superb track.

By 1974, the second solo of "Straw" began to distinguish itself. You can hear Jerry restlessly pecking away, searching to expand the boundaries of the "Straw" framework. My favorite version from this era is from the Philadelphia Civic Center on 8-5-74. "The City of Brotherly Love" became a hotbed for blazing "Straws." The Grateful Dead took a twenty-month break from touring and returned with a new batch of originals. As they explored the new material from their last three albums, as well as Weir's and Garcia's solo efforts, "Jack Straw" was put on the shelf until it reemerged in the rotation on May 3, 1977, in New York City's Palladium. On that evening, there was a tremendous roar from Deadheads when they realized that their favorite outlaw from Wichita had returned.

As the Dead focused on jamming within the structure of their new arrangements and cut back on freeform improvisation, "Jack Straw" soared. But unlike songs like "Sugaree" and "Music Never Stopped," which became instant instrumental blockbusters in '77, "Jack Straw" grew in increments. There are several impressive versions from '78, but "Straw" stepped into beast mode in '79, and awesome versions continued to flourish in 1980.

As the '80s rolled along, "Jack Straw" became a reliable powerhouse opener and the length of the second jam varied from show to show. From October '84 through April '85, there was a sensational run of "Jack Straws." During the East Coast fall '84 tour, the Dead played "Jack Straw" in unusual spots: fourth song of the second set in Worcester on October 9, seventh song of the opening set in Hartford on October 15, and the first-set closer in Syracuse on October 20. The offbeat song placement helped the band attack the big "Straw" jam with a renewed sense of urgency.

When the band returned to touring in 1987 after Jerry's near-fatal coma the summer before, "Jack Straw" had a glorious run. As Garcia's virtuosity declined during the band's final years, "Jack Straw" persevered anyway, a musical force to be reckoned with. It always pumped up the crowd, even if the jam didn't impress on the audio tape. Except for 1976, "Jack Straw" was always an essential ingredient in the Grateful Dead repertoire every year.

10-20-84 Carrier Dome, Syracuse, NY: The Carrier Dome, an indoor stadium with an inflatable roof, hosted home games for the Syracuse University football and basketball teams, and it became a popular destination for touring rock bands, although, based on my experience, the acoustics were far from optimal. On this last night of the East Coast tour, the Dead were locked in tight, playing the devil out of routine tunes. The eighth song of the set, "Birdsong," came off like a fusion firecracker. Transcendent music was on the verge of taking flight in the strangest of settings.

After "Birdsong" lands, Garcia's restless fingers suggest "Jack Straw." The opening licks sound like they could slice and puncture. The budding momentum is staggering as Weir howls, "Cut down a man in cold blood, Shannon. Might as well be me...Me!!!" Bone-crunching bass blasts are met with furious guitar strumming during the brief opening jam. The essence of the Jack Straw character firmly takes hold of Weir as he venomously hollers, "One's for sport and one's for blood at the point of a knife! Now the die is shaken. Now the die must fall!" As the song settles into the "Fourth day of July" verse, the upcoming rampage is palpable. Anyone with an ear for the Dead knows they're about to witness something unforgettable.

Weir ignites the final assault: "You keep us on the runnnn, RUN!" A Lesh bomb that would have collapsed a smaller venue sets Garcia on the warpath. The licks are coming fast and furious as Jerry changes flow by adjusting a few knobs without dimming the forward thrust. This is a group exorcism as they bash away in unison—physically letting it all hang out. Compressed and controlled pandemonium fills the dome. Jerry Bond 007 blazes away and creates a new guitar language. My friends told me that Jerry leaped in the air during this jam. You might hear a landing thud at the 5:47 mark.

There's no traditional chord fanning as the band passes the point of no return yet somehow, the mojo keeps rollin'. Phil's relentless bass bombs set off seismograph detectors in central New York. This could be the most explosive and primal jam in Dead history. If you pick this "Straw" up mid-stream, it doesn't sound like the Dead—or any other band. All the anger and evil inherent in the song is unleashed, and the effect on the listeners is cathartic and euphoric as it all rolls back to the starting point: *We can share the women, we can share the wine.*

"We're going to take a short break. Everybody move back," says Weir, as if he's Jack Straw and he's still pissed off. The Carrier Dome, which is louder than most indoor stadiums, is deafening. I can only imagine how ecstatic I would have been if I was there. I had caught all ten shows of this tour prior to the Syracuse finale. I had to attend my brother's Bar Mitzvah on 10-20-84. There's nothing I love more than a crazed "Jack Straw." Instead, I was dancing the hora as the Murray Fields Band played "Hava Nagila." I should have been there. With all the hard traveling and touring I put in, I earned that Syracuse "Straw." Well, at least we have the tapes. I've relived the thrill of that "Straw" thousands of times.

8-30-80 The Spectrum, Philadelphia, PA: Here's another Straw that closes an opening set, and it comes on the heels of Garcia's hottest guitar solo ever in an "Althea." The opening set was possessed from start to finish. Every aspect of the band's performance was extra-crisp, so the dazzling "Straw" was logical. Other standout performances include the "Feel Like a Stranger," "Peggy O" opening, and the mid-set "Cold Rain and Snow."

"Jack Straw" was the ideal choice to benefit from the heat of a smoking "Althea." There's a smooth pressure cooker flow to the music as the band struts through "Straw" with an eye on the big jam. Searing intensity bubbles throughout as Garcia wheels from segment to segment with brazen attitude and conviction. Just when it sounds like the band's ready to step into chord-fanning overdrive, Garcia stuns everybody in the Spectrum with an improbable piercing tirade. Extra effort dances with perfection as the band sticks a thunderous finale. Was it performance-enhancing powder, or the rowdy Philly diehards pushing the band beyond the brink? This jam's worthy of instant replay on each listen.

10-19-80 Saenger Theatre, New Orleans, LA: In the middle of their 1980 acoustic/electric run of the Fox Warfield Theatre and Radio City Music Hall, the Dead enchanted New Orleans with a pair of shows utilizing the same format. After "Ripple" closed a gripping acoustic set, Bayou Deadheads awaited more inspiration. This was the ninth anniversary of the first performance of "Jack Straw," and the Dead delivered a definitive "Straw" to commemorate the occasion. It's hard to believe that anyone in the band was aware of this historical tidbit, yet some force propelled this improvisational blitzkrieg.

A successful "Straw" jam has two parts of varying length: the creative lead flow from Jerry and the finale, where the band hammers a dramatic chord progression. Garcia and the Boys steamroll both parts more than sufficiently in New Orleans. As Weir is about to sing "Jack Straw from Wichita cut his buddy down," Garcia's fingers slide south, uncorking a series of shrieking notes that redirects the jam. Ideas flow as he adds another paragraph to the musical narrative. Happy birthday, "Jack Straw"!

12-31-79 Oakland Auditorium Arena, CA: The Oakland Coliseum explodes as the Grateful Dead take the stage to kiss goodbye to the '70s and welcome a new decade of decadence. New Year's Eve revelers are enthralled with the "Jack Straw" opener. The music thunders, although the vocals are unusually subdued. Weir sings, "You keep us on the run," without his trademark enthusiasm, but his guitar strumming's fierce. The combined effect of Garcia and Weir's playing comes off like a buzz saw effortlessly mowing down a forest. The jam is dramatic as the music ricochets across the auditorium. Jerry's scalding chord-playing is wildly imaginative as Phil's concussive punctuation accelerates the tension. Straw segues into an equally unhinged "Franklin's Tower." This is a stunning one-two punch that exceeds anything else the Dead played during this strong three-set extravaganza.

11-6-79 The Spectrum, Philadelphia, PA: In the next to last slot of the opening set and in front of their Philly devotees, the Grateful Dead shred "Straw." Garcia's garrulous guitar gobbling is consistent as Phil's bass blasts disorientate. These fall '79 soundboards are phenomenal; you can clearly hear the fantastic playing of everyone in the band. Within this jam, all contributions are vital.

After Garcia unloads a connected series of quick-picking runs, Mickey, Billy, and Phil pound a foundation for the chord-fanning crescendo. Weir and Garcia are strumming madly—it's a frantic dance and a deadly duel, and Brent's hanging in, chopping away at his organ is if his existence depends on it. The power of the jam is terrifying, and when the Dead return to the serenity of the final refrain, "We can share the women, we can share the wine," the crowd's roar can be heard clearly through the soundboard. The energy of Philadelphia inspires another dynamic "Straw."

1-11-79 Nassau Coliseum, Uniondale, NY: This version, the tenth song of the first set, features an improvised lyric from Bobby, "We used to play for acid, now we play for Clive." That was a shout out to Clive Davis, head of the Grateful Dead's new record label, Arista. There's a bit of sloppiness and Weir cuts Jerry off too soon, but Garcia unloads an unprecedented speed run that's relentless—lightning strikes cascade across the Uniondale night—sonic waves hotter than Kung-Pao chicken. If there were a device that could record notes per minute, it would have malfunctioned. Jerry had a predilection for quick-picking "Straw" jams in 1979. If it were not for a ragged return to the final verse, this "Straw" might rank at the top of the heap. "Deal" follows to close the opening set.

4-4-85 Providence Civic Center, RI: A fiery "Alabama Getaway" sparks a frenzied "Straw" in the second spot. There's extra length in the opening "Straw" solo, and Jerry continues his piercing barrage in the alpha jam. "Straw" once again benefits from not being in the opening slot. Garcia and mates streak ahead. The leads pile up fluidly as if the band's speed skating on autopilot. I don't know; it might have been the yeyo. These sparks ignited an aggressive evening of adventurous music. A Lost Sailor > Saint of Circumstance > Deal ending combo perfectly balanced the best opening set of 1985.

9-9-87 Providence Civic Center, RI: Providence inspires another standout "Straw" in the two-hole after the debut of "Hey Pocky Way" to open. With the success of *In the Dark* and "Touch of Grey," and Jerry's recovery from the coma, these were blessed times for Deadheads and the band. Feeding off the energy in the arena, the band elevates the jam in consistently digestible chunks that are hotter with each round. As it goes on and on, Jerry seems to toy with his devotees—this is what you love—I know how to push the buttons. Pocky Way > Straw was a tasty one-two punch that was paired on two other occasions.

4-6-87 Brendan Byrne Arena, East Rutherford, NJ: "Jack Straw" is the eighth song of the first set, and this is Jerry's first appearance in the New York City area since the coma. The joint is ready to erupt. Weir sets the jam in motion by howling, "You keep us on the run-uh-un!" With collective aggression the band slams down a thunderous chord that rattles the walls and halls. A volatile outburst from Garcia is matched by tenacious input from Brent and the drummers, yet the tapestry is wonderfully weaved. The playing is very intense, and the jam reaches an early climax. The over-ambitious crowd roars. The band is giving them everything as expected, and then Garcia extends the jam with a blistering run, unlike anything heard before in "Jack Straw." All the Garcia aficionados howl in approval. Ironically, this twenty second segment starts at the 4:06 mark of "Jack Straw." Bobby, Phil, and Brent take turns mimicking Jerry's outburst as best they can. Garcia finishes the jam off with a chord-fanning crescendo. *We can share the women, we can share the wine!* And thanks to the tapes, we can share the spontaneous genius of Garcia and the Dead. "Deal" closes the set.

4-14-82 Glens Falls Civic Center, NY: The band started late. Weir announced that "certain members of the rhythm section didn't make it here on time." The "Jack Straw" opener more than makes up for the tardiness. The urgency in this "Straw" jam is unbelievable. It's not long, but if a jam can start off as a ten and maintain that breathless intensity throughout, then this is it. Phil is blasting as Bob and Jerry strum madly—a demonic release. The percussionists are forgiven. The instrumental is at the same time elegant and as subtle as a wrecking ball.

3-25-85 Springfield Civic Center, MA: The Dead came out as if they had a score to settle in Springfield. And maybe they did. This tour got off to a lackluster start in Hampton. Like the 4-4-85 Providence "Straw," the opening Springfield solo is extended. Solo two could ignite a barroom brawl. Weir's slamming the whammy bar and Garcia's slicing and dicing. It's a frenetic workout that sets the table for a bombastic "Sugaree."

11-6-77 Broome County Arena, Binghamton, NY: This top-notch '77 "Straw" follows a blazing "Mississippi Half Step." For a song that made its reputation as a show opener, only four of the twelve "Straws" listed here were played in the opening slot. This suggests that the Dead performed their best "Straws" when they were warmed up and riding momentum. This logic can be applied to just about any jam anthem.

This is the last East Coast show of '77, and the rowdy Binghamton faithful inspire the musicians. "Jack Straw" is alive and kicking. The rhythmic flow is breathtaking, and the group harmonizes with a soulful feeling. Bobby hollers, "You keep us on the run." The fuse is lit, a cannonball of sound is fired with signature Binghamton high-pitched fanning to close out the jam.

SUGAREE

There were few show-opening combinations as powerful as Jack Straw > Sugaree, and their early evolutions in the Grateful Dead scheme were similar. A Hunter/Garcia composition from the band's most prolific songwriting era, "Sugaree" was born on July 31, 1971, in New Haven's Yale Bowl. After a "Truckin'" opener, "Sugaree" was debuted in the second slot, a position it would often appear in through the years. The New Haven version is a crisp performance that lasts a shade under seven minutes.

For the next three years, "Sugaree" consistently checked in between seven and eight minutes in length as it became a crowd favorite. The studio track appeared on the album *Garcia*, and a live version from Winterland '74 was released on *Steal Your Face*. With "Jack Straw," the band was stretching the instrumentals by 1974 as it began to emerge as a jam anthem. "Sugaree" started to blossom when the band resumed touring in '76.

The instrumental expansion of "Sugaree" fit in with the band's new philosophy of focusing on jamming within the songs. Garcia experimented with various "Sugaree" motifs as '76 progressed. There were high-pitched, thick, emotional leads—patient in nature. And towards the end of the year, Jerry put together patterns of quick-picking runs in conjunction with thunderous chord fanning. The last two "Sugarees" of the year, 10-9-76 Oakland Coliseum and 10-15-76 Shrine Auditorium, were the best.

The ascension of "Sugaree" blasted through the heavens in May of 1977. During this month, the Grateful Dead performed epic versions of "Sugaree" in New Haven, St. Paul, Atlanta, and Hartford. The collective will and power of the band was scary as they accelerated to amazing crescendos that defied time—unconscious group brilliance.

These '77 "Sugarees" unfolded systematically. Jam one was inspired and devilish, hinting of the impending mayhem to come. Jam two was epic, pure lunacy, a band pushing it to the brink. Jam three could either be a soothing jazzy balm or another barnburner if the Dead felt as if they had to expand upon the previous jam.

If someone were to list the seven best renditions of "Sugaree," and they were all from '77, it would be hard to argue against that list.

"Sugaree" peaked in 1977, whereas the history of "Jack Straw" was a series of rolling peaks over a substantial timeframe. In 1978, Weir introduced slide guitar playing into the "Sugaree" jams. Weir developed into an incredibly gifted guitarist with distinctive voicing, but his slide guitar playing in "Sugaree" was an abomination. Often, when Jerry would get on a roll, Bob's primitive slides would clash against the superb virtuosity flowing from Garcia. As a listener, this made it tougher to enjoy what Garcia was doing, and it also may have impacted Jerry's flow. That being said, there are still many excellent "Sugarees" from '78 and '79.

We have several impressive "Sugarees" from 1980, and then the consistency of the instrumentals varied. You could always count on one noteworthy outburst from Garcia, but on too many versions from 1982, the band bailed on doing anything substantial during the third solo. "Sugaree" was only played seven times between '83 and '84, but many of these are full-bodied versions. The 10-17-83 Lake Placid version unfolds ideally. Each solo is substantial, and each solo is hotter than the one that precedes it.

After 1985, Garcia's virtuosity in "Sugaree" diminished a bit. It's one of those songs he never reestablished with authority after his coma. Brent Mydland, and then Bruce Hornsby, helped pick up the slack in the instrumentals as the Dead continued to play one of their classic numbers consistently through the years. The Grateful Dead played "Sugaree" 357 times. I'm sure some fans might disagree with my assessment, but I've yet to hear a "Sugaree" after 1985 that would be in the same class as the ones I've listed here.

Backing my post-coma "Sugaree" theory would be the Jerry Garcia Band's performance history of the song. "Sugaree" was a glorious Garcia Band number year after year until the coma. It was only played once after the coma, on 5-30-87. JGB dropped several of their hard-hitting jam songs and replaced them with spiritual numbers. Garcia was still shredding solos, but these numbers didn't have the same jam intensity as "Sugaree," "Rhapsody in Red," or "After Midnight." Regardless, the Grateful Dead left us a legacy of blazing "Sugarees" to cherish.

5-19-77 Fox Theatre, Atlanta, GA: The fabled Fox "Sugaree" comes on the heels of a "Promised Land" opener. There's a slight shake to the velvety tone of Jerry's voice. Garcia's just walking the dog as he glides into jam one. The music's unified, and a positive tension quickly builds. At the same time, the band's playing it cool and bursting at the seams. Garcia's guitar suddenly snatches a loud, soulful feeling. Everyone on the stage can sense that a transcendent moment is imminent, but it won't happen during this jam.

Garcia croons the "You thought you was the cool fool" verse and passes the baton to Keith, who opens jam two. Sorry to interrupt, Keith...here comes Jerry! Guitar licks fly as Phil rumbles, Weir strums, and the drummers pound.

Suddenly, Garcia opens the door to a new realm of madness. It sounds like a million bluebirds are singing inside the funnel of a cyclone. The cohesiveness is remarkable. Garcia pulls the trigger and the band bites the bullet. If there was any means of measuring the sound, the Grateful Dead would be breaking world records for velocity and intensity. The band reaches the highest level they can, and they sustain it for as long as they can without giving an inch. The Fox roars, and Garcia sweetly sings, "You know in spite of all you gave, you still have to stand out in the pouring rain."

To be or not to be, that's the question as Garcia steps in for his final licks. It begins insignificantly, as if the band might offer some nice atmospheric music before heading for an exit ramp. However, Garcia strums some choppy chords and the band is alert, aware that Jerry might go for the jugular at any moment. This jam escalates. Garcia's in beast mode and Billy, Mickey, Bobby, Keith, and Phil fan along on the same frenzied frequency. It's a breathtaking sequence and wisely, they pull the plug to avoid coming off as overindulgent. As they reach the end of the line in synchronicity, Keith takes one last swipe at his piano and the rebellious jam obediently drops back into the last verse. Incomparable perfection!

5-28-77 Hartford Civic Center, CT: On the final stop of their legendary May tour, the Grateful Dead rampaged through a Bertha > Good Lovin' opener. In lieu of tuning up, they segued right into "Sugaree" as if this was a holy mission. For those Deadheads in attendance who hadn't seen the New Haven show earlier in the month, "Sugaree" was probably still an enchanting seven-minute song. "Sugaree" had undergone an astounding metamorphosis—a lovely tune was now a tour de force that would be worshipped evermore.

Garcia rolls into the first solo and discovers a big, juicy note that pleases him so he fixates on it, repeating it seven times, lovingly bending his guitar string in the same manner. It's a beautiful moment, something that will capture your attention on every listen. Then Garcia starts racing through scales, his fingers tapping strings as if he's Hunter Thompson pounding typewriter keys on mescaline. Chez Garcia tosses a psychedelic salad here as he effectively mixes fanning, strumming, and picking, and reins the jam in before it gets out of hand.

Smooth piano rolls set jam two in motion. Keith's intro is longer than usual. When Garcia joins the fray, a wall of sound thunders—the collective will of the band guides the journey. The typical "Sugaree" funnel develops and the band savors it as they inch ahead at warp speeds. The music blurs forward, lurching and snatching simultaneously, and Garcia accents the jam with sharp hiccups and burps. This may be longer than any other "Sugaree" solo, but it's never overstated. After the second jam, this Hartford version holds a slight edge over the one from the Fox.

An attempt at another wild crescendo probably would have flopped, so the band eases into the third jam with some nice bass from Phil. However, Garcia's in no mood to mail anything in. His noodling develops into a substantial solo without any fireworks, just pretty picking that's focused. Garcia sings the final verse and there's a quick, climactic flourish before the final chorus—an exclamation point to the epic Hartford "Sugaree."

10-17-83 Olympic Center, Lake Placid, NY: Pumped to play in Olympic Center, the Dead come out blazing with "Sugaree." Garcia seems particularly fired up as he steps into the opening solo with more substance than most from this era. The next jam starts off hot, and after Jerry moves through several phases, nothing but molten lava pours out of his Tiger. The band's doing their thing, but Garcia isn't waiting for any cues as he breaks out the full assortment of quick-picking runs in his "Sugaree" arsenal. Garcia shifts gears with petrified chord fanning and a sneaky/ornery run before singing, "You know in spite of all you gave, you still have to stand out in the pouring rain."

This would have been a great "Sugaree" even if Garcia mailed in the third solo. But Garcia was an American hero in an enchanted venue. There's no hesitation or deception as Jerry attacks with the galloping chord > peeling onion lick motif. Garcia's gone mad. There's more guitar soloing in the Lake Placid "Sugaree" than any of the epic '77 versions. The reason I rate the 5-19-77 and 5-28-77 "Sugarees" ahead of this one is that on those occasions, the band is discovering how far they can go with "Sugaree," blowing away any preconceived notions of the song. And the '77 jams are crafted in a sophisticated manner where the band is improvising and clicking as one. On 10-17-83 Garcia is possessed, clearly the most inspired musician in the band, and it's a beautiful thing.

If you place this masterpiece alongside the 10-12-83 Help on the Way > Slipknot! > Franklin's (MSG) and the 10-14-83 Scarlet > Fire (Hartford), you're looking at one of the special weeks in Dead history.

9-6-80 Lewiston State Fairgrounds, ME: In the city were Ali "shook up the world" again by knocking out Sonny Liston with a phantom punch in the first round, the Grateful Dead shook up those at the State Fairgrounds with a five-alarm "Sugaree" following an Alabama Getaway > Greatest Story opener. Jerry comes out swinging in the first solo. A substantial run is followed by the best Weir slide guitar in any "Sugaree." Instead of clashing with Jerry, here he complements him with a fine flourish to end jam one.

Jam two is the end of innocence. It commences with playful ping-pong between Jerry and Brent. Garcia rips into some high-voltage leads and the rout is on. It's as intense as "Sugaree" can get. A bull stampede transitions into a Chernobyl meltdown as Phil's seismic pounding accentuates the madness. Jerry has one of those moments where he expands the improbable. This may be the most impressive "Sugaree" jam. It's definitely the scariest. The third instrumental is dreamy and brief.

6-21-80 West High Auditorium, Anchorage, AK: The Anchorage "Sugaree" rumbles and rambles like the one from Lewiston. For years I've confused the two, probably because they are standouts from the same year, yet the jam sequences are vastly different. "Sugaree" opens the musical jubilee on this occasion. A lean lyrical opening solo is followed by a spirited intro for jam two. Brent's the catalyst and Jerry responds by stepping on the gas. There's a gripping sweep to this segment that doesn't overstay its welcome. High-velocity picking ignites the last jam. This "Sugaree" flows very organically; the jams materialize like a preordained rhapsody. Phil and the band drive the last part of jam three as Alaska gets shaken down to the very marrow, evoking memories of the Anchorage earthquake of 1964.

5-5-77 Veteran's Memorial Coliseum, New Haven, CT: "Sugaree" is the second song of the evening, and Garcia does his best to incite a riot. Something's burning as the band gets pushy with the first instrumental. The solo escalates like a panic attack and then dashes off to a fanning crescendo. This "Sugaree" is the embodiment of the powerhouse '77 sound—it will obliterate anything in its path.

Keith leads the way into solo two with a series of spicy piano runs. Phil's bombs raise the tension as Jerry's sharp twangs become the focal point. All lights are green—the music soars—torrents of compressed wildness are unleashed. The band rides an explosive and dangerous surge, yet they have control and power over the beast. Symphonic waves fill the coliseum. The pressure cooker jam advances logically and ends with a brilliantly timed piano sweep. Back in the beautiful ballad Garcia sings, "You know in spite of all you gave, you still have to stand out in the pouring rain."

Accomplishing all of their objectives with two blockbuster jams, the third solo is serene. Phil thuds some lead bass as soft piano and light guitar strokes gently swirl and float. New Haven was the birthplace of "Sugaree" back in the Yale Bowl on 7-31-71. Whether they were cognizant of the fact or not, the Dead went on to create a legacy of outstanding "Sugarees" in New Haven and Hartford through the years. Connecticut should make "Sugaree" the state song.

4-12-82 Nassau Coliseum, Uniondale, NY: Here's to the wizardry inside a subdued "Sugaree." This is the second tune of set two. As usual, the band loosened up with the first solo, and Garcia rallied with impressive virtuosity towards the end of the second solo. To solo or not to solo? That was the question facing Garcia and those hardcore Deadheads who obsessed over the tapes. I haven't done any official research on the topic, but I'll estimate that Jerry skipped playing a third solo of any substance 75 percent of the time in '82. A two-solo "Sugaree" isn't necessarily better than one where Garcia strikes three times, but more usually equals better with Jerry.

Solo three materializes softly as Garcia repetitively chord-fans at low volume against mesmerizing keyboards from Brent. There's a sizzling/bubbling undercurrent to the sound. The rest of the band deftly mirrors Garcia as they incrementally increase volume, tempo, and intensity. This instrumental has a relaxed, masterful vibe that reminds me of the 3-18-77 Winterland "Sugaree." As the solo rolls on, Garcia breaks out of the controlled fanning mode and delivers a resounding finale, turning this "Sugaree" into a jamming jubilee.

3-25-85 Springfield Civic Center, MA: This "Sugaree" benefited from the hot "Jack Straw" that preceded it. A determined surge permeates the first two solos, and the searing run at the end of jam two hints at Garcia's intentions. Jerry's scratchy voice doesn't have much bark, but his leads inspire as solo three ascends.

Garcia hits a peak and breaks the jam down. It sounds like it's over but he's just playing possum with the audience. His repetitive leads regenerate and charge ahead full steam. Jerry's picking velocity mathematically escalates in increments as his scale variations slightly adjust—skittle-skattle squared! It's a mad dash—clinically insane—on and on, faster and faster—a stunning, hypersonic collage of sound as the rest of the band admirably scrambles to keep pace with the maestro. The Springfield "Sugaree" is a well-orchestrated example of execution and desire.

12-28-79 Oakland Auditorium Arena, CA: Sloppy, bombastic, and awesome are the adjectives that best describe this sixteen-minute "Sugaree" a few days before a new decade. A week before this performance, the Jerry Garcia Band delivered a ferocious "Sugaree" to open their show in the Keystone Palo Alto on 12-21-79. This Oakland version, which also kicks off the festivities, is cut from the same cloth. Solo one is heated, and perhaps the longest opening solo of any "Sugaree." It's disorientating in a good way. The Dead are disregarding the standard flexibility of the arrangement. You can easily get confused as to where you are in the song during this version.

Slide guitar and pitter-patter bass set the mood for jam two. Garcia dances around the fretboard and then drops into overdrive. Weir continues to do his thing on slide guitar, but Jerry turns up the volume and shreds. Jerry drops into chord-fanning mode to give Bobby room to do his thing. Jerry concludes another long jam with cute fanning and a few rounds of bubbly leads. The band quickly bails on the third jam. This is a sixteen-minute version. If the band opted for another instrumental, the Oakland "Sugaree" would have set a new world record for length.

3-18-77 Winterland Arena, San Francisco, CA: Dead jams tended to be more pressure-packed in the heat of the moment in places like New York, New Haven, and Philadelphia, in venues where exuberant fans fueled the fire. On their home turf, the tension is eased; the music twists, turns, and crashes in gentle waves. This playful searching does wonders for the fourth song of the night, "Sugaree." There's a whole lotta soulful picking in the first two solos. It's compelling and satisfying, yet this never kicks into typical "Sugaree" overdrive. Everything about the third solo is delightful and unique—the individual chords that Weir strikes throughout, the rich, almost comical sound of Phil's bass, the banjo-like sounds of Jerry's guitar as he converses with Keith. After a gripping jazz moment, the "oom-pah" of Phil's bass leads back to the final verse. Only in the Winterland!

HELP ON THE WAY > SLIPKNOT! > FRANKLIN'S TOWER

Dark Star" is widely acknowledged as the Grateful Dead's original improvisational masterpiece from the '60s. If I were to bestow that honor on a '70s creation, I'd choose the opening trifecta from *Blues for Allah*: Help on the Way > Slipknot! > Franklin's Tower. Over the years it has featured the band in their prime, jamming within the structure of the compositions. This distinctive combo smoothly fuses the crisp instrumentals in "Help on the Way" and "Franklin's Tower" with the jazzy, freewheeling improvisation of "Slipknot!"

After a few years of devotion to Help on the Way > Slipknot!, "Franklin's Tower" connected with other dance partners. The seductive groove and singalong chorus of "Franklin's" could instantly entice a crowd of Deadheads into a dancing frenzy and inject any show with a shot of euphoric energy. "Franklin's Tower" was played 108 times with Help > Slip, and 113 times without it. There are several outstanding pairings of Dancin' in the Street > Franklin's and Mississippi Half-Step > Franklin's. However, "Franklin's" shined brightest in its original configuration; therefore, I'll focus only on the *Blues for Allah* magnus opus.

On June 17, 1975, in the Winterland Arena, the Dead debuted "Crazy Fingers" to open the show. The first performance of Help on the Way > Slipknot! > Franklin's Tower closed the set. "Help on the Way" was performed as an instrumental in the Winterland. Robert Hunter's evocative lyrics were added to "Help" at the Dead's next show in the

Great American Music Hall on 8-13-75. Help on the Way > Slipknot! formed an almost exclusive partnership with "Franklin's Tower." On only a handful of occasions did the band tinker with the magic of the first two *Blues for Allah* tunes.

Through 1976 there was a loose, spacey feel to "Slipknot!" that suggested possibilities outside of "Franklin's Tower." The seven 1977 performances of this dynamic trio were performed with possessed certainty. That's what makes the Help > Slip > Franklin's hiatus puzzling. After the Dead opened their Norman, Oklahoma, show with it on 10-11-77, the dynamic trio wasn't played again until they broke it out in Compton Terrace on 3-25-83.

During this hibernation, "Franklin's" continued on in other pairings. I can only hypothesize that the intricate chord changes and structure of Help on the Way > Slipknot! was tough to return to after the band stepped away from it. And with new songs from *Shakedown Street* and *Go to Heaven* entering the live rotation, the band's will to reacquaint themselves with Help > Slip vanished until '83. They practiced it in the studio before reuniting the *Blues for Allah* masterpiece to start set two in Compton Terrace.

After a few cautious versions, "Slipknot!" morphed into a monster jam, from the summer of '83 through 1984. The only causality of this return was the between-verse "Help on the Way" solo, which was shortened from three or four rounds down to one predictable round.

Help on the Way > Slipknot! was only played twice in 1985. After four years on the shelf, it returned to active duty in the Hampton Coliseum on October 8, 1989. The sanctified trio never went into hibernation again, yet it was never overplayed. From the anticipatory allure of "Help on the Way" to the spiraling brilliance of "Slipknot!" to the delightful redundancy of "Franklin's Tower," this trifecta always challenged and pleased both the band and audience.

10-12-83 Madison Square Garden, New York, NY: My preferred viewing spot for a show was about ten rows up on the opposite side of Jerry, but when set two started on 10-12-83, I was watching from behind the stage. I was awed by the sight of the crowd as "Help on the Way" kicked off the set. Wide smiles spread across the faces of 20,000 Deadheads as they hopped to the beat and merrily focused on the musicians. The building was bouncing. To see the joy of the crowd from the band's perspective was awesome

This became a time-out-of-mind experience as the band segued into "Slipknot!." It was hard to comprehend how a band could create such intimate and sophisticated music at a rock concert while captivating and mesmerizing a hedonistic New York mob.

Garcia's playing has a dark and stormy aura. Genius rages as group synergy blazes. "Slipknot!" improved with each outing since it was returned to the lineup on 3-25-83, and this is the culmination of those efforts. Jerry explores and extends all possibilities in the arrangement as his guitar buzzes like swarming bees. The signature line leading to the bridge delivers maximum suspense.

As Garcia leads the ascension, Phil's blasts rattle the faithful and Weir smashes down on the whammy bar, forming a stunning collage of sound. In the slight pause before the bridge, Brent teases the melody to come. The bridge between Slipknot! > Franklin's is gonzo execution without the slightest stumble as the Garden blasts into "Franklin's Tower."

Before the first verse, Garcia lays down a beautiful solo and reestablishes the "Franklin's" beat and wallows in it. A deafening roar fills the Garden, and Garcia concedes that it's time to sing, "In another time's forgotten space." Between the last-sung line of "Help" and the opening line of "Franklin's," ten minutes have elapsed. Those ten minutes comprise the best instrumental jam I ever witnessed from the Grateful Dead.

And there's more good news because this is one of the hottest "Franklin's Towers" ever played. There are six solos from Garcia, and each one is gripping. Even on inspired versions of "Franklin's" you won't hear anything like this. Garcia was master of his domain, on top of the guitar world on this tour. And this was a wise and passionate NYC audience. Listen to them react after the "Listen to the music play" solo and following the final foray. New York and the Dead were perfect together, especially in 1983.

6-9-77 Winterland Arena, San Francisco, CA: This revered rendition received an exotic introduction. Following "Samson and Delilah" to open set two, Weir announces, "Our highly efficient and trained crack equipment team is busy at work making sure everything is just exactly perfect." This is good news for fans of the "Funiculi Funicula" tuning. In the divine scheme of things, if everything happens for a reason, then "Funiculi Funicula" was born for this moment. The instrumental's buoyant and carefree. It's obvious the band's getting off, and everybody in the Winterland has a happy heart. Technical difficulties never sounded so sweet. The little waltz winds down and Weir proclaims, "Ladies and gentlemen, we have a winner!" Indeed! The night of 6-9-77 wouldn't be the same without the "Funiculi Funicula" bridge between "Samson" and the beloved *Blues For Allah* opener.

"Help on the Way" kicks in like a heart skipping a beat—soulful anticipation rings sharply—jazzy riffs pound—*Paradise waits. On a crest of a wave her angels in flame.* Garcia and Hunter—inspired. This "Help on the Way" is as good as it gets, and then the "Slipknot!" ascension begins.

Jerry, Bobby, Phil, Keith, Mickey, and Billy dart off to lands where only jazz legends roam: Coltrane, Miles, Monk. This summertime Winterland exploration is metallic and dark, a spiritual voyage linked to something past but not forgotten—the continuation of an eternal jam. The ghosts of Coltrane seem to find their way into every "Slipknot!." I envision Coltrane in a dark suit blowing his horn through a smoky haze in a dimly lit lounge on 52nd Street.

Suddenly, we're back in the Winterland Ballroom and the Dead are whipping through the intricate transition to "Franklin's Tower." No band delights in a segue like these guys, and this segue is July 4th fireworks and the New Year's Eve countdown rolled into one. The ensuing "Franklin's" is a seventeen-minute breakout aerobics session. Garcia's singing is hyped towards the end: "I want you to roll away the dew.

Yoouuuu better roll away the dew. Come on, come on, roll away the dew!"

2-26-77 Swing Auditorium, San Bernardino, CA: After kicking off the second set with three stand-alone songs, including a hot "Music Never Stopped," the Grateful Dead unveil their *Blues For Allah* masterwork in all its congruent glory. This Betty Board recording that began to circulate in 1986 is a precious audio jewel. "Help on the Way" smokes, and the group harmonizing excels. Garcia's possessed playing puts the exclamation point into "Slipknot!." A cascading range of sound boils within—moody guitar probing uninhibited by indecision—crackling fusion. Lesh thumps bass lines that tickle body and soul.

The Grateful Dead are in rarified air, operating as one master organism. The definitive jam of the night bursts into "Franklin's Tower." Garcia's in the swing of things as he peppers away on each solo in a loosey-goosey manner. On one solo, Garcia discovers a guitar phrase he likes and he repeats it three times; on each round, he slightly varies the timing and emotional texture of the phrase. This elite version takes flight during the first show of 1977.

10-9-76 Oakland Coliseum, CA: This was the show of the year. Set two commences with St. Stephen > Not fade Away >St. Stephen. Following Donna and Bobby's "NFA" chant, a smooth chord vamp leads back into "St. Stephen." Our beloved saint lands with its Q & A finale: "Can you answer? Yes I can! But what would be the answer to the answer man?" A suspenseful second of silence is glorified by the band's bouncing beat proclaiming the arrival of "Help on the Way." It's an exhilarating handoff: the past, *Aoxomoxoa*, shakes hands with the future, *Blues for Allah—Paradise waits, like a crest of an angel in flames.*

Garcia's guitar twangs pierce through the Oakland Coliseum like the sound of a marching brass band on Benzedrine during "Help on the Way." The musicians blaze forth—a unified psychedelic stand. A subtle "Slipknot!" slowly and sweetly spins into a drum solo that introduces "Samson and

Delilah." This gorgeous loop finds its way back home with the resurrection of "Slipknot!"

The Slipknot! > Franklin's Tower bridge is crafted patiently and precisely—one more tantalizing segue to the last number of the loop. And what a grand finish to the set "Franklin's Tower" provides. Each solo is an opportunity for Jerry to paint, and he fills the canvas with plush brush strokes. The Who were waiting in the wings to follow the Dead. Nobody should have had to follow The Boys on this night.

4-17-84 Niagara Falls Convention Center, NY: To ease the crush of the crowd, the band starts the second set with a "Take a Step Back" march, lots of echo and reverb. Almost every time the Dead asked the audience to take a step back, they would follow that by playing something outrageous, sending the crowd in a state of delirium. If you're going to be smashed by the masses, you might as well experience transcendent music. After their plea to the audience, the Dead bounce into "Help on the Way."

Garcia's guitar dominates with a demonic tone as the band soars into "Slipknot!." Garcia's playing is borderline belligerent—in a redeeming way. His communique to his fellow bandmates is "follow me if you can." Fragments of the "Slipknot!" melody are explored and magnified. Garcia's zipping through scales, striking up dark chord riffs and milking the licks that he likes during this aggressive, nine-minute "Slipknot!."

"Franklin's Tower" isn't as pretty as it is gritty. The band sounds a little detached in the first half, but they rally late. Garcia's final solo astounds—a ballpeen hammer to the collective cranium of his New York state devotees who howl their approval. This is the top Help > Slipknot! > Franklin's of 1984.

9-2-83 Boise Pavilion, ID: "Citizens of Boise, SUBMIT, for you are a conquered people!" growled Phil Lesh when the Dead took the stage for their one and only appearance in Idaho. After getting comfortable with the nuances of Help > Slipknot! > Franklin's over the spring and summer tours, Garcia and company are prepared to take this trio to higher ground. This is the first of three outstanding versions on this tour; the others are from Red Rocks 9-6-83 and Santa Fe 9-11-83. All the Help on the way > Slipknot! > Franklin's Towers from '83–85 opened the second set.

At times, "Slipknot!" would get a little sloppy or disorganized, and in most cases that was a good thing. The Boise "Slipknot!" is a glorious, eight-minute adventure, fully explored and focused. Brent and Jerry are finishing each other's thoughts. Brent leads the way during the Slip > Frank transition. Garcia and Weir accentuate the joy of the segue bridge with clever chords and licks. "Franklin's Tower" is an even-keeled monster. Each instrumental is a patiently crafted musical paragraph—sizzling *Blues for Allah* for Boise.

10-17-84 Brendan Byrne Arena, East Rutherford, NJ: Help on the Way > Slipknot! > Franklin's Tower was a gem of an opener to kick off set two, although it didn't make a grand impression on me that night. This "Slipknot!" isn't as long or majestic as the one from 10-12-83 Madison Square Garden, but Garcia tees off. His clever leads swirl around and bounce off Phil's pounding bass attack. Garcia's guitar licks ramble on impressively as the band's foundation dissolves behind him. Jerry galvanizes this version with the signature line prior to the Slipknot! > Franklin's bridge. It's a stunning statement, and Garcia finishes it with a devilish, plinking twang.

Jerry leads his mates to the bridge and abruptly double-times the melody as the band scrambles to stay with their inspired leader. The hair-raising transition explodes into "Franklin's." It's as exhilarating a start to "Franklin's" as there is. Garcia accentuates the moment with shrieking leads before the first verse. His voice is bolstered by echo and reverb, courtesy of Dan Healy. The sharp guitar tone combined with Jerry's aggression makes this an invigorating listen, although this "Franklin's" suffers from blown lyrics and sloppy execution. Still, as a whole, this trifecta is one of those imperfect masterpieces, loveable and noteworthy.

THE MUSIC NEVER STOPPED

"The Music Never Stopped" was born on *Blues for Allah*, the Grateful Dead's organically created 1975 studio album. *Blues for Allah* was an artistic success, but several of these songs were destined for further expansion once the band brought them to life on stage. The spry sax solo at the end of the studio track barely hints at the instrumental surge that would make "Music" one of the band's beloved first-set closers. This Weir/Barlow composition was debuted live in San Francisco's Great American Music Hall on August 13, 1975. It was played at thirty of forty-one of their shows in 1976. And like several new tunes worked on that year, it grew in stature on a nightly basis until it exploded in 1977.

The lyrics and upbeat tempo of "Music" made it instantly irresistible, but for the purpose of this endeavor, I'll focus on the jam. For the first year and a half, the tune's closing instrumental consisted of some jazzy noodling before the band turned it over and steamrolled the melody line. Towards the end of '77, the brief jazzy noodling began to expand, and eventually it became a substantial building jam prior to the turnover. To simplify matters, I'll refer to these two different parts of the instrumental as the "building jam" and the "turnover."

There's a plethora of hot "Musics" from '77–'81. During those years, the song had a consistent sizzle factor. During 1982, "The Music Never Stopped" was only performed four times, and then seemed to slump between '83–'86. I saw several "Musics" during those years, but they didn't burn like previous versions. Luckily for "Music" fans, Jerry rediscovered the euphoria of the jam after his coma. Two versions from 1987 can stand toe-to-toe with any best-ever contenders.

"Music" remained in the Dead's rotation and was played 234 times, although I've yet to be blown away by any versions after 1987. "The Music Never Stopped" jam is a one-of-a-kind thrill, the Grateful Dead in transparent rock 'em, sock 'em mode. After its introductory phase, it was never overplayed, and it was always a feel-good blast to any show. My fondness for this tune is intense. The jam torches my soul and rocks me down to the very marrow.

5-9-77 War Memorial Auditorium, Buffalo, NY: When it was first introduced, "The Music Never Stopped" was an uplifting number that closed out with a spirited guitar jam, a song that worked in several key spots in either the first or second set. Night after night in '77, "Music" was on the rise. It seemed like the length of jam was increasing by twenty seconds every show as the crescendo intensified with each performance. And every night, Garcia was in his glory, racing through scales and carving out new paths on the road to musical ecstasy. The "Musics" from 5-5-77 New Haven and 5-7-77 Boston are extraordinary versions; stepping-stones for the Buffalo masterpiece.

The jazzy riffs that precede the "Music" turnover are almost nonexistent in Buffalo. There's unified determination as the band hammers away with striking precision—wave after disciplined wave, each round incrementally faster and more intense. Garcia was a master of this type of soloing, but it's striking to hear the Grateful Dead locked in and moving forward individually, yet unified.

As the jam ricochets longer than any other "Music," there's nothing left for the band to do but hop into a fanning crescendo. This is where Garcia gets creative, and steps outside of the logical progression to invent a round of bawdy licks that are playfully taunting—a distinctive stamp to mark the jam as extraordinary.

And then, they release the barking dogs. This jam has swagger and presence, and clearly states that the Grateful Dead rock like Golden Gods.

If you seek out a version of the Buffalo "Music," it's essential to find an audience tape, because there's a nasty thirty-seven-second cut in the jam on the soundboard tape—the best part, where Garcia does his playful taunting. One of my first tapes was a great audience recording of 5-9-77. I was thrilled to get the soundboard many year later, but I was outraged when I heard the cut. It's a smooth cut, almost unnoticeable for someone not familiar with the audience recording. They often play the soundboard version of the Buffalo "Music" on the Sirius Grateful Dead Channel. Even with the cut, it's an elite version, but you're missing out if you don't listen to the audience recording or a soundboard with the audience patch.

10-9-77 McNichols Sports Arena, Denver, CO: Archivist Dick Latvala brought fame to the band's next performance in Norman, Oklahoma, on 10-11-77, calling it one of the three examples of primal Dead. I'm not sure what criteria I would use if someone asked me to list three shows that embody the concept of primal Dead, but I believe this Denver show is more primal than the one in Norman, and this "Music Never Stopped" is as primal as a band can get.

A Lazy Lightning > Supplication, "Sugaree" onslaught precedes this set-ending "Music Never Stopped." Whether or not this was due in part to the mile-high atmospheric conditions, the band is ripping and energy's crackling through the arena. The timing is right as the band funnels supernatural forces into this "Music."

Garcia unleashes a wild build-up jam that sears and soars before it gives way to the feel-good finale. Build-up jams would become longer, but wow, this is fabulous, easily the best to date. The turnover jam pulsates rapidly, shrieking guitar leads in the fast lane. I wish a video of this existed. Garcia had to be jumping, bouncing, and imploring his mates. Garcia pounces on an imaginative riff and repeats it backwards and forwards—looney tunes.

The band's in the zone, answering Garcia's inspiration with ferocious playing while skillfully maintaining synchronicity. Denver is ten miles high as Phil, Bobby, Billy, and Mickey pound away. Garcia's ready for some fanning and Weir joins in as they pull off the mother of all incendiary crescendos. If this jam had a little more length, it may have topped the Buffalo "Music."

10-1-77 Paramount Theater, Portland, OR: After the triumphs of the East Coast tour in May, the Winterland run of June, and the mega success of the Englishtown extravaganza on Labor Day Weekend, the Dead were an extremely confident band, and one could say they were playing with an edge of arrogance in October. This was good news for songs like "The Music Never Stopped," the last number of the first set during the first of two nights in the Paramount Theatre.

There's a brief build-up before the turnover, and then the jam takes off—a barrel ride down Niagara Falls. The musical ideas line up in a swirling rotation. There's a smooth flow and orgasmic progression to this instrumental, and the band sticks a perfect landing. It's another great '77 "Music," and as if Jerry realizes this, he decides to separate this one from the pack by redirecting the jam out of its landing. This could have been messy, but the band picked up Jerry's thoughts and suddenly, it's a daredevil adventure again. The band sticks one more flawless landing and we have ourselves another charismatic and distinct "Music Never Stopped."

3-27-87 Hartford Civic Center, CT: The arrival of this "Music Never Stopped" is surprising. There were few extraordinary "Musics" from '83–'86, and then there was Jerry's coma. This was the Grateful Dead's first East Coast tour after the coma. I was on hand for this Hartford show. The crowd was stoked, but through seven songs, a bland first set of mediocre performances unfolded. There was no momentum or reason to expect magnificence from the band. Maybe set two would be better. And then I heard Jerry suggest "Music Never Stopped." A rush of adrenaline surged through me. It's the type of song that could instantly deliver unforgettable thrills.

There's obvious joy in Jerry's voice as he croons his backing harmonies, "Who-who-who-who-ew-who-who." Audible anticipation buzzed in the Hartford Civic Center. Emotions were on the rise and if Jerry were up to the task, the ingredients for a great "Music" were there. A confident and steady building jam readied the band for takeoff.

Garcia launches the pinball and one of the hottest turnover jams since '77 ensues. Start to finish it's a screaming barn burner, emotionally delivered in measured increments. Anyone who witnessed this was in awe. Jerry was finding those seemingly impossible pathways to raise the temperature of the jam when it seemed to be maxed out. There were a few transcendent jams like this in 1987 that led me to believe the Grateful Dead were back and better than ever. Sadly, these were fleeting moments, but decades later, I'm eternally grateful.

9-23-87 The Spectrum, Philadelphia, PA: "Desolation Row" and "Big Railroad Blues" precede and fuel the fire for this act of Grateful Dead wizardry. There's barely a pause as Phil and Bobby charge into "Music Never Stopped." After Bobby sings, "Fish are rising up like birds," Brent plays a riff that sounds like "Fish rising up like birds." Weir chuckles as he continues, "It's been hot for seven weeks now," and in response to Brent's riff, hollers, "Did you hear what I just heard?"

There's a great vibe as the ending jam develops. You know Jerry's going to rip it. As the temperature rises, Garcia latches onto a startling run in an impossibly high frequency that separates this "Music" from any that has ever been performed. Jerry quickly eases the intensity so he can redirect the jam. But why redirect when you can charge back into that rarified air? And that's exactly what Jerry does as he leads the band back to the previous high-frequency run and improbably builds upon that—lightning strikes twice. The Spectrum roars in awe. At the conclusion of this majestic "Music," Weir slyly announces, "And we'll be back in a little bit." You mean there's more?!

5-18-77 Fox Theatre, Atlanta, GA: This is a night of mellow Jerry ballads and inspired Weir offerings. The first set doesn't generate much heat until "The Music Never Stopped" blows the roof off of the Fabulous Fox. Garcia's turnover solo is wildly imaginative: high notes, low notes, repetitive runs juggled and jumbled, sudden changes in tone and volume, chord fanning and dramatic windup, all masterfully spliced at excessive speeds. There's a herky-jerky yet possessed flow to the jam that makes it a standout.

7-5-81 Zoo Amphitheater, Oklahoma City, OK: The imperfections and quirkiness of this version seem to spark the explosive jam. After "Samson and Delilah" and "Don't Ease Me In" kick off set two, the Boys break into a surprise "Music Never Stopped" in the third hole. A spacey vibe permeates the build-up jam as it sounds like it might drift off into another song. The instrumental dissolves into some cool noodling from Brent and Bobby, and Jerry sparks a fiery run as Bobby leads the turnover, but the suddenness of it seems to surprise Jerry.

After the missed cue for the turnover jam, which sounds cool anyway, Garcia picks the right moment to step back in with authority. This leads to an impossibly exciting run of repetitive leads from Jerry—*a rainbow full of sound...fireworks, calliopes, and clowns*. The beat pulses on but the melody dissolves and mirrors the build-up jam. There's exquisite balance to this jam as Jerry strikes up another rousing round of repetition and Weir's mad strumming rallies the band to climax. To make sure everybody's on the same page, Garcia's guitar shrieks a piercing exclamation point. The final chord progression lands with a touch of uncertainty as Garcia seems like he might want to noodle into another song. There are better "Musics," but few shine like this crazy diamond.

MISSISSIPPI HALF-STEP UPTOWN TOODLEOO

Although it didn't receive the critical acclaim of *Workingman's Dead* or *American Beauty*, *Wake of the Flood* contains several songs that became essential live pieces of the Grateful Dead experience. "Mississippi Half-Step" kicks off *Wake of the Flood*. It's a truncated version that fades away during the "Rio Grande" chorus, and superfluous violin noodling doesn't add to its luster. By the release of *Wake of the Flood*, "Half-Step" was a beloved tune that thrived live in the band's rotation, and it was well on its way to immortality in Grateful Dead folklore.

July 16, 1972, was the day "Mississippi Half-step" was born in Dillon Stadium, Hartford, and it was played twenty-five times by year's end. Inspired energy bursts through these early versions. With five chances to solo, there is plenty of opportunity for the band to experiment within the framework of the arrangement. The evocative lyrics and up-tempo shuffle made this an instant favorite. As the band delighted in experimenting with the instrumental execution within "Half-Step," the song popped up all over the map from '72–74; early or late in the opening set, inside of song loops, or on its own in the second set. "Half-Step" was included on *Steal Your Face*, the double album from the Winterland '74 run.

Like "Sugaree" and "The Music Never Stopped," "Mississippi Half-Step" underwent creative expansion as '76 rolled into '77. The eight "Half-Steps" of '76 gave us a blueprint as to how the band would like to open up the instrumentals.

However, Deadheads couldn't imagine the extraordinary leap "Half-Step" would take the following year. The jams before "Rio Grande" were startling, climactic, and way longer than before. Deadheads devoured the sparkling improvisation and cheered madly before heading across the Rio Grande. And you couldn't overlook the outro jams, which came close to matching pre "Rio" intensity.

As in "Sugarees" from this period, the synergy of the band was sublime. The mighty presence of "Half-Step" continued to make crowds swoon in '78 and '79, but the group mastery had slipped a bit. Deadheads like to debate what the band's best years were, and I'm not suggesting '77 was their best year, but the band seemingly created masterpieces in autopilot mode. These were the dividends of mastering their craft on the road.

"Half-Step" history took an intriguing turn on May 14, 1978, in Providence. This was the first Mississippi Half-Step > Franklin's Tower. The next "Half-Step" was a standalone production. After that, the next 34 "Half-Steps" segued into "Franklin's Tower," and the duo primarily opened shows. As exhilarating as a Half-Step > Franklin's opener was, "Half-Step" fared better on its own. It was as if the band knew "Franklin's" was waiting in the wings and they had to conserve some energy for it.

There was considerable shrinkage during the pre "Rio Grande" jams. The Half-Step > Franklin's streak ended when Help on the Way > Slipknot! > Franklin's Tower was reunited in 1983. Amazingly, the great "Mississippi Half-Step" was not played once during the next two years. It returned in various spots in 1985, but it was more of a mad dash than a jam anthem. Most versions were less than eight minutes long.

After the coma, "Half-Step" returned in '87 and then soared in 1988, starting with the spring tour. Garcia found the mojo again, especially in the outro, ripping solos that reminded fans of its glory days. "Half-Step" found a new dance partner in "Feel Like a Stranger," although it remained flexible in where it may appear during a show. Bruce Hornsby's tenure with the band helped revive the spirit of "Half-Step." It was a beautiful song, but the mighty jam swagger was gone.

9-3-77 Raceway Park, Englishtown, NJ: Weir urges the surging crowd to take a step back as the musicians play a light-hearted shuffle. This is a game-changer. As we already know, the "Take a step back" plea is often a prelude to a transcendent masterpiece, as it is here during the fourth song of the opening set in Englishtown. The Dead confidently advance into one of their signature gems of '77. Jerry's trembling voice merrily sings the verses, and his solos ignite a mass dancing frenzy on a track built for drag racing and funny cars. Jerry belts out the chorus one more time, "Half-step Mississippi uptown toodleloo. Hello, baby, I'm gone goodbye. Have a cup of rock and rye. Farewell to you, old Southern skies, I'm on my way, on my way, on my way-ay-eee!" Immortality beckons.

This instrumental revs into high gear as if it's feeding off the acceleration and burnt rubber expended on this gnarly turf. Harnessing the abundance of energy at their command, the band slams into a quick climax, and then Keith and Jerry take a sharp left turn and charge the mountaintop again, doubling the exhilaration. Phil's bass bubbles brilliantly between the aggressive drumming. Already, this is one of the finest pre-"Rio Grande" jams. Elated by the rapture of the music, the crowd hoots and hollers as one.

The musicians take a moment to soak in the love of their smitten fans as they ease their way towards the bridge. Inspiration strikes the gifted hands of Mr. Keith Godchaux. He begins to twinkle a lovely melody. Garcia's listening, and he's pleased with what he hears. He bends his strings to mimic and play off of Keith's notion. A sonic rainbow is forming—the aesthetic is gorgeous—cooling waterfalls—grasshoppers and butterflies in a dewy meadow. Phil's bass rumbles like a yawning lion. Billy, Mickey, and Bob assimilate to the sublime sound and guide the jam until it hits the sweet spot. Group wisdom vetoes another rousing crescendo; it would have cheapened the allure of this masterful creation, which is unlike anything they had conjured up during any previous "Half-

Step." A monstrous audience roar fills the humid skies over Englishtown as the instrumental simmers.

The "Rio Grande" bridge is harmonized to perfection and followed by a dazzling outro. There was a myth floating about that the Grateful Dead failed to rise to the occasion when the bright lights were shined upon them on the biggest of stages. It may have been true, but that myth was officially debunked on September 3, 1977. The Englishtown "Mississippi Half-Step" is that great.

11-5-77 War Memorial Auditorium, Rochester, NY: The Englishtown "Half-Step" changed my perception of music. It was my first bootleg tape, and after hearing Jerry go off on that "Half-Step," I understood why people followed this band, and that Garcia was the greatest guitarist with no equal. The 9-3-77 "Half-Step" was my go-to version for decades, but I'm now smitten with the "Uptown Toodleloo" from Rochester.

When the Grateful Dead take the stage in Rochester, the crowd surges to greet them, and Weir promptly asks them to take a step back. Oh baby! Here we go.

An extraordinary "Half-Step" beckons, but only after the band opens with "New Minglewood Blues." It had been eight shows since the Dead last played "Mississippi Half-Step," and the band's fired up. Pure joy permeates this performance. The between-verse solos are hypnotic, and Jerry's golden voice belts out, "I'm on my way!" with maximum emotional commitment. He's promising to deliver on the song's theme of escape. The audience will transcend. Everybody will be freed from their troubles and woes.

I could dance across a pit of burning coals while listening to this pre-"Rio Grande" adventure. Garcia's leads are astounding out of the gate—an escalating stream of aural jubilation. The band is unified, and Garcia can do as he pleases in this compressed cocoon of sound. With Phil and the drummers confidently guiding the jam, this isn't a foray to a new frontier as much as it's assured virtuosity. The momentum never waivers or hesitates. The band rides this beast for as long as they can, and Garcia finds an impossibly climactic lead that extends the instrumental for another round. The band must be jumping out of their shoes at this point. When the wave crashes, Rochester goes berserk. This jam blows my mind every time.

Jerry and Donna harmonize "Rio Grande" attentively; hard to believe in the heat of this performance. They sing the mesmerizing bridge to a whisper and crank it up again. This band is unreal! Garcia and mates crush the outro.

As the first set continues, there's two more "Take a step back" pleas. People may have been getting crushed, but nobody was feeling any pain. The power of this "Half-Step" inspired the band to play it again the following night in Binghamton. It's another extraordinary version, and the last time "Half-step" was played on successive nights.

5-7-77 Boston Garden, MA: On the seventh day of May 1977, during the seventh song of the show, the Grateful Dead pull off their first epic performance of "Mississippi Half-Step." Jerry croons this tale of impending adventure with the spirit of an eternal optimist. The drumming is up-tempo and absolute. As the band hops into a jam that will lead them to the "Rio Grande", Keith plays a dreamy organ that sets a surreal mood as Garcia takes flight, and Phil mixes rattling blasts with stealth carpet bombing. Garcia bends all the euphoria that he can out of his guitar strings. Jerry works overtime on a gorgeous, flowing narrative, and his mates are with him every step of the way. There's some dramatic chord fanning before it all simmers into the exquisitely sung bridge: "Across the Rio Grande-ee-oh, across the lazy river." "Mississippi Half-Step" has officially ascended into the realm of *Masterpiece Theatre.* The final instrumental steams into "Big River."

9-21-72 The Spectrum, Philadelphia, PA: In the middle of set two, in the thick of a legendary show, the Dead transform South Philly into a honkytonk saloon as they shuffle through a ragtime rendition of "Mississippi Half-Step Uptown Toodleloo." This music's spirited and infectious. There's an appealing wildness to this version and others from '72. Garcia's guitar has a razor-sharp tone and the group vocals are emphatic. Two raunchy solos split three verses. The final verse segues right into "Rio Grande" and Garcia cuts loose, as per the "Mississippi" motif in '72. Jerry's in guitar-string-bending heaven before the reprise of the "Rio Grande" bridge. And then the Dead gently rock this baby to bed.

9-1-79 Holleder Stadium, Rochester, NY: Fifteen Dead shows in Rochester yielded two "Half-Steps." You're familiar with the other one from '77. A fluid "Half-Step" opens this evening. Through the "Rio Grande" bridge this is a slightly above-average rendition. And then the ghost of Rochester '77 kicks in. Garcia peels away from the last "across the lazy river" chant with a searing guitar surge. The band is amped up as they join Jerry in a hasty and impressive fanning crescendo.

This wouldn't be a noteworthy version if the story ended here. Garcia pulls a kangaroo out of his hat, redirecting this jam with a manic run, one of those moments that's so stunning, it's impossible to miss even if you weren't focused on the music. It's Evil Knievel in flight—but sticking the landing might cost him a few fractured ribs. This is one of those moments when you know that the only guitarist on the planet who could have created these licks was Jerome John Garcia. These amazing outbursts had us flocking back for more and makes listening to this stuff eternally compelling.

3-24-88 The Omni, Atlanta, GA: I'd been touring for seven years, but I had never seen a hot "Mississippi Half-Step" until they opened the second set with it on this night in Atlanta. Jerry's voice is a bit scruffy, and there's a blown lyric or two. Nice texture and flow precedes the "Rio" phase, but one could hardly expect the ensuing fireworks. This is the first "Half-Step" of the year, and Jerry attacks it as if he had recently listened to a '77 version and thought, "Wow, I used to do that!" Brent is turned up loud in the mix and his inspired playing is supporting and spurring Jerry to take it to higher ground. And so the Magnificent One rises to the occasion again. It's a stunning give-and-take that has The Omni roaring. This is the top "Half-Step" of the '80s.

5-17-77 Memorial Coliseum, Alabama University, Tuscaloosa, AL: "New Minglewood Blues" opens the show and then restless fever yearns in Jerry's presentation of "Mississippi Half-Step." He sings in an emphatic cadence, and his guitar talks double time. Ol' Jerry smokes a tight pre-"Rio

Grande" solo, and his vocals continue to bubble and burst through the bridge. Whatever Jerry was doing for kicks before the show was accelerating the pace of his performance.

As Garcia kicks the last jam into overdrive, the drummers are trying to keep pace, trying to follow the muse. After a few passionate passes, the band is ready to wrap things up. It's only the second song of the show, but Garcia's running down a dream and he uses his veto power to singlehandedly extend the jam with spectacular leads and dramatic fanning. "Mississippi Half-Step" neatly slips into "El Paso," continuing a symmetrical geographic journey that starts with the outlaw who is wanted down in Texas.

3-10-81 Madison Square Garden, New York, NY: This is an outlier. A speaker blew as Jerry was about to step into the first solo. This disruption changed the flow, tempo, and structure of the song. As the Boys move forward, there's not much in the way of backing vocals; it's almost all Jerry. The pre "Rio" jam is the best of the decade. Jerry weaves his magic patiently, admiring and paying attention to the sound coming out of the new speaker, which is squeaking/squawking with unusual feedback. Instead of fighting the audio difficulty, Garcia savors it as he works the long solo down an untraveled pathway. This show and the night before in MSG (my first show) are rewarding must-listens. This distinctive show opener is a pleasure, and Madison Square Garden dances and grooves as "Half-Step" glides into "Franklin's."

LET IT GROW

"Let it Grow" was born on September 7, 1973, a little more than a month before it was released on *Wake of the Flood* as part of the "Weather Report Suite." The Dead debuted the entire "Weather Report Suite" on September 8. The fetching "Prelude" and "Part One" of the suite was retired at the end of '74. Aside from its debut, "Let it Grow" was played by itself one other time during this period, on 5-25-74.

When the band returned to touring, "Let it Grow" was played frequently, although the Dead were still trying to find the right spot for it to flourish. Was it a second-set song that could be part of larger song loops, or was it a first-set powerhouse? "Let it Grow" vacillated in the lineup until it was put on the shelf for a year after it was played on 10-2-76 as the next-to-last song of the opening set.

"Let it Grow" had epic potential. It was a powerful Weir/Barlow tune that gave Garcia a green light to plant, cultivate, and harvest. There was a between-verse solo and two major instrumentals—a can't-miss jam anthem. In 1977, the Dead had taken "Sugaree," "Mississippi Half-Step," and "Music Never Stopped" to monumental heights. "Let it Grow" returned to the lineup at the end of the first set between "Sugaree" and "Franklin's Tower" in Seattle on 9-29-77. The next seven 1977 versions are monsters, and this tune finally found a home at the end of the first set as a closer on most occasions.

By '82, the second instrumental after the "rise and fall" bridge morphed into a sophisticated jam with three distinct movements. "Let it Grow" was the jamming highlight of many of the shows it appeared in before Jerry's coma. It continued to be a desirable jam number through the Dead's final days, but Garcia never recaptured the wild intensity he used to bring to it. The big instrumental after "rise and fall" seemed to conclude with repetitive chord sequencing as opposed to the high-flying improvisational genius that boggled the mind. And there was a period where Jerry opted for the Midi wizardry. I preferred when Jerry broke it wide open with old-school guitar shredding. Still, "Let it Grow" always delivered jams that satisfied the jazz, blues, and rock aficionado in us all. The Grateful Dead played their agricultural anthem 276 times.

8-7-82 Alpine Valley Music Theatre, East Troy, WI: Alpine Valley sounds like the type of place where the Grateful Dead would cultivate a memorable "Let it Grow," and Deadheads reaped a bountiful harvest on 8-7-82. From the opening riffs to the final chord, this is as perfect as live improvisation gets. Weir's on top of his game singing with conviction and Brent is a major improvement over Donna on background vocals, especially during "Let it Grow." In 1982, the Dead tended to play cocaine crisp, and this hyped rendition is the best of that milieu. The between-verse solo is streamlined virtuosity that carries on after Weir howls, "Seasons round, creatures great and small, up and down, as we rise and fall!"

The life-sustaining joys of planting, plowing, and harvesting surge through glistening sonic streams— photosynthesis at the speed of sound. The scary thing about this alpha jam is the smoothness of the segues. The machine plows effortlessly. Phase two takes flight. Crops, take heed! The temperature and intensity of the rhapsody is on the rise.

Moving into phase three is a cross between ecstasy and a nightmare. Bob's orchestrating, and Brent's pounding the fertile fields. It's all silky-smooth. Garcia's guitar overboils, and Brent's there to pound out the warning on his keys. Alpine Valley, beware! Here comes the Great Garcia with a climactic run, wrapping it up with a bold lightning strike. The Boys touch down smoothly as they ease back into the melody line. All the crops of Alpine Valley stand proud and tall.

The focus is uncanny as Weir leads his mates through the chorus reprise, and Garcia blazes from the last-sung words, "Listen to the thunder shout I am, I am, I am…I am!" The jam is astounding without overstaying its purpose. There's not a sour note anywhere in this performance. They duck back into the final melody line as Garcia and Weir's guitars sigh in unison. Garcia approaches the last chord by striking each string individually, and then he digs in for the mother of all final chords—one gorgeous strike packed with fertile heart and soul. Let it grow indeed!

7-29-74 Capital Centre, Landover, MD: This prenominal "Let it Grow" is the best ever within a "Weather Report Suite." Prelude > Part 1 is sweet, and Donna sounds so-so here. I'd recommend the 5-19-74 Prelude > Part 1 as my favorite. I find Donna's singing alongside Weir a little unnerving on 7-29-74, but Sweet Jumping Jesus…Jerry goes off! The between-verse jam roars, and after "Rise and Fall" Garcia goes nuclear. Phil and Billy are doing ridiculous things as Jerry dances around the moons of Neptune. Human and plant life revel in harmony, and the Cap Center "Let it Grow" shares the miracle of it all.

It sounds like the outro jam will whittle or wisp away in the wind, but Señor Garcia digs in for a brazen tangent. This is surreal stuff, and Billy Kreutzmann's percussion playing is urgent and elegant. Unbelievably, Garcia matches the intensity of what he created in the first solo. The Landover "Let it Grow" is leader of the '74 pack.

10-29-77 Field House, Northern Illinois University, De Kalb, IL: "Morning comes, she follows the path to the river shore," sings Weir as Jerry's licks flood the terrain. The band's off and running with a "Let it Grow" for the Heartland. Garcia's voice is bombastic during the "Might As Well" show opener, and now his guitar's possessed as he responds to Weir's plea: "Listen to the thunder shout I am, I am, I am!" The dam bursts and the sound gushes.

After its allotted go-round, the genie is briefly bottled. At Bobby's command, the impending jam will rise and fall. Garcia navigates his way through a series of intricate arteries and the band shifts gears with ease to accommodate the impulses of their leader. Garcia's got a lot of bones to pick, and on this extreme journey, he pieces together a boiling patchwork of improvisation. It's a standout performance, the undisputed heavyweight champ of '77 "Let it Grows." From this day forward, "Let it Grow" was untouchable, a revered first-set closer that aroused the palettes of discerning Deadheads.

11-4-77 Cotterrell Gym, Colgate University, Hamilton, NY: This set-ending "Let it Grow" is phenomenal, right up there with the one from DeKalb five nights earlier. After Weir bellows, "Rise and fall!" Keith steps up to lead the instrumental. The sonic landscape is elegant and jazzy as Garcia smoothly connects the dots in a vacuum of high-velocity picking and strumming. Weir, Lesh, and the rhythm devils shift gears precisely, and Garcia and Godchaux have all the answers. This jam doesn't explode like DeKalb. It's an improbably fluid display of elaborate improvisation. And the outro jam is the longest of any '77 version. The Boys are hot, and Jerry noodles on until "Let it Grow" recedes into its final signature line.

9-7-73 Nassau Coliseum, Uniondale, NY: There's double-edged distinction here. This "Let it Grow" is an outstanding performance, and it's one of the most remarkable debuts of any Grateful Dead song. The band's on fire in the Nassau Coliseum. There's a pleasing, twangy tone to Garcia's quick picking as he navigates his way through "Let it Grow" for the first time. The entire band shines as they conquer a tricky musical arrangement. Jerry's fancy strumming and phrasing resembles what he had cooked up in some heated "Dark Star" segments. Billy's intricate drumming helps extend and glorify the outro jam, which segues into "Stella Blue." If you heard this without introduction on the Grateful Dead Channel, you would never guess it was the first performance of "Let it Grow."

12-5-81 Market Square Arena, Indianapolis, IN: Before a show in Providence, I met a guy from Indianapolis who was at this show. He recalled this "Let it Grow" and told me that the house lights were on during the entire song. It makes sense when I listen to this performance. The tone, texture, and velocity here reminds me of 8-7-82 Alpine, but there's a few minutes less jamming in Indy. Regardless, the Dead reach remarkable peaks early in the big jam. Weir leads the charge with blazing rhythm as Garcia unleashes shrill leads in gleaming batches, and Mydland's organ phrasing splashes in at the right moments. The final solo under the house lights comes off like a victory lap in the Indy 500. This ended a consistent first set with desirable song selections.

9-11-83 Santa Fe Downs, NM: On Mickey Hart's 40th birthday, after kicking the second set off with Help on the Way > Slipknot! > Franklin's Tower, the Dead thrill the faithful with "Let it Grow." It was an apropos choice in the high deserts of Santa Fe, a pleading prayer to the gods. The "rise and fall" jam is longer than usual on this occasion. The three-pronged attack is still there, with expanded boundaries. In Santa Fe, Garcia just puts his head down and plows the fields without much regard for structure. More Garcia is always a winning formula, even if it comes off a tad chaotic at times. This doesn't have the framed brilliance of the '82 Alpine Valley "Let it Grow," but the Dead rocked on for fifteen minutes—another abundant harvest for "Let it Grow" fanatics.

EYES OF THE WORLD

The Grateful Dead gave birth to "Eyes of the World" on February 9, 1973, in Roscoe Maples Pavilion in Palo Alto. Six additional originals were also played for the first time on 2-9-73: "Row Jimmy," "Loose Lucy," "Here Comes Sunshine," "They Love Each Other," "China Doll," and "Wave That Flag." By the time a pleasant but truncated version of "Eyes of the World" was released on *Wake of the Flood* in September, this jam anthem was already legendary and transcendent.

Where and when an "Eyes" would arrive during a show was unpredictable. It could come out of a "Dark Star," "Other One," or "Truckin'"; segue into "Sugar Magnolia" or "China Doll"; or pop up out of nowhere in the first set. Several of the spectacular early versions materialized out of the between-song calm in the opening set. "Eyes of the World" was played 381 times. Only seven of those performances were in the first set.

I was tempted to make this entry Estimated Prophet > Eyes of the World, but "Eyes" had an illustrious history before it hooked up with "Estimated" in 1977. And conversely, "Estimated Prophet" veered from "Eyes" on many occasions. When "Eyes of the World" returned after the Dead's touring hiatus, the elongated "Stronger Than Dirt" outro was sliced off. On the bright side, the Dead poured all their energy into the intro and the between-verse solos. If you could take a '77 "Eyes" and combine it with a '74 outro, you'd have the immaculate version.

Along with Scarlet > Fire and Help on the Way > Slipknot! > Franklin's Tower, "Eyes of the World" embodied that distinctive Grateful Dead sound that combined imaginative and optimistic lyrics with fetching musical arrangements that provided ample opportunities to jam within. The grooves of these tunes instantly had Deadheads dancing.

As "Eyes" whirled through the '80s, the pace quickened and the versions shortened. It remained an undeniable favorite of live audiences, but the noteworthy versions were few and far between. However, when the Dead were in the zone and riding momentum, they could still thrill and captivate the toughest of critics with "Eyes" in the '80s.

In the following decade, the band's approach to "Eyes" became more patient, and they took the time to explore the jams within. *Wake now, discover that you are the eyes of the world.* When that Brazilian beat filled the air, aural ecstasy was imminent, regardless of the decade.

8-6-74 Roosevelt Stadium, Jersey City, NJ: In the middle of this twelve-song first set, the Grateful Dead played a standalone "Eyes of the World" tucked in between "Jack Straw" and "Promised Land." It's almost unprecedented for a royal rhapsody of this magnitude to emerge at this point of a show. Out of the post-"Straw" stillness the "Eyes" groove emerges naturally, almost understated. Jerry's sweet vocals match the subdued flavor of the groove.

Intensity surges as Bobby and Donna join in on the chorus. Weir's voice leads the way, and Donna sounds sweet. Billy and Phil are locked in tight as Jerry fills the opening solo with sublime perfection from the first note. For sixty-six seconds, the inspired musicians are one with the universe. They *are* the eyes of the world. Garcia finishes this surge dramatically, a piercing string of aural adrenaline. Following the last euphoric twang of Garcia's guitar, the infectious rhythm of "Eyes" returns in all its understated glory. You can hear Roosevelt Stadium roar through the soundboard recording.

That opening solo would be far and away my favorite between-verse solo of an "Eyes" from this era if it were not for the ensuing solo. "There comes a redeemer, and he slowly too fades away." Jerry's singing sweet and true. This wheel's on fire and the greatness of what's to come is evident before it materializes. The only intrigue is how it will unfold. As solo two emerges, Jerry pauses for a second; oh, how he plays the silence! The silky-smooth leads flow as he expands on the ideas from the previous solo. This is how the ninety-four-second instrumental unfolds: stutter-step > loading the cannon > fireworks galore > spooling yarn finale. Kreutzmann's drumming fortifies and fills the sonic landscape. There would be longer between-verse solos as the structure of "Eyes" changed in 1976, but the compressed creative genius of the 8-6-74 solos is unmatched.

Phil's in lead bass heaven and the band swings loosely behind him as the "Eyes" outro commences. After a year and a half of improvising on this "Stronger Than Dirt" motif-jam, the intricate chord changes are crisp and perfectly timed. Intent listening and the instincts of the group mind combine as the Dead segue to a series of careening chord progressions. Garcia's leads whirl like a spinning top as the force of each new riff resonates. Jerry's rampaging as Weir strums madly. The Grateful genius is grounded in stone-cold musical logic. A tornado of sound dissipates as "Eyes" hits the eighteen-minute mark. Garcia's guitar sobs in disbelief. This is a major masterpiece that grabs our attention all the way through and shines a bright light on what this band was capable of when they were in peak performance mode.

10-19-74 Winterland Arena, San Francisco, CA: This is another first-set "Eyes" that comes after "Mama Tried" as the twelfth song of an epic fourteen-song set. One of the highlights of the iconic *Grateful Dead* movie, this "Eyes" features intimate footage of the band wailing as their devotees gyrate and whirl to the sonic muse. However, the movie version is missing six minutes of prime-time jamming. There's an excellent version of this "Eyes" in its entirety on the *So Many Roads* box set, with a superb audience recording precisely spliced in to fill the missing gap from the soundboard tape. This eighteen-minute "Eyes" is pure bliss. The band's on the verge of a touring hiatus so they treasure every second, and their palpable joy seems to indicate that maybe this retirement from the road idea is a mistake. A band this hot can't retire—it goes against the natural laws of physics and reason.

A casual excellence radiates throughout this version. The between-verse solos are crisp, and Jerry's attentive vocal phrasing brings out the buoyant vibe of "Eyes of the World." The music is sparse and hypnotic after the last verse. Phil's bass leads resonate as Bobby and Billy strike a seductive groove. Jerry's leads are exquisite. This has a much different aura than the Roosevelt Stadium "Eyes." It's very organic and West Coast cool. The "Stronger Than Dirt" motif is intense yet graceful—a bittersweet jam that screams we don't want to say goodbye.

9-7-73 Nassau Coliseum, Uniondale, NY: I first came across this version as a bonus track on the reissued *Wake of the Flood* CD that was part of the *Grateful Dead: Beyond Description 1973–1989* box set. Hearing the 9-7-73 "Eyes of the World" for the first time was like receiving high-voltage shock therapy. This offering of "Eyes" is sandwiched between an "Other One" jam and "Sugar Magnolia" to close the second set in Nassau. The band is amply warmed up as a turbocharged "Eyes" takes flight. Jerry's picking away and there's a sharp, twangy tone to his guitar—electrified folk/bluegrass. The outro is an outrageous rampage, and Garcia's orchestrating the assault. There's some nice work by Keith here as he plays off of Jerry's improvisational sizzle. The jam is fearless, fierce, and remarkably consistent. At times it's uneven and overambitious, but any Jerry junkie will be in awe of his fretwork.

3-29-90 Nassau Coliseum, Uniondale, NY: We're back in the Nassau Coliseum again, seventeen years later, but the song remains the same. Saxophonist extraordinaire Branford Marsalis joins the Grateful Dead for the sixth song of the opening set, "Birdsong." Branford wasn't too familiar with the Dead's material, but he was at ease trading licks with Jerry. Mission accomplished; Branford was ready to split. Phil and Jerry convinced him to stay for the second set.

Set two kicks in with "Eyes of the World," and Branford knocks down sweeping melody lines as the song begins. His confidence is astounding. The "Eyes" tempo is perfect; slower than the speedy versions throughout most of the '80s. The band creates space for Branford to drop in as he pleases, and as Garcia sings, Branford's applying brush strokes.

Stepping into the first solo, Jerry's sound is robust and spirited, and at the same time, intentionally subdued. As Branford plays in rhythm with the band, Garcia's sharing the genetic makeup of "Eyes" with his musical brother. Everything Branford needs to know is there: the emotions, colors, texture, and temperature of the tune. All great improvisers are keen listeners. Although Branford wasn't familiar with "Eyes" when he stepped onstage, he absorbed the professor's lesson.

Without any visual or verbal cues, Garcia steps off and Branford glides in at the 3:35 mark. The next 90 seconds comprise my favorite solo by anyone not named Jerry Garcia. With the ease of Coltrane, Branford's blowing and everyone in the Nassau Coliseum is glowing. Branford's connecting riffs and licks in a rapturous vacuum à la Garcia in a language that any Deadhead can relish.

After scaling crescendo mountain, Deadheads roar and Jerry and Brent pick up the conversation. Jerry throws out a lead, Branford answers, and Brent pounces on that cue. Brent's at his best here. This sublime give-and-take lasts ninety seconds, and there's a final blast of joy from Branford right before Jerry sings, "There comes a redeemer, and he slowly too fades away."

The first seven minutes of this "Eyes" is so spectacular, it obliterates the remaining ten minutes. Garcia switches on the MIDI effect in the middle of solo two. If you have Branford onstage, I'm not sure why you'd want your guitar to sound like a flute, but that's the way Jerry was rolling in 1990. Commenting on Jerry's MIDI experimentation, Branford said, "Jerry found a way to adapt to whatever the situation was and add a color. When he switched to the [MIDI] guitar synth, I never felt he needed it. Intrusion is too strong a word. It obstructed his sound."

The outro solo contains clever fiddle-faddle between the musicians. The 3-29-90 "Eyes" is extraordinary and transcendent, and it's also unbalanced because the opening segment soars into another dimension and then gravity pulls it back to the Nassau Coliseum. What goes up must come down. A few different versions of this masterpiece have been officially released. My favorite mix is the superb recording that appears on the *Without a Net* compilation.

5-15-77 St. Louis Arena, MO: Jerry teases "Eyes of the World" before the band leaps into "Estimated Prophet" to start set two. It reeks of conspiracy, as if the Dead discussed the never-before-played combo of Estimated > Eyes before they took the stage. The "Estimated" outro explodes like a Roman candle lighting the sky, and the smoldering sparkles ignite "Eyes of the World." Phil embarks on tasty lead bass before passing the baton to Garcia, who knows just what to do. Jerry fills St. Louis with the spirit of "Eyes" and when there's a lull in the chord progression, he chimes, "Right outside this lazy summer home."

Ecstasy pours from Garcia's wand in the aftermath of the first chorus. *Wake now, discover that you are the song that the morning brings*. The temperament and tone of Garcia's solo matches the sentiments of Hunter's prose. Garcia soars as if within this musical vacuum lies the secrets to carefree and joyous living. The band works up a skimming stones chord progression followed by Garcia's playful taunting. The St. Louis crowd is engaged and boisterous; an eruption of gratitude follows each solo. When the final words are sung, Garcia casts his rod again and he hooks onto a gorgeous run—his strings sing in ascension—those shrill, piercing notes that make every dog and Deadhead in the area bark.

6-9-76 Boston Music Hall, MA: Deadheads anxiously welcomed back the Grateful Dead for their first East Coast show after their elongated break from touring. On this magical evening, set two begins with the return of "St. Stephen," the first one since Halloween 1971. *What would be the answer to the answer man*? As the final line touches down, the shamans whirl into a hyper "Eyes of the World," although there's no rush to sing the first verse as they cast an enchanted spell over Boston. The intro spins forward—layered passion. The Grateful Dead and "Eyes of the World" are back.

After several satisfying rounds, Phil delivers a few lines as if he's leading the band into the "Stronger Than Dirt" motif. The jam simmers before it's brought to boil again. I believe this eight-minute jam before the first verse is the longest one on tape. It was as if they were kissing goodbye and paying tribute to the majestic '74 versions of "Eyes" at the same time. There's nothing like this jam! Moving forward, the extended and brilliantly developed 'Eyes" outros were cut. On the bright side, the early solos of "Eyes" became longer and more compelling. This was a superb transition version.

11-4-77 Cotterrell Gym, Colgate University, Hamilton, NY: Phil introduces the band at the start of set two as the Jones Gang. On this wild night, the third song of the set is "Playin' in the Band." The roulette wheel spins—where and when she will stop, nobody knows. Deep inside the beast, Weir introduces some "Eyes of the World" chords and Garcia peels off some "Eyes" licks, but it sounds like this thing will swing into "Uncle John's Band." But the "Eyes" seed has been sown, and Garcia latches onto it. Yes! They're storming into "Eyes."

"Eyes" whips ahead at a terrific tempo as an amused Garcia riffs this way and that way before breaking into piercing leads. Weir strikes up some interesting-sounding chord progressions that aren't synching with what Garcia's doing, but the clash of rhythm and pitch sounds brilliant and gives this "Eyes" a unique tension. Garcia unravels a tasty intro before things settle into a hyped groove. Any instant now, Garcia's going to sing the opening verse . . . but it appears he's transfixed by the rolling rhythm, so he decides to reel off another cascading solo and eventually he ducks back into the chord motif. The crowd roars.

After Donna, Bobby, and Jerry harmonize the opening chorus, the band storms ahead—a shuffling staccato beat. This is loony tunes! Wile E. Coyote is chasing the Road Runner. Garcia's solos are aggressive, and there's no indecision as he channels the muse that only he has access to. At the end of the first solo, Garcia introduces the repetitive, taunting licks I so admire. For the most part I prefer an "Eyes" with a slower tempo, but this is an extraordinary display, a standout in a year of excellence.

10-14-83 Hartford Civic Center, CT: I've overlooked the greatness of this "Eyes of the World" due to the colossal Scarlet > Fire at the beginning of the set. Thankfully, we have eighteen minutes of "Eyes" to deal with here, by far the longest of this era. The Scarlet > Fire on this night receives royal treatment; every jam is fully explored. As "Estimated Prophet" winds down, it sounds like there may be no "Eyes." But once they jump into it, the Dead methodically dig into every nook and cranny. Jerry takes each solo as long and as far as he can in accordance with the laws of jam mathematics. Solo two is a marathon. Garcia extends the ladder of creative genius. This is the hottest Scarlet > Fire, Estimated > Eyes before Drums. Only 9-2-78 comes close to Hartford.

SCARLET BEGONIAS > FIRE ON THE MOUNTAIN

This is the mother of all Grateful Dead combos. Scarlet > Fire gives us seven instrumental segments, if you include the song intros. It's twice as long as most China Cat > Riders, the hypnotic transition's guaranteed to fry your mind, and the lyrics and danceable beat fit the Grateful Dead scene like a glove. "Scarlet Begonias" was born with the first Wall of Sound show of 1974 in the Cow Palace on March 23. Jerry's voice is overcome with joy as he lets "Begonias" fly for the first time. "Scarlet" was a powerhouse on its own, but that sweet noodling outro was searching for a dance partner. In Roosevelt Stadium on 8-6-74, "Scarlet" was tucked inside "Playin' in the Band." Anything can work within the "PIB" framework. Yet "Scarlet" was willing to be on its own until the right partner arrived.

"Fire on the Mountain" was adapted from a Mickey Hart composition, "Happiness Is Drumming," which was played in Chicago on June 28, 1976. Hunter added his lyrics and the first "Fire on the Mountain" emerged from "Scarlet Begonias" on 3-18-77 in the Winterland. It was a sloppy version, but swayed by the infectious beat, the crowd roared approval. The next performance of "Fire" in Philly on 4-22-77 clicked.

Scarlet > Fire peaked in May '77 with several outstanding versions, including the legendary performance in Barton Hall (5-8-77). We have the invigorating intro solo of the Chicago "Fire" (5-13-77), a full-bodied Scarlet > Fire adventure in Tuscaloosa (5-17-77), and the smooth grace and relaxed transition of the Lakeland combo (5-21-77).

Scarlet > Fire was an instant favorite and fixture in the rotation, but it seemed to hit a bit of a creative malaise towards the end of '77 and through parts of '78. These versions lacked the creative spunk of May '77. After Scarlet Begonias > Goin' Down the Road Feelin' Bad was played in the Palladium on 4-29-77, the Dead played twenty-two consecutive Scarlet > Fires before switching things up with a Scarlet > Dancin' on 4-18-78. Scarlet > Fire returned the following night and help was on the way. On 9-2-78 in Giants Stadium, the "Almost a blaze still you don't feel the heat" verse was added to "Fire." This provided another opportunity for the band to jam, and it gave Garcia the opportunity to build on the theme he established in the first solo or change direction with the second solo. Including intros and outros, Scarlet > Fire now had seven jams. Brent's addition to the band sparked the flow of Scarlet > Fire as the Dead stormed into the '80s.

Eclectic versions of Garcia's dynamic duo popped up all over the place in 1981. The following year, the Dead had a cocaine-crisp sound, and consequently, several tight Scarlet > Fires were finished in under twenty minutes. A new golden age for Scarlet > Fire flourished in '83 and lasted through most of the following year. The band took their time and thoroughly explored all the passages within as Garcia relished the opportunity to lose himself in a world of noodling, doodling, and steaming guitar forays.

Bad news for Scarlet > Fire fans arrived on May 8, 1984, in Eugene, Oregon's, Hult Center when Scarlet > Touch of Grey broke a streak of 110 consecutive Scarlet > Fires. Ironically, this was the seventh anniversary of the revered '77 Cornell Scarlet > Fire. For the next year and a half, the band also paired "Touch of Grey" and "Hell in a Bucket" with "Scarlet," as well as "Fire." The outro of "Scarlet" suffered when it wasn't heading into "Fire" and of course, "Fire" was a better instrumental jam than either "Touch" or "Bucket."

On the other hand, "Fire on the Mountain" fared well when it wasn't paired with "Begonias." Two examples of this are the One More Saturday Night > Fire from 7-13-85 Ventura and Cold Rain and Snow > Fire from 7-4-86 Buffalo. "Scarlet" built anticipation for "Fire," so it was a disappointment when it segued into a lesser song. When "Fire on the Mountain" arrived out of nowhere, it worked because it was an unexpected pleasure.

Scarlet > anything but Fire became a rarity after '85, although the instrumentals in "Scarlet Begonias" became shorter after the coma. "Fire on the Mountain" enjoyed a major resurgence in early 1988 as Garcia teed off on several outstanding versions. Scarlet > Fire was performed 251 times. There are noteworthy versions of this pairing as late as 1994. Regardless of the year, a sense of euphoria would rush through the crowd whenever the band tuned up for "Scarlet Begonias" at the start of set two.

5-8-77 Barton Hall, Cornell University, Ithaca, NY: When the Dead returned from intermission, the crowd surged towards the stage, causing Bob and Jerry to implore them to take a step back. Another mystical performance beckons. As snow flurried outside the windows against the bluestone façade of Barton Hall, the Grateful Dead stormed into "Scarlet Begonias." There's a magnetic pull to this version—the pronounced heartbeat bass, irresistible rhythms, pitch-perfect harmonizing, dreamy lead guitar accompanied by twinkling keyboard fills. Jerry sings like an angel as "Scarlet" marinates at a perfect pace. As the heavens open and mind leaves body, the Dead transport their followers to another realm with the "Begonias" outro.

Donna's scat-singing at the onset of the outro is ear candy, and it's a catalyst for a transcendent jam. Jerry noodles in response to Donna, and Keith's stealth piano runs add to the luxurious sonic landscape. A stunning twenty-second drumming vamp turns up the heat. Garcia's in an inspired zone as notes descend and ascend in steady flurries, conjuring up a winter wonderland—*Not a chill to the winter but a nip to the air*. Everyone in Barton Hall, including the musicians, are sucked into the blissful vortex of this sonic seduction.

Weir's first to make the move towards "Fire on the Mountain" with a lazy riff that doesn't disturb the delicate balance of the jam. Garcia's still building, bubbling, and boiling in transition paradise. The band is seamlessly playing "Scarlet" and "Fire" at the same time. The fine line between songs has been eviscerated. I like to think of this segment as "Begonias Mountain." When the entire band clearly crosses into "Fire on the Mountain," Garcia engages his guitar filter and pierces the groove with a lush melody line.

The hypnotic musical flow continues during the between-verse jam on their way to the completion of the second and final verse. And then, the greatest guitar solo of any "Fire" materializes as Jerry reels off a series of surging runs and orchestrates an unprecedented bridge to the coda's trademark melody line. This segment is unshakable and certain of its royalty. The ensuing guitar leads are colorful and lively—anticipation unbearable. Intuitively, the band knows where they're going, even though they've never been there before. When Garcia can hold back no longer, his right hand becomes a strumming, chord-fanning blur creating a torrent of sound that bombards Barton Hall. The Dead double down. Garcia opens another passage to a second chord fanning that eclipses the previous one and then the band surfs into the "Scarlet" refrain. This Scarlet > Fire is the defining masterpiece of Cornell, and one of the greatest segments of live music ever created by any band.

10-14-83 Hartford Civic Center, CT: The magnus opus of this evening begins with the "Scarlet Begonias" intro as Brent introduces a xylophone synthesizer lick at exactly the right moment and continues to tap all the right notes before Jerry sings the first verse. It's the ultimate signature lick, the one that will have any fan of this Scarlet > Fire salivating instantly. It's a warm performance of "Begonias" with a between-verse jam that's a slight cut above most of the Scarlet > Fires from this golden era for the combo. There are some excellent percussion exchanges between Billy and Mickey as the outro takes flight, and Garcia's blazing leads unfold like strings of pearls, one finer than the last, in a controlled manner. The music swirls around Jerry as if everything's predetermined. The leads seem to regenerate as "Scarlet" precisely winds down.

There's a fractioned second of silence as the band begins to build "Fire" note by note and chord by chord. The regeneration that tapered off "Scarlet" will now be used to stoke the flames of "Fire." The pulse beats steady and slow and accelerates smoothly. The Hartford Civic Center claps along in a trance as they anticipate the first verse. Jerry's in no rush as he lets the beat resonate before singing, "Long distance runner, what you standing there for?" There's a yearning kick to Jerry's voice—he's poised to take this up a notch.

The first solo of the 10-14-83 "Fire" is a masterpiece on its own. Garcia's lyrical playing instantly grips the imagination. And with each ensuing round, the velocity and sonic pressure rise incrementally. As Garcia deftly accentuates different parts of these passages, he gives off the illusion that he's going all out and holding back at the same time. The solo has legs as it impossibly keeps getting hotter and more compelling. The crescendo goes where no "Fire" goes, yet it's not as startling as the finale of the next solo. It's one of my favorite guitar solos yet; it still leaves room for the ensuing jams—pure genius.

Solo two takes off with a rapturous glow, like its predecessor. Garcia scales the mountain quicker, and it seems like the band's ready to land for the third verse, but Jerry redirects the trajectory of the jam and a mighty climax ensues. Every instrumental passage in this Scarlet > Fire receives special treatment. The Hartford "Fire" is topped off with the best outro solo since 5-8-77 Cornell. As the band returns to the "Scarlet" coda, Brent checks in with more xylophone punctuations to balance and crown the pièce de résistance.

9-1-79 Holleder Memorial Stadium, Rochester, NY: Before kicking off the second set with Scarlet > Fire, Weir announces, "This next set is respectfully dedicated to all the little mice and rats who are trapped in laboratories all over the world." This is a lovely performance of "Scarlet" with sublime singing and a robust groove, but surprisingly, the intro and between-verse instrumentals are both brief. The "Begonias" slowly boils for a while, and about ten minutes into "Scarlet," the band pivots towards "Fire." Garcia boldly rejects that advance with a noodling "Begonias" reprise that goes on for several minutes—

flashbacks to Cornell and "Begonias Mountain." There must be something in the upstate New York air.

The even flow of this performance continues until Garcia steps into the solo after the second verse of "Fire." Along the way, Garcia digs into a guitar line that he likes, and he repeats it three times with slightly more passion on each round—trouble ahead. Jerry and friends accelerate into a crescendo that burns like the one from Cornell. Instead of heading back to the final verse, Jerry plays a lead that Brent receives as an invitation to solo. Jerry returns with some bubbling licks to bring this monster jam to the last verse. An exhilarating outro tumbles into Drums without the signature "Begonias" ending lick.

5-17-77 Memorial Coliseum, University of Alabama, Tuscaloosa: After twelve songs, the Dead treat Alabama to a Scarlet > Fire to close the set. This was the band's first concert in Alabama, and they were determined to make it memorable. Garcia's got the holy mojo rolling on the between-verse "Begonias" solo, a cut above the rest of the pack. The drummers and Jerry are driving the train here. Donna has a funny vocal hiccup as she leads the Boys towards "Fire." No version can be like Cornell, where every move by every band member is magically placed and spaced. But Garcia's doing things with strings—masterful fretwork on a "Begonias" that lasts longer than most from May '77.

"Begonias" loosely swings into "Fire," and then comes one of the greatest song intros you'll ever hear. The truculent beat indicates the band's on a mission. Garcia rips off a perfect melody line and chases that with a swirling solo of cascading notes—precise in length, breathtaking in its euphoric effect. However, Mr. Garcia is appreciating the amazing pulse and beat of the band, so he settles into the groove. To accentuate his pleasure, Garcia stomps on the effects pedal and strums a definitive "Whap!" One, two, three, four, "Whap!" One, two, three, four, "Whap!" One two, three, four—no whap. This sequence is repeated eight times. Alabama is under Garcia's spell. This is one of the sickest rhythmic adventures I've ever heard. Stunning synchronicity with minimalist playing.

Garcia's on a creative binge as he redirects the middle jam three times, making for a meaty rendition. The outro steams, although it lacks the authority of Cornell. The rousing ending to the marathon set establishes it as the elite opening set of '77.

4-20-84 Philadelphia Civic Center, PA: It was Saturday night. Jerry was in red and I was there in the second row. A thousand cough drops couldn't have soothed Jerry's sore throat. It sounded as if he had a bran muffin lodged in his esophagus all night. Jerry was in physical dire straits all year, but on many nights his guitar playing was heroic. This was one of those nights.

The first "Scarlet" instrumental thrills the Deadheads in Philadelphia. Garcia unleashes four rounds of slicing/searing fretwork, and the band finishes it off with a pounding round of chord fanning. Immobile during this entire presentation, Garcia mesmerizes the audience with "Begonias" runs—bright-colored leaves falling from trees. The line between songs disappears. It is an unconscious transition by the Grateful hypnotists. *Long distance runner, what you standing there for? Caught in slow motion in your dash to the door / The flame from your stage has now spread to the floor.*

Phil's booming bass has the entire audience clapping in time as Jerry begins to sing. Jerry's notes roll out thick, juicy, and slow. Each line sucks you deeper into an aural web of intrigue. This is the mother of all jams that tease. The solo is filled with deep feeling, but there's no quick-picking—the ladder of hypnotic guitar leads extend beyond what's possible in shrill frequencies. This jam is cut from the same cloth as the first "Fire" solo of 10-14-83 Hartford.

Garcia hits the quick-pick runs we crave in the second solo and the outro is adequate. There's a million negatives attached to smoking Persian, but for good or ill, I don't think this type of Scarlet > Fire could have been created any other way.

9-2-78 Giants Stadium, East Rutherford, NJ: A rambunctious Scarlet > Fire initiates set two. Garcia and Lesh attack the between-verse "Begonias" solo and there's more brute force on the road to "Fire." Garcia peels off squawking/squeaking runs that are backed with surging sonic intensity from Phil and the drummers. Time disappears as the band mesmerizes itself with this motif until Jerry's licks set off the smoke alarms and the beat glides into "Fire on the Mountain."

The 9-2-78 "Fire" debuts the "Almost ablaze still you don't feel the heat" verse. After a sensational run of "Fires" in May '77, the jamming became mundane on certain versions. The extra verse gives us a double dose of Jerry's "Fire" creativity, since the outro solo is structured and ends with a predetermined "Begonias" riff. The extra solo also gave Jerry the option of building on what he did in the first solo or taking the second solo in another direction. An abundance of jamming fills the 9-2-78 "Fire." A touch of hubris is evident in the Dead's performance as the best band in the land jams the night away during their Giants Stadium debut.

10-19-81 Sports Palace, Barcelona, Spain: There are better Scarlet > Fires than the one that opens set two in Barcelona, but few are as addictive. Over the last five years, I've probably listened to this one more than any other. The opening chord progression and tempo of "Scarlet" is sensuous. The lush swirl of Brent's keyboard ignites an uplifting groove. Jerry blows a lyric early on, but his vocal phrasing is sweet and the vibe is right for a memorable Scarlet > Fire. This is also Señor Garcia's one and only performance in the land of his ancestors.

The "Begonias" outro is substantial without overstaying its welcome. The last few minutes linger in elegant sophistication. Garcia guides the improv with soft leads in a lower register as the band eases the tempo and softens the volume. Garcia's licks touch down like drizzling rain as Brent and the drummers attentively play off the maestro's direction. It's a wonderfully subdued jazz moment.

WHOMP! The passive suspense explodes into the glorious groove of "Fire on the Mountain." The beat ticks along like a healthy heart, and it never could have flourished like this if it weren't for the "Begonias" foreplay. The Barcelona "Fire" is lean and combustible. At the tail end of the second solo, Garcia unleashes a barrage of piercing notes with extreme velocity— the type of surge that'll overwhelm the most passive of listeners. The tantalizing nuances of the music combined with the rich, high-end audio mix of the soundboard infuse the Barcelona Scarlet > Fire with its alluring charm.

10-14-94 Madison Square Garden, New York, NY: On the eleventh anniversary of the Hartford Scarlet > Fire, the Dead added to the legacy of this dynamic duo in Madison Square Garden. This is the best Scarlet > Fire I've heard from the '90s, although I haven't heard them all. The rippling electricity of Madison Square Garden helped the Dead launch a lively "Scarlet."

It seems as if the band's racing to help Jerry through it. The handoff to "Fire" is seamless in the fast lane. According to those who split the tracks, the ensuing "Fire" clocks in at over twenty-three minutes. If I was splitting the tracks, I would add two minutes to "Begonias" and subtract two from "Fire," but either way, the duration of "Fire" is historic.

This is a case where the tempo plays the band. The infectious, upbeat groove won't be denied as Billy and Mickey keep the Garden rocking. Garcia's guitar work and singing is inspired through the first solo. It lacks the brilliant design of the Hartford "Fire," but all Garcia has to do is add licks to keep things interesting. The Garden is buzzing because they know they're participants in a memorable moment, and they're inspiring Jerry. This version has three between-verse solos. The length of the jams confuses Jerry. He sings the last verse twice. Screw creative purpose; Jerry and the band ride the rampaging pulse as a magical performance emerges.

2-5-78 Uni Dome, University of Northern Iowa, Cedar Falls, IA: This is one of the shows featured on *Dick's Picks Vol. 18*, and what a pick it is. After opening set two with the hottest "Samson and Delilah" ever played, the Dead explode into "Scarlet Begonias." The between-verse solo pulsates with Phil's hyper bass lines. An aggressive outro jam transitions to a massive "Fire" intro.

Mesmerized by the sound of his guitar, Jerry wails away like a mad fiddler. With only two verses, the action-packed, sixteen-minute Cedar Falls "Fire" never becomes over-indulgent—merrily lost, yet focused in the majesty of their luxurious creation. The second set of this show is up there with the best of '77. The Dead played Iowa nine times, and they always brought their A game to the Heartland.

SUGAR MAGNOLIA

The sweet Southern serenade, "Sugar Magnolia," was played 591 times. Despite it being an extremely popular tune, I never felt it received proper respect from Dead aficionados when compared to other major Dead tunes. "Sugar Mag" might be the Rodney Dangerfield of jam anthems.

"Sugar Magnolia" was released on the band's second studio album of 1970, *American Beauty*. It was the most joyful jingle on the record, but it lacked instrumental punch. When the Dead played "Mag" live it became a dynamic force with a heated but structured instrumental. Out of the massive sampling of live performances, there's an abundance of raging Cajun jamming to dig into.

"Sugar Magnolia" was born in the Fillmore West on June 7, 1970. It segued out of an instrumental "The Main Ten Jam," which was the precursor to what would soon become "Playin' in the Band." It was a raw debut with incomplete lyrics, yet the delightful groove that would make the song irresistible was present. By the time "Sugar Magnolia" was played for the first time in the Fillmore East on 9-18-70, it was wholly formed with a raunchy jam and a brief "Sunshine Daydream."

"Sugar Magnolia" was Bill Graham's favorite song and it was played fourteen times on New Year's Eves, usually after the ball was dropped. During an eight-year span that ended with the closing of the Winterland on New Year's Eve 1978, the Dead played "Sugar Magnolia" twenty-six times in the Winterland. Many of these versions are spectacular. If the

Winterland were still around and it was to be renamed, it would have to be called Bill Graham's Sugar Magnolia Auditorium.

After a few years of bouncing around the second set, "Sugar Magnolia" settled into its position as an authoritative set closer. The band pounded out terrific versions regularly between '72 and '74. I did my best to list some standout versions here, but without a doubt I've missed a few. If you love a hot "Mag"—and who doesn't—I'd suggest paying attention to every version from this era. Through the years, "Magnolia" has had a more structured arrangement than most jam anthems. The most noteworthy change in the song came during the Brent years when a second, shorter instrumental emerged in the middle of "Sunshine Daydream." At any point in the band's career, a hot "Mag" could be the exclamation point of a hot show, or it could single-handedly salvage a show sliding south.

11-19-72 Hofheinz Pavilion, Houston, TX: The first time I heard this tape, I pegged this "Sugar Magnolia" as the best I've ever heard. At one point I placed the 11-11-73 "Mag" ahead of this, but I've reconsidered. Every instinct by each band member works, and there's not a misplaced or dull note on the 11-19-72 "Mag." Even the brief between-verse instrumental has extra pizazz. Following the final verse, Weir turns away from the mic and howls, "Whoooooooo!"

The band's locked in—emotional and cognitive synergy. This jam will explode and everyone in Hofheinz Pavilion can sense it. I see smiles on the faces of the musicians as they bop with certainty to the chord progression. Whatever drugs are circulating through the minds of the musicians is irrelevant; they're all riding the same high. Phil's playing out of his mind, and this is a bass-heavy recording.

As the jam moves forward, the band builds anticipation without blowing the lid off the pot. Once the jam is fully loaded, the fuse is lit and steady streams of aural fireworks bolt from Jerry's guitar as the rest of the band propels this fuel-injected ride. This instrumental is impossibly logical and dramatic, with extra credit for duration—thunderous rock executed flawlessly.

I usually find listening to "Sunshine Daydreams" from this era to be a task due to Donna's over-emphatic vocals, but on this night it's enjoyable, and the momentum accelerates into a scorching "Goin' Down the Road Feelin' Bad."

11-11-73 Winterland Arena, San Francisco, CA: This version proudly presents, without doubt, the hottest series of leads from Jerry in any "Mag." Weir's hyped vocals and Billy's crisp drumming trigger this onslaught. Garcia's leads progress as one might expect. Around the five-minute mark, Jerry unleashes the brightest guitar run you'll ever hear. The beautiful sound and searing intensity make you wonder how Garcia got to this place. And now that he's in this euphoric pocket, he strings together quick-picking runs and inexplicably keeps this thrilling ride alive. All the band can do is support Jerry because he's picking on a level beyond crescendo mode.

As the amazing cliff dive ends with a smooth splash, the Winterland faithful roar and Phil holds a bass note until "Sunshine Daydream" is launched.

10-10-82 Frost Amphitheater, Stanford University, Palo Alto, CA: Bass blasts rumble. Weir's singing in raging glory as the Boys wrap up a brilliant two-night stand in the Frost. There's an East Coast cocaine-crisp intensity as this version develops. Phil bombs create musical craters as the instrumental takes off. Blitzkrieg music fills the space between craters. Jerry attacks and the band pulls back without stepping off the gas so Garcia can strike again. Power thunder chords introduce each segment. Each run from Garcia picks up where the last one left off. Just when it seems like the band will wrap this up with a chord-fanning crescendo, Garcia rallies with his finest surge before the band brings it on home.

Before "Sunshine Daydream," Weir says, "Vote on proposition ten if you can vote." The Dead's furious playing rips through "Daydream." Weir's howling lots of "An hahhhs!" and "Cabba cabba hahhs." There's a brief romping chord progression that must have had Weir prancing around the stage. I confess that I find Weir's antics here charming. This is a great version that stands alongside the best from the '72–74 era.

12-6-73 Municipal Auditorium, Cleveland, OH: This is an ideal ending to a set that featured a sensational "Here Comes Sunshine" and a forty-four-minute "Dark Star." For this tour, the Grateful Dead were a five-man band; no Donna. They roll out the jam with a warm, bouncy feel. Jerry starts to bend notes in a mischievous manner. The music becomes thicker in steady waves. And then Jerry finds that improbable lick zone as he did during the 11-11-73 "Mag." The sound of his guitar is the defining characteristic of these versions. Garcia's pathway to ecstasy is more playful here: repetitive licks, speed-picking intensity, and redirection. The canvas is full, and the band frames it with a quick chord progression. Amazing artistry! Weir's vocals are fine during "Sunshine Daydream."

8-6-74 Roosevelt Stadium, Jersey City, NJ: This is an understated gem, rich in ambiance and texture. The band pumps out a solid groove, and Garcia opens with sophisticated runs as he seems to revel in the warmth of the Wall of Sound. Everything's lined up for a mighty outburst like on 11-11-73. However, Jerry works up a unique chord progression, a shuffling staccato pattern that mesmerizes—a reggae-like plinko/planko stream. And when Jerry strikes gold, he knows how to milk it.

The ending of this jam is glorious, and perhaps the most danceable thing I've ever heard. Jerry was still in pretty good shape these days and I'm sure he had to be hopping and bopping as he played this. The band skillfully latches onto this moment. Usually "Sugar Mag" comes off as a definitive rock and roll statement. On this occasion, the Dead tap into the pure pleasure of the rhythm minus the aggression.

12-31-72 Winterland Ballroom, San Francisco, CA: It's New Year's Eve '72 and the Grateful Dead are on top of the world. Weir thanks Bill Graham, and then announces that they will play Bill's favorite song. This "Sugar Magnolia" follows a wild Truckin' > Other > Morning Dew. The Dead harness their creativity and rock the Winterland in wonderful waves. These are good times, and they thank Uncle Bill with a version that surpasses previous time barriers. Garcia spearheads the advance, noodling incrementally heated passages as the band plunders and pounds. There's a stop-and-go flow to this charming presentation. It's another notch of "Sugar Magnolia" immortality on the Winterland belt.

6-25-85 Blossom Music Center, Cuyahoga Falls, OH: Sometimes a sensational "Sugar Magnolia" can be a show's salvation, as it was on this occasion. This was a fine show that rocketed out of the gate with Day Tripper > West LA Fadeaway. Out of a calm "China Doll" outro, Garcia slams down on the "Sugar Mag" chord and everybody is psyched—a dance-off finale to celebrate the Grateful Dead's twentieth anniversary on this summer tour.

When the band's on stride with "Sugar Mag," the outcome seems predetermined. The jam on this version is relentless. It starts in overdrive and explodes through the sky. Garcia's en fuego as the band storms through phases until they reach the highest ground. During this jam, my taper friend placed duct tape across my lips just in case I had an uncontrollable outburst that might ruin the audio integrity of the recording. I think he sealed his own mouth shut as well. It was that hot. Weir kept his cool with a subtle "Sunshine Daydream."

10-15-77 Moody Coliseum, SMU, Dallas, TX: One of the Grateful Dead's strongest attributes was their ability to latch onto an infectious groove and let it roll. The rhythmic pleasures of "Sugar Magnolia" are irrefutable—it instantly set bodies in motion and put a collective smile on the audience. On this occasion in Moody Coliseum, the "Sugar Magnolia" beat is bouncy and joyous—nobody wants to leave the warm comfort of the womb. The Boys rock out over three minutes of happy time before Weir sings the opening line. I'm sure nobody would have complained or ceased to dance if the intro lasted an hour.

After a pleasant stroll through the lyrics, the final jam smokes. Phil's blasts rattle Mustang country. But it's the leisurely intro that makes this version elite.

7-4-81 Manor Downs, Austin, Texas: This is a song of celebration, and Austin, Texas, experienced a lethal "Magnolia" dosing on Independence Day. Garcia shreds early, inspiring Weir to turn up his guitar to show off his rhythmic abilities. Picking up on the escalating competition, Lesh bombs away, running commentary on the dueling guitarists. Weir's strumming is awesome throughout as he forces Jerry to outmaneuver him. Garcia gets in the final blows on this "Mag," blurry fingers scurrying on the bottom of his fretboard—frantic, celebratory sound. The clashing sonic surge makes this "Mag" special. Weir closes out this Saturday night set by singing, "Hey, another Fourth of July."

MORNING DEW

In 1961, as the Cold War between the Soviet Union and the United States intensified, Canadian folksinger Bonnie Dobson wrote "Morning Dew," a post-apocalyptic conversation between a man and a woman. "Morning Dew" captured the fear of the times as Dylan would do with "A Hard Rain's A-Gonna Fall" a year later. "Hard Rain" is a lyrical masterpiece from the poet laureate of his generation. Dobson's shorter iconic anthem cuts to the bone, yet it packs a similar emotional punch, making it a great song to improvise on. "Morning Dew" was covered by many, including Jeff Beck, the Allman Brothers Band, and Robert Plant. But it was the Grateful Dead who brought "Morning Dew" to the next level, turning it into a near-religious experience and the holy grail of their performing repertoire.

Those at the Human Be-in in Golden Gate Park's Polo Field heard a "Morning Dew" born on January 14, 1967. It's an outstanding first performance with an impressive ending jam, and a much better version than the studio track from the band's eponymous debut album. "Morning Dew" magnified Garcia's talents and his musical vision. He took a deeply moving song and extended it by slowing the tempo and summoning deep emotion as he sang. This made the explosive instrumentals more dramatic as they spiraled to climax. There are many outstanding versions, from the Polo Field debut through the last version of 1971 on August 6 in the Hollywood Bowl. If the Dead never played another "Dew," it had secured its place as a legendary jam anthem. But the best was yet to come for "Morning Dew."

After not playing "Morning Dew" for fifty-nine shows, the Dead returned Dobson's beloved song to the rotation at the start of set two in Rotterdam on 5-11-72. This was Keith's first "Morning Dew," and his solemn piano playing imbued the "Dew" with deeper emotional character. The song now had an element of transcendence and royalty that was displayed on the performance captured for *Europe '72* in London on May 26.

"Morning Dews" from '73 and '74 consistently delivered magnificence. The band had to be in the right mood, and the timing had to be right. This wasn't the type of song that could be played on an off night, or if the vibe from the crowd was off. The last "Dew" of '74 from the Winterland was captured in the *Grateful Dead* movie. The year I saw my first two Grateful Dead shows, I must have seen this movie a dozen times at various midnight matinees and at the Student Activity Lounge at Rockland Community College. When the time came for "Morning Dew," my friends and I would spring to our feet and swoon and sway in reverence as if this were our national anthem. Seeing the "Dew" was a religious experience, and I hungered to see my first one.

There was a "Dew" drought when the band returned to touring in 1976 until it was played at Duke's Cameron Indoor Stadium on September 23. There were five spectacular "Dews" played in 1977 (six if you count the version from 12-31-76, which technically was played in '77). The "Morning Dew" from 5-8-77 is the most revered and popular version of this anthem, and it's hard to argue against that perspective, although a nice list of candidates is up there with 5-8-77.

After an epic "Dew" in the Winterland on 6-7-77, it wasn't played again until 4-15-78 at William and Mary College—ghosts of "Dews" past. The Dead performed a superior "Morning Dew" in William and Mary on 9-11-73. The "Dew" was only played once in both '78 and '79, and four times in 1980.

Everything materialized perfectly on the night I saw my first "Morning Dew" in the Philadelphia Spectrum on April 6,

1982. On that night, they played the four songs I wanted to hear: "Shakedown Street," "Terrapin Station," "Morning Dew," and "Sugar Magnolia." It was the only time in the band's history those four songs were played together in the same show.

The other three tunes were exciting, but experiencing "The Dew" was surreal ecstasy. However, this life-changing "Dew" doesn't qualify as an all-time great. The '82 "Dews" aren't overwhelming. The jams picked up steam in '83 and peaked on the spring '84 tour. Jerry appeared gravely ill at the time, but he channeled everything he had into the "Dews" from that year.

The next "Dew" resurgence came after the coma. Jerry had survived and the Dead were thriving. "Morning Dew" no longer seemed like an apocalyptical anthem as much as it sounded like a song of survival from a beloved legend who, in the eyes of the faithful, had taken on deity status. The emotional outpouring from Deadheads packed into large sports venues spurred Jerry to dig deep when singing "The Dew." Perhaps the greatest interaction between Jerry and the audience happened on 9-18-87, when "Morning Dew" was played in Madison Square Garden. The revered anthem remained in the rotation and delivered chilling thrills almost every time it was played.

9-2-80 War Memorial Auditorium, Rochester, NY: Bedlam erupts in the War Memorial as a rare "Iko Iko" segues into "Morning Dew." This is one period in Dead history when the "Dew" was truly a scarce commodity. The entire show was building to this moment, although nothing was predetermined. Garcia sang each line as if it were Holy Scripture, and his voice could heal and comfort the survivors of apocalyptical tragedies. Bobby's striking rhythm, Phil's bass bridges, and Brent's solemn organ-grinding all fall into place. Jerry only belts out: "I guess it doesn't matter anyway," twice. The last one is as heartfelt as any he has ever sung. The emotional control, temperature, and texture of this performance makes this one of the most gripping "Dews" to listen to.

All ears are on Jerry as he pinches his guitar strings to produce the sound of a lonely robin singing, and Weir strikes a chord that finishes one of Jerry's thoughts—the group mind flourishes. The band knows where Jerry's going and exactly what needs to be done, even though this is a unique improvisation. Garcia's runs are delivered with maximum feeling as they maintain a mathematical quality. The escalating tension is almost unbearable as the band rises to the crescendo. Garcia unleashes a wild torrent of speed licks as the band rolls into chord-fanning mode and then Jerry joins the thundering madness, which ends with a mighty bass blast and a final "Guess it doesn't matter anyway" blessing from Reverend Garcia. There's something about this "Dew." Every note, lick, and vocal embellishment is perfectly pitched with precise emotion—silence and thunder balanced. This scores a perfect ten on the "Dew" scale. Other "Dews" might be hotter in spots, but the totality of the Rochester "Dew" makes it supreme.

9-10-74 Alexandria Palace, London, England: Of all the elite versions, this one from *Dick's Picks Vol. 7* is the most underrated. The London "Dew" rises solemnly out of "Dark Star," the next-to-last time these two anthems would hook up. The hypnotic crawl is redirected by a beguiling solo that wobbles and trembles. Weir's fine strumming stands out against Garcia's barrage. It's a conversation they will pick up in the next jam.

Heading into the big jam, Keith's electric piano playing sets the stage like heavy humidity before a thunderstorm. Garcia's early leads are authoritative and patient. The waves of escalation are remarkable as Billy the drummer orchestrates. Jerry turns up the heat (he's always messing with the thermostat). As the lava flows, Weir's on fire and inspiring Garcia to the next plateau. It sounds like dueling lead guitarists as Bobby challenges Jerry with rapid chord strumming. Garcia accepts the invitation and obliterates what's possible at the speed of sound. My mind is boggled by this showdown. It's the best Weir/Garcia guitar moment side by side. And then this monster "Dew" bounces and pounds to climax. If any jam could sonically simulate an atomic explosion, this is it. This is the most exhilarating instrumental in any "Dew," but by a hair, the overall presentation ranks second behind Rochester.

5-8-77 Barton Hall, Cornell University, Ithaca, NY: After a drum detour, Jerry's purposeful noodling leads back to a "St. Stephen" reprise. Jerry, Bobby, and Donna harmonize the immortal final lines: "Can you answer? Yes I can. But what would be the answer to the answer man?" Garcia strikes the holy chord signaling "Morning Dew." Barton Hall erupts into pandemonium as lucky Deadheads experience the only St. Stephen > Morning Dew the band would ever play—a distinguishing characteristic that hurls Cornell towards instant immortality.

This "Dew" is emotionally and artistically intense. Jerry's first solo is subtle, as if he knows the mayhem that will be released later. After singing, "I guess it doesn't matter anyway," Garcia offers shrill lead guitar as the band restlessly thumps behind him. What ensues is perhaps the finest group effort in Grateful Dead history.

As the instrumental escalates, there are six Garcias in sync. It's an all-out blitz—scientifically precise, yet wild—an earthquake of a performance that's tough to comprehend. Jerry cries out a final, "I guess it doesn't matter anyway!" Framing the magnificence of "The Dew," the Dead end the set. And then, they come back for an anticlimactic "One More Saturday Night" encore.

12-31-76 Cow Palace, Daly City, CA: As an instrumental "NFA" fanfare rings out, Phil hits the unmistakable blast announcing "Morning Dew." "Walk me out in the morning dew, my honey." Jerry's voice covers the Cow Palace like a velvet blanket. The patient devotion of the band is admirable bordering on heroic. At the end of a marathon set, the band digs in and commits to each note with heart and soul. Keith's piano playing sets the sacred tone. They say it takes ten years to truly master your craft, and perhaps that explains how brilliant this "Dew" and the ensuing '77 versions sound.

This Cow Palace "Dew" offers a steady barrage of unrelenting magic that places it in the pantheon of killer "Dews." This must be the longest "Dew" jam as Garcia taps into all his creative genius and the band reads his thoughts.

Jerry scurries along, slicing and dicing like a hibachi chef. If you like lobster meat, that's what Chez Garcia's serving.

As the jam boils, Cow Palace is enchanted, engaged, and fully under The Dead's spell. Jerry concludes the ceremony with a final sigh, "I guess it doesn't matter anyway," and the set is closed with a thunderous instrumental exclamation point. The one thing that this "Dew" is missing is an incredible closing crescendo like Cornell. Yet the Cow Palace "Dew" is exceptional. And like Cornell, this "Dew" closes an immortal set.

9-11-73 William and Mary College Hall, Williamsburg, VA: For the most part, the William and Mary "Dark Star" is a delightfully understated journey, atmospheric and embracing. Seventeen minutes pass before the first verse. Phil takes command of the next jam, and early on I hear hints of "The Dew." As Phil carpet-bombs Williamsburg, the rest of the band seemingly cowers in fear and prepares for the inevitable. This bass-driven jam is as much a "Morning Dew" prelude as it is a continuation of "Dark Star." William and Mary College, the second-oldest American institution of higher education, founded in 1693, is about to experience an aural sensation and molecular transformation that can't be explained in any lecture hall.

The musical terrain has been eviscerated, and out of the rumbling ruins of Phil's bass, "Morning Dew" is born. Jerry's solemn voice sings respectfully, as if he's comforting survivors. It's eerie, and ultimately moving as Garcia connects with the spirit of the lyrics. Suspense is born out of the stillness of this version.

Keith and Jerry carefully walk out in the morning dew to Phil's sobbing bass. Garcia's emotional playing comes through in soft, rolling waves. The band's executing in conjunction with their leader, and the music swirls and intensifies naturally—the laws of physics are in play. Yet, the thickness of the bass and the temperature and velocity of these guitar notes can't be charted. As the shit's about to hit the fan, the soundboard recording cuts out, as if it couldn't handle the heat. Luckily, a Deadhead is out there making a decent audience recording, and this is wonderfully spliced in—not one note is lost. Garcia's guitar runs squeal like sirens and then he pulls back as Keith bangs away and thunderous bass clears the way for the final run. Jerry's chord-fanning sequence climbs the high-frequency ladder faster and faster, with Weir matching him in a lower register every step of the way until the last witness sighs, "I guess it doesn't matter anyway."

6-7-77 Winterland Arena, San Francisco, CA: "Terrapin Station" winds down and rolls into the holy grail, "Morning Dew." This is the last "Dew" of '77, and it's the final Terrapin > Dew ever. Garcia's not messing around as he shreds the mid-song solo—kinetic energy compressed in a succession of shrill notes. Billy, Mickey, and Phil simulate a musical heart attack, pumping away as they keep pace with Garcia. It's the best opening solo of the '77 "Dews." Great versions have distinguishing characteristics, and another tell-tale sign of the 6-7-77 "Dew" is that Jerry only sings "I guess it doesn't matter anyway" once before the ballistic ending. Jerry's calling the shots and escalating the urgency of the jam. It's as inspired as it is technically flawless. In rolling climax mode, the band chases Jerry in unified bursts. It's a brilliant "Dew" all the way, and it challenges the Cornell version for '77 supremacy and bragging rights.

9-18-87 Madison Square Garden, New York, NY: I was there. "Watchtower" fizzled into a few seconds of no man's land. If the next song was "Black Peter," "Stella Blue," or "Wharf Rat," it would have been a letdown. The moment demanded immortality. Garcia had no path but the "Dew," and he bent a warning note before striking into the sanctified anthem.

To be in the thick of that audience and to experience the collective ecstasy is the realization of the ultimate power of music, which is beyond anything from any other realm. It was as if New York was healing Garcia, and Jerry had just announced that everyone had a winning lottery ticket. These were deeply emotional times in the Grateful Dead universe. Garcia was in the thick of his first MSG stand since the coma, "Touch of Grey" had just cracked the top ten of the Billboard pop charts giving the Dead their first hit single, and this was the first All Along the Watchtower > Morning Dew.

Jerry sings soulfully and spiritually, bestowing "The Dew" upon his devotees like a soothing prayer. This is where the enthusiastic wisdom of New York Deadheads factors in. They know every nuance of the song and treat it like a religious anthem, only expressing their joy in response to their spiritual leader. You can hear a pin drop as Jerry growls, "Where have all the people gawwwwn TODAY!" And then the silence is parted by the unified roar of his flock. "Morning Dew" was more moving than ever before for both the singer and the audience in the aftermath of Garcia's comeback from a near-death experience.

Phil's bass rattles the arena as Garcia leans forward and shreds a screeching solo between verses. Singing from the heart of humanity, Jerry croons: "I guess it doesn't matter anyway," four times, each cry more sorrowful than the last and each ensuing eruption from the audience louder. Madison Square Garden is shaking from the last roar as it never has before. It is as if a Knick just hit a three-pointer at the buzzer to win the NBA Championship.

Usually Garcia builds his "Dew" solo deliberately, but due to the overwhelming emotional explosion, he goes for the jugular—down on the lower part of the fretboard, a blizzard of notes. Standing there fifteen rows from Jerry was surreal. To make sure I wasn't dreaming, I bent over and slapped the cement floor with the palm of my hand three times.

How is Garcia going to execute and extend this jam when he started with a climactic tirade? Simple. He invents pathways. At one point he makes a circular motion with his hand, as if he's waving a magic wand, and then seemingly discovers a frequency that never existed before, hitting the highest possible notes on the fretboard and peeling them off with speed and precision before the band joins in for the final fanning blitz. The Garden explodes again as Garcia croons the last line. Heroic!

10-12-84 Augusta Civic Center, ME: Coming out of Space, the noodling sounds like a return to "Playin' in the Band," even though the song hasn't been started. The theme swirls around in preparation for the blastoff into what will be the first standalone "Playin'" reprise. The band pounds an authoritative charge to the final chorus . . . or the opening verse, on this occasion. Jerry and Bobby tee off as "Playin'" rampages to its next destination, an "Uncle John's" reprise. Temperatures rise in the Augusta Civic Center as the music surges to the great sing-and-clap-along: "Whoa oh what I want to know oh oh, is how does the song go?" The place is electrified, and as everybody's singing "Come hear Uncle John's Band" I'm thinking, *Here comes "The Dew"!*

"Morning Dew" was inevitable and unprecedented in this sequencing. Uncle John's > Dew had happened before in '73 and '74 in the center of a few "Playin'" loops. Those were crafted masterpieces. Augusta was the ultimate in on-the-fly improvisational execution. The rush of the Playin' > Uncle John's reprises dramatically frames the moment. This would be the only "Dew" of the tour, and Garcia sings it with deep emotion, overcoming any vocal limitations brought on by decades of smoking anything that wasn't nailed down. Phil rattles the Augusta Civic Center repeatedly, opening up the pathway for a rousing between-verse instrumental.

The final journey commences with sweet-and-sour Jerry—thick, juicy notes. The band has control of the tempo as Jerry shifts the creative flow. As the jam accelerates, there's a series of high-frequency guitar leads that are searing and soothing at the same time. The crowd's roaring in steady waves, and Phil's bombs set the pace like a timekeeper ringing a bell. Garcia's playing has legs as the band rises through the crescendo. Garcia sighs, "I guess it doesn't matter anyway," and as they did in Cornell and the Cow Palace, they lay their instruments down. "The Dew" said it all.

9-21-72 The Spectrum, Philadelphia, PA: Towards the end of a wild "Dark Star" ride, the Dead rise into a jam that loosely resembles "Feelin' Groovy" and for the next five minutes, they ride an intergalactic trail. This is September 21, 1972, and the show must go on, so the band nonchalantly tumbles into "Morning Dew."

It's a concert once again as Jerry's soulful singing stirs deep emotion alongside his mates' astute playing. The band is relaxed and bold as they play in one of the major East Coast sports venues as the main event for the first time. The final "Dew" jam is a steaming wave of cascading heat—pure aural paradise and the best version of the year. This is a D Star > Dew for the ages, and the second set has only reached the halfway point.

4-26-84 Providence Civic Center, RI: This was the third "Dew" of this Northeast tour, making it almost anticlimactic, if that's possible, and it materialized after Space. Jerry's shredded voice struggles all the way through. It's painful to listen to, and it's hard to imagine how Jerry rallied this to pure ecstasy. A sad yet energetic tone emerges as the jam takes flight. The screeching licks materialize like lightning. As if Jerry understands the fragility of his own mortality, he digs in to give it his all. Every segment is more exciting than the last, and this performance is heroic. Jerry scales all emotional barriers, and his stunned mates keep the wheels turning. All the pain is released in this cathartic outburst. This is in my top three "Dew" jams, and if the rest of this version was worthwhile, it would rank much higher.

6-24-83 Dance County Coliseum, Madison, WI: On the other side of Drums, the "Truckin'" jam peaks and casually unwinds into "Morning Dew." Everything is as it should be. Madison's going nuts, Phil's blasts rock the coliseum, and the first solo sets the table for a dramatic final jam that's as unique as it is long.

The expedition starts deliberately. Tension builds as Phil's bass shakes the foundation underneath Brent's swirling chords. Usually Jerry goes for the emotional jugular at this point, but as the cyclone spins, he pauses to let Brent lead him to another plateau. The band is all ears as Jerry lets Brent set him up for guitar strikes that are fiercer with each round. Garcia masterfully extends the funnel cloud portion of the jam as he juggles intensity and creativity. It's an exhaustive performance, and the best "Dew" of 1983.

7-10-89 Giants Stadium, East Rutherford, NJ: The Neville Brothers joined the Dead during Drums. An adventurous "All Along the Watchtower" that veers between rock, jazz, and anarchy follows "Iko Iko." Out of nowhere, the Dead are on the verge of salvaging an uneventful evening. The Neville Brothers provide the impetus, and the Dead are eager to show them what it's like to stop time in its tracks in a football stadium with 80,000 witnesses as they ring the bell for "Morning Dew."

When the Dead played the first Watchtower > Dew in Madison Square Garden on 9-18-87, it was the most thrilling live moment of my years following the Dead. The next one I saw at Oxford, Maine, on 7-2-88, was almost anticlimactic. Seeing the "Dew" was always colossal, but in the late '80s, this once rare anthem had become commonplace.

Garcia's vocals are engaging on the 7-10-89 "Dew." The middle solo rises like a tsunami and folds back into Giants Stadium. Garcia finishes the last verse and shrieks: "I guess it doesn't matter anyway!" four times. What happened next was absolutely brilliant—the last mind-blowing solo I'd hear from Jerry (I only saw four more shows in the '90s).

The majestic jam emerges with frisky licks that cascade through the swampy Jersey night. At the 9:10 mark, Jerry strikes a chord that rings out as if he's punching a time clock. The creative direction of the solo changes as Garcia's fingers scramble through scales, east and west, north and south, and then he retraces his footprints in reverse. It's a stunning sequence, unlike anything in any other "Dew."

Garcia easily slides into the climactic crescendo, but the musicians are a step behind. Perhaps they were induced into a trance by the Bearded One's virtuosity. As Garcia rams this across the finish line with rapid chord fanning, I envisioned myself paying my taper friend a visit the following day to dub a copy of the show. I knew that this was a moment I'd cherish. Since 7-10-89, I've listened to this solo at least 1,000 times.

CHINA CAT SUNFLOWER > I KNOW YOU RIDER

C hina Cat Sunflower," a trippy studio track off *Aoxomoxoa*, might have slipped into obscurity if it had not connected with "I Know You Rider." The "Cat" was performed live for the first time in the Carousel Ballroom on January 17, 1968. The Dead stopped playing "China Cat" after March, and then it reappeared in the rotation in early 1969, around the time it was recorded for *Aoxomoxoa* in the studio. The fortunes of "China Cat Sunflower" changed when it segued into "I Know You Rider" on 9-30-69 in Café au Go Go, New York. "I Know You Rider" was a traditional arrangement the Dead rocked in 1966, but it fell out of the rotation until this fateful night in New York. Listening to this ragged debut, it's hard to imagine that the band had just struck gold. China Cat > Rider would become the most played combination in Dead history.

More than any other song, I think "China Cat" is a barometer for whether someone is, or could be, a Deadhead. Tunes like "Touch of Grey," "Sugar Magnolia," and "Ripple" can be enjoyed by a wide audience of music fans who will never become Deadheads. If somebody loves "China Cat," they understand and appreciate the sophisticated nuances of the Dead's artistic approach. From the mysterious lyrics, to the funky beat, to the exotic music that's a mix of jazz, blues, and rock served in the Grateful Dead's secret sauce, those who are moved by "China Cat" are likely to embrace the band's experimental ways. Garcia said, "We're like licorice. Not everybody likes licorice, but the people who like licorice really like licorice." "China Cat" is the song that best represents licorice in this equation.

The unlikely pairing of China Cat > Rider ended up making perfect sense. After the Dead take you *out there* with the pleasurable weirdness of "Cat," they ground you in the charging certainty of "Rider." The inevitability of "Rider" enhances "Cat." No matter where "Cat" roams, there's a breadcrumb trail that leads to "Rider." And what a powerful celebration "Rider" is in the aftermath of "Cat." After uniting for the first time on 9-30-69, there were only two times "Cat" was separated from "Rider": 3-9-85 China Cat > Cumberland Blues, and 7-29-88 China Cat > Crazy Fingers.

Cat > Rider maintained a rambunctious/psychedelic vibe as the band played it fifty-five times in 1970. By the time the Dead headed to Europe with Keith Godchaux in '72, "China Cat" was a polished jewel. The transitions within were crisp as the music radiated with an exotic jazzy vibe. "China Cat" stepped into its prime halfway through '73 and blew the minds of Deadheads as it rang out from the Wall of Sound in '74. After the "Cat" crescendo, the group added a segment known as the "Feelin' Groovy" jam. The addition of this segment made the "Cat" jam epic, and it made for a sweet transition into "Rider." For me, "Rider" doesn't start until the band clearly lays down the rhythm for "Rider" and the band sings the opening chorus.

China Cat > I Know You Rider was played on October 20, 1974, at the final show of the Winterland run. When the Dead returned to touring in 1976, Cat > Rider was nowhere to be found until they broke it out in the Winterland on 12-29-77. There was much rejoicing on that night, but the "Feelin' Groovy" jam was scrapped, and "Cat" lacked the mojo and length of a '74 version. The "Cat" went into hibernation again until it returned to the rotation to stay in 1979.

Although it's best known for kicking off set two, Cat > Rider appeared in various spots upon its return, and in the fall of '79, it opened up three shows. Although "Cat" would rarely approach its '74 heights, "Rider" raged, better than ever, in the early '80s as Weir (*The sun will shine in my backdoor someday*) and Garcia (*I wish I was a headlight on a northbound train*) sang their signature lines with conviction. "China Cat" could always whip the crowd into a frenzy, and that was part of the problem in later years. The crowd would go bonkers in these large stadiums and arenas as soon as Garcia ripped the "Cat" crescendo, and that usually meant a quick transition into "Rider." Regardless, it was still one of the Dead's prime-time jam anthems in their final years.

6-16-74 State Fairgrounds, Des Moines, IA: This "Cat" supreme arises late in the first set after "Jack Straw." The jam leading to "Rider" scorches—indisputably one of the best. The pristine soundboard recording makes it all the more enjoyable. You can marvel in what the musicians are doing individually and collectively through the Wall of Sound. Sonic brilliance and terrifying energy are unleashed hand in hand. Guitars growl and grind against jackhammer bass patterns as Billy's drumming blends jazz and rock, propelling the jam forward and filling up the soundscape.

There's a unique urgency to this instrumental as it evolves through a series of rolling peaks. The music swells and contracts. At points, it's almost out of control as it threatens to break free from the "China Cat" framework. This jam stops you in your tracks and demands your attention; it's impossible to listen to it passively as background music. Garcia's on the rampage as the band skids off the "Feelin' Groovy" exit ramp. Hide the women and children and run for shelter. This "Cat" leaves burn marks. On this occasion, a quality version of "Rider" is anti-climactic. The Dead always shred in Iowa.

6-26-74 Providence Civic Center, RI: After "U.S. Blues" and "Me and My Uncle" start set two, a jam emerges, and out of that jam the Dead pounce on "China Cat." The quirky hook of the infectious melody takes hold of the band for four minutes before Jerry starts to sing: "Look for a while at the China Cat Sunflower, proud-walking jingle in the midnight sun." That instrumental is a precious gift—a swirling, aural painting dripping with bright colors and exquisite taste. No other "Cat" is blessed with this type of regal introduction.

As the band moves through the verses of "China Cat," Phil's efforts are extraordinary. He's playing lead bass and supporting the band's direction at the same time. A typically great '74 Cat > Rider continues with all the necessary ingredients: fanfare > Feelin' Groovy > smokin' Rider. This isn't as hot as Des Moines, but that transcendent intro makes the Providence "Cat" one for the ages.

3-9-81 Madison Square Garden, NY: This 1981 China Cat > Rider is up there with the best of '74. Confession: 3-9-81 is dear to me because it was my first show. Regardless, this pairing to open set two is remarkable. As "Cat" opens, Garcia's guitar has a sharp tone, which Brent effectively mimics on organ. During the longer of the brief between-verse solos, Garcia hits a jarring change of direction note, and on my favorite audio recording of this show, a young lady lets out an orgasmic scream. Sure, this has nothing to do with the majesty of the performance, but sometimes crowd participation can enhance our listening experience.

This is the first of a two-night MSG stand that features some of the Dead's most sophisticated playing of the decade. Brent and Jerry free-flow creatively to an early fanfare. The playing is relaxed yet fiery as Garcia's leads regenerate and bubble to the next plateau. In the shuffling madness of New York City, Garcia and the Boys are in the lab, weaving a psychedelic potion on a leisurely timetable. There's an indirect approach into the next "Cat" fanfare, which lets off more steam than its predecessor. Thanks to some additional fiddle-faddle, this "Cat" extends for ten minutes prior to the start of "Rider." Many '74 "Cats" with the "Feelin' Groovy" jams aren't as long. It's easy to simply extend the length of a jam, but the way the Dead layer and weave this unique improvisation together baffles the mind.

"I Know You Rider" rocks hard. Weir jumps the gun and emphatically belts out the "Sun gonna shine" line verse prior to the first ripping solo. The Garden rumbles and roars as Jerry serenades the "Headlight" verse. The band doubles down with another grinding and growling jam.

When "Rider" was fully explored in the '80s, it had more presence than versions from the previous decade. This is a powerhouse Cat > Rider all the way through, although I was too much of a novice to fully appreciate it in the moment.

8-5-74 Philadelphia Civic Center, PA: Phil peppers and pounds incredible bass through the Wall of Sound. A feisty Philly vibe consumes Jerry's leads. Some of Weir's finest guitar work is from the "Cats" of this era, and 8-5-74 is no exception. The jamming is very festive; I imagine a lot of swinging, spinning, and chaotic dancing in Philly that night. It's a very fluid and smooth instrumental, even as Garcia fights off the notion of heading towards "Feelin' Groovy" too soon. When the going gets "Groovy," the band fires away in unison. At the 9:45 mark, the transition to "Rider" is complete. A robust "Rider" concludes another extraordinary '74 "Cat" combo.

11-11-73 Winterland Ballroom, San Francisco, CA: Even in a band that attempts to consistently alter their sound, a certain amount of familiarity sets in. Garcia attacks this "Cat" as if he's painting on a fresh canvas. His guitar strings ring in a fetching manner. Perhaps Jerry's banjo playing for *Old and In the Way* (1973) helped him vary his approach. He also recently started playing the Wolf guitar. Anyway, there's a pleasing attentiveness to all the nooks and crannies inside the short jams, as well as the big one. Billy's drumming guides and inspires the band as they move from scene to scene. Jerry peels off some quick licks after the "Cat" fanfare, and then fixates on a tasty lead that he repeats three times before the band slips into "Feelin' Groovy." It's a gorgeous performance that unfolds organically—the audience is awed. A smooth "Rider" closes this presentation, yet there's still another half-hour of music left in the opening set—the joys of '73.

10-12-81 Olympia Halle, Munich, Germany: After the "Cat" verses are sung, Garcia's off to the races as his guitar hisses, snarls, and purrs all the way through the jamming fanfare. The velocity of the music is off the charts. Brent's fluid playing facilitates a swirling, psychedelic ambiance. Too many of the best "Cats" from this decade have a very satisfying rush to the signature instrumental fanfare before ducking hastily into

"Rider." This Munich version is a different tale. Garcia keeps pecking away until a second fanfare is regenerated. And then Jerry stamps this wonderful version with some thoughtful noodling. Two scorching "Rider" instrumentals cap off a rousing twelve-song opening set in Munich.

8-7-82 Alpine Valley Music Theatre, East Troy, WI: On a beautiful summer's eve in the Midwest, set two opens with the confident "China Cat" strut—Jerry's thick opening riffs cushioned by organ mounds of Brent sound. Second-set "Cats" from this era have a patient vibe; it's the start of an adventure, as opposed to a closing statement when it was played at the end of set one.

Jerry's line of attack is focused. Expressive leads pour from his Tiger into the Alpine Valley night. This version is technically perfect, one of several fine performances from this show, which is immortalized on Vol. 32 of the Dick's Picks series. The extracurricular activity makes this a standout Cat > Rider. The band is slowly heading toward "Rider," but Jerry is having "Cat" flashbacks. We must be in segue paradise—the Dead are playing both songs at the same time. "Rider" stands tall all the way through.

DEAL

Played for the first time in Port Chester's Capitol Theatre on February 19, 1971, "Deal" instantly established itself as a crowd favorite. Through the first decade of its existence, "Deal" pleased the faithful with its ripping between-verse blues-based jam and sing-along ending. A timely arrival of "Deal" could easily energize a lackluster set. Primarily, it was a first-set song that could land in just about any slot. As consistent as it was, "Deal" never would have been one of the great jam anthems unless the structure and mission of the song was altered.

Prior to their acoustic/electric residencies in the Warfield and Radio City, the band rehearsed. During this time, they decided to add a second instrumental to "Deal." The Jerry Garcia Band had used this dual instrumental format earlier in the year. The Dead debuted the revamped "Deal" on 9-25-80 to end the first electric set in the Warfield. Of the 419 performances of "Deal," 180 of them would feature the double jam format.

The second instrumental started as a chord-driven acceleration; a pressure cooker as opposed to the lyrical pizazz of the first solo. A version of the new "Deal" was released on *Dead Set* (1981), the lame electric release from this Warfield/ Radio City run. I never pass on an opportunity to bash *Dead Set*.

The second "Deal" instrumental started out as a two-minute affair. By 1983, it had become a monster jam that often exceeded four minutes in length. Now Jerry had a first-set closer with a showstopping jam that could stand up to the likes of "Music Never Stopped" and "Let it Grow," match them blow for blow or lick for lick. Brent's organ playing helped Jerry redirect his solos and take them to new heights. "Deal" remained a set-ending barn burner, fixed in its majesty until the final deal went down.

10-17-83 Olympic Center, Lake Placid, NY: This building became an American shrine after 1980. The band and their devotees revel in that patriotic energy through the opening set. This "Deal" jam taps into the Olympic spirit. As I listen to this improvisation, I can envision ice skaters performing triple lutz and axel jumps to the sonic barrage. Garcia sends Deadhead nation airborne as the drummers and Phil push the pace. The relentless jam also has an aura of unhinged celebration: "Do you believe in miracles?" It sounds like the band has had enough around the eight-minute mark, but Garcia wants to impress the judges with his long program. The energy radiated by Garcia is surreal when one considers his subpar physical condition. The rhapsodic momentum of "Deal" sounds as if it's emanating from an extremely athletic band. The robust mound of sound from Brent's organ clears the way for Garcia's final foray. After ten minutes of card-shuffling madness, a gold medal opening set is history.

4-4-85 Providence Civic Center, RI: This "Deal" follows a blazing "Saint of Circumstance" and ends one of the best opening sets of 1985. There's a cocaine-crisp blast of excitement evident throughout the set. Jerry's missing lyrics left and right all night, but his ripping solos bring instant redemption. The between-verse "Deal" solo has extra sizzle in Providence, and then Jerry sings something that sounds like, "Since it cost…ham, and tightened up my shoes." None of this matters, because the band's on a rampage. From Jerry's opening licks, everything is sharp and combustible. Jerry lays out a short paragraph with a climactic conclusion, and then throws out a longer paragraph with another smoking exclamation point. Garcia makes a sharp left turn and picks up the narrative. The band blows the third section up like Mt. Fuji.

This is not a long "Deal," but the blowtorch effect is irresistible. The Dead craft a gripping version—every lick is crucial.

3-23-86 The Spectrum, Philadelphia, PA: March 23, 1986, was my 100th Grateful Dead show, and I knew it would be special, as if somehow, while onstage in the Philadelphia Spectrum, Garcia would pick up on this vibe and play something to commemorate the occasion.

To a thunderous roar they opened the show with "Gimme Some Lovin'" and stunned the delirious crowd with "Deal" in the second spot. During this decade, "Deal" was almost exclusively the last song of the first set. The crowd knows the band's every move and they voice unhinged excitement as Jerry triggers the big jam. When Garcia starts to peel off some screeching climactic notes, Deadheads hoot and holler. Now Garcia knows what this crowd likes and builds an increasingly emotional solo around that motif, and everyone in the Spectrum goes nuts. It's a remarkable performance, especially this early in the set, and those of us who cherish the tapes knew this was a thriller jam that we'd rewind many times.

3-27-83 Irvine Meadows Amphitheatre, Irvine, CA: This was the year "Deal" extended in length and ascended into the pantheon of essential jam anthems. This was the third show of 1983. The night before Irvine, the Dead ended the first set with a hot "Deal" in Las Vegas—a fitting choice for the Mecca of gambling. Apparently, what happens in Vegas doesn't always stay in Vegas. It was extremely rare that the Dead repeated a tune that had been in the rotation on successive nights in the '80s, but luckily, they closed the opening set with "Deal" on 3-27-83.

When a song gets played often through the years, the sung verses can become robotic, as the true exploration happens during the jam. But Jerry's singing is very attentive on this night and the band is playing it anew. Garcia steps into this jam with uplifting leads and his creative vision is expansive yet focused. Leads formulate smoothly, mathematically, and in a seemingly circular motion. After an impressive and long run, Garcia climbs that fleeting stairway to the stars, bending, squeezing, and holding climactic notes before releasing the tension with a reverse flurry. It's a jaw-dropping yet sly climax that's wildly imaginative. This was the best "Deal" up to this point in Dead history.

6-30-84 Sports and Music Center, Indianapolis, IN: "Deal" comes on the heels of Lost Sailor > Saint of Circumstance. There's nothing like an LSD combo to close a set. Lazy Lightning > Supplication > Deal produced psychedelic sparks as well. In Indy, Jerry sings "Deal" as if he's rediscovering the joys of gambling and risk-taking. The jam flies high—a massive collage of pulsating sound—relentless in its desire to please the most discriminating Deadheads. This version is as long as the one from Lake Placid, but not as overwhelming. There's great teamwork in Indy. Jerry gracefully whirls through scales as Phil's concussive bass and Brent's racing organ-grinding provide comfort. Billy and Mickey control and push the pace. There are many jammed-out versions from this era, and the 6-30-84 "Deal" hangs in with the best.

6-9-84 Cal Expo Amphitheater, Sacramento, CA: If this set were closed with "Might as Well" or "Don't Ease Me In," it would have been a forgettable seven-song presentation. "Deal" salvages what ends up being a fine set. A tight groove is established as the band maneuvers through "Deal." The band hammers the blues as Garcia rolls out a succession of ascending scales with aggressive efficiency. Phil's digging in as hard as Jerry, and it sounds like they're dueling. It's a stunning display of clashing virtuosity that can validate a grueling cross-country road trip to see the Dead.

After a generous and gripping exploration, the band moves towards a chord progression that will lead to the final "Don't you let that deal go down" chorus. Phil and Brent try to put the finishing touches on the jam, but Jerry, the Energizer Bunny on this night, undermines that effort with one more volley of fireworks. You must respect a ten-minute "Deal."

6-21-89 Shoreline Amphitheatre, Mountainview, CA: June 21 was the Summer Solstice, and Deadheads who couldn't make it to Mountainview were able to watch this show on pay-per-view TV. I was in my college town of New Paltz, hosting the party from my crash pad. I treated my guests to fish tacos, banana daiquiris, and psychedelic goodies. Bobby Weir was in short shorts and Jerry looked like the gray god of sumo wrestlers. Garcia looked reasonably healthy and played great all night long. A ten-minute "Deal" gloriously concludes the opening set.

Jerry's works up a touch of sweat as his devotees dance and spin wildly. Garcia's dealing as the band digs in. After several raucous rounds the band settles down, thinking Jer might be through. Forget about it. Our hero is relaxed and confident as he cuts loose with blistering leads again. There's another lull as Jerry prepares to dig in for more mayhem. The crowd is wiped out and ready for a break. After charging up the mountain three times, Jerry concedes, but not after rallying the band to a sprawling exclamation point after the last sing-along—nonchalant brilliance on the longest day of the year.

UNCLE JOHN'S BAND

As flexible a tune as the Dead ever performed live, "Uncle John's Band" served many roles, and it segued in and out of many songs as it remained a potent option in the band's live repertoire. After a pair of "UJB" instrumentals, the first version was played in the Fillmore West on December 4, 1969. An acoustic "Uncle John's Band" was recorded for *Workingman's Dead* in February 1970. Thanks to Hunter's sublime lyrics, a catchy composition, and fine group harmonizing, "Uncle John's Band" was one of the Grateful Dead's first songs to receive a decent amount of airplay on FM radio. The first acoustic version of "Uncle John's Band" was performed in the Fillmore East on February 13, 1970, and the last acoustic version was played later in the year in Port Chester's Capitol Theatre on November 8. When the Dead revived their acoustic act for a tour in 1980, "UJB" wasn't part of the reunion. It had been firmly established as a beloved jam anthem.

"Uncle John's Band" slowly stretched out as it became an electric favorite during its early years, and it often ended up in the encore slot. There were subtle variations in the length of the two instrumental passages. Several "Uncle John's" in the second half of 1972 smoked. The jams were bursting at the scams, and after putting "UJB" on the shelf for forty-seven shows in '73, the Dead thrilled the Dane County Coliseum with an "Uncle John's" encore on October 25. Four shows later in Evanston, Illinois, on the first day of November, the Dead unveiled this combo for the first time: Playin' in the Band > Uncle John's Band > Playin' in the Band. The hookup of these

"Band" tunes was inevitable. Call it destiny, although it was a liberal marriage.

Playin' > UJB would never get as steady as Scarlet > Fire or Estimated > Eyes, but they were always there for each other, ready and willing to jump into any loop or sandwich the band might be cooking. The "Uncle John's" from the '73–'74 era took on an air of royalty as the instrumentals expanded. The merging with "Playin'" opened up pathways for "UJB."

"Uncle John's Band" was one of several tunes temporarily dropped from the rotation when the Dead returned to touring in 1976. "UJB" returned as an encore for the magnificent New Year's Eve affair in the Cow Palace on 12-31-76. "Uncle John's Band" was a key ingredient in several legendary '77 shows. The last of twelve versions from this year was played in Tempe, Arizona, on October 6. Amazingly, tapes from this show don't exist. What happened? Where was Betty Cantor? Where were the tapers? There must have been a crack squad of super-security people patting Heads down that night in Tempe.

A strange thing happened after Tempe. "Uncle John's Band" was not played for 170 consecutive shows until it opened the second set on 12-26-79. As with the previous black holes in "UJB" history, the song returned stronger than ever. The 1979 New Year's Eve run ushered in a golden era for "Uncle John's." Just about every version from 1980 is a must-listen. The band raised the intensity level on the jams with frenzied chord riffing. It also maintained a mysterious elusiveness. You could never predict or pin down where or when it may appear in a show, although it was primarily a second-set tune. Despite it being performed 330 times, Jerry and Bobby usually found a way to butcher a line or two in "UJB." For the remainder of their touring days, the Dead never took "Uncle John's Band" for granted, yet they never overplayed it. *Dah-dah-dah-da-da-da...dah-dah-dah-da-da-dahhhh!*

5-19-77 Fox Theatre, Atlanta, GA: In the thick of set two, a legendary song loop commences with "Playin' in the Band." Garcia and crew are steering the ship around the moons of

Neptune when Jerry introduces a brief "Uncle John's Band" riff at the 8:30 mark. The jam continues to blossom and spark. The rest of the band is ready to jump on board the next time Garcia introduces the "Uncle John's" reprise eleven minutes in. To the amazement of Deadheads in Atlanta, they're hearing the familiar ending to "Uncle John's Band," and the song hasn't begun. The music stops on cue, and as if they've done this a million times before, Jerry, Bob, and Donna step to their respective mics and harmonize:

"Whoa oh what I want to know, oh, oh, is how does the song go?"

Instead of continuing on with the last chorus, they slam into the beginning of "Uncle John's" with stunning conviction. Oh, that's how the song goes! It's one of those absurdly thrilling moments that seemingly only the Grateful Dead could produce, as if they alone were the keepers of the mystical musical theatre playbook. Garcia rips the intro solo and the singing is gorgeous throughout. Both instrumental passages contain pleasing outbursts. There's additional noodling as "UJB" tumbles into Drums. The "Playin'" loop is closed with The Wheel > China Doll > Playin'. Despite this amazing UJB conquest, the band would never play it this way again.

12-26-79 Oakland Auditorium Arena, CA: After two years and 170 shows since it was last played, "Uncle John's Band" returns to open set two. Phil's bass is dominant during a graceful intro, and Brent sounds smooth on organ and vocals during his first "UJB." Garcia soars into the first solo and he may never return. Jerry rediscovers the joys of "UJB" jamming: *pickity-packity-pickity-packity-pooh*. Turn it up and take it higher and higher! After the longest first solo in "UJB" history, Jerry beautifully works his way back to the "It's the same story" verse.

It's off to the land of "UJB" bliss again as Jerry and mates crank out another inspired jam. The instrumental segues into "Estimated Prophet." On its own, this is a top-notch rendition. The rest of this set is filled with surprises and bold improvisation, but no reprise of the last "UJB" chorus. This development wouldn't be uncommon in future versions. As ecstatic Deadheads in Oakland are dancing to the "Shakedown Street" encore, the song's about to return to the last chorus but the band makes a sharp left turn and dashes to the "Uncle John's" reprise. The high-flying chord strumming and the final sing-along are sublime. It is a sensational surprise ending, and the beginning of a new era for "Uncle John's Band."

10-12-84 Augusta Civic Center, ME: This "Uncle John's Band" ignites one of the most impressive musical segments of 1984. You can watch a grainy video of this on YouTube. The bootlegger was filming from an area close to where I was enjoying the show. Videos like this help recreate that hazy vibe that makes you feel as if you are there. Jerry's dressed in black t-shirt and jeans and his long, frizzy, gray mane makes him look like a grizzly guitar god as he stands like a mountain and wails away. He may have been in abysmal health and stoned on Persian, but the virtuosity of his playing is breathtaking. He's not smiling or gesturing as he applies all his focus and energy in these two "UJB" solos.

The outro solo is one of the best, and longest that's part of any "UJB." After a finger-picking onslaught, the band ricochets a chord progression as if they're coming back to the final chorus, but Jerry takes this as a cue to step on the gas and blaze away. This jam transitions into a pre-Drums jam heavily influenced by the previous number. After Drums, Augusta catches a thrilling finale: Space > Playin' > UJB > Morning Dew. Any reprise always enhances the standing of any "Uncle John's Band," especially this monster presentation from Augusta.

12-1-73 Boston Music Hall, MA: Playin' > Uncle John's magic flourished right away from the first time they hooked up a month earlier. The Boston Music Hall "UJB" boils right out of the transition. It's impossible for a stand-alone "Uncle John's" to start this hot. The intro feeds directly off the "Playin'" mind melt. The audience is in awe, and so is the band as Garcia shreds tiger-like licks over the "UJB" theme. Like the opening of the 5-19-77 version, the playing is distinctive, and the band takes time to revel in the creative process. The singing and playing rolls along brilliantly, à la '73. And the segue back to "Playin'" is tasty. However, it's the magnificent intro that places this "UJB" in the elite stratosphere.

5-10-80 Hartford Civic Center, CT: Most 1980 "UJBs" contain jarring bursts of virtuosity from Jerry. This Hartford performance is solid yet unassuming until the final instrumental. Following keyboard sparks from Brent, Garcia goes off on a wild tangent—shrill leads seared and compressed. This shocking display is about ninety seconds in length and unlike anything in any "UJB." Then the jam rolls on in a more subdued fashion as Jerry pecks, pokes, and squawks for another three minutes before Drums.

8-6-74 Roosevelt Stadium, Jersey City, NJ: As I research for this project, my affection for this Roosevelt Stadium show continues to soar. Set two opens with a masterful performance of "Uncle John's Band." It's a joy to hear this anthem through the Wall of Sound. There's also a unique motif to Jerry's playing on 8-6-74 that sounds like brush strokes touching down on masterpieces in progress. It's mesmerizing to hear Phil and Jerry create individually as the music meshes harmoniously. As the final jam heads toward the chord ending sequence, Jerry takes a detour bound for euphoria. This is an impressive eleven-minute version, and another notch of greatness for 8-6-74.

9-27-72 Stanley Theater, Jersey City, NJ: It's hard to compare versions of "UJB" from this year because the musical arrangement rarely varied. The improvisational length was generally the same show to show. However, this version jumps out. The guitar solos go nuclear, and every aspect of this performance is perfect and compact, like this analysis.

7-4-86 Rich Stadium, Buffalo, NY: Selected from the heart, this "UJB" comes to us at the end of this trifecta, which was simulcast for Farm Aid: The Wheel > I Need a Miracle > Uncle John's Band. The Dead opened this second set with a rambunctious Cold Rain and Snow > Fire on the Mountain > Samson and Delilah, and the ensuing Farm Aid segment was an exercise in crisp perfection. Jerry was struggling with dehydration and an abscessed tooth, but his "Uncle John's" vocals were gorgeous. The band nailed every twist and turn of this performance. Petrified chord strumming leads to a shooting star solo from Jerry. The final "Come hear Uncle John's Band by the riverside" sing-along is as moving as any I've ever heard. After the Dead's next two shows in Washington, DC, Garcia fell ill and lapsed into the coma. The Buffalo "UJB" was the last noteworthy performance before Jerry's illness.

TRUCKIN'

For many classic rock fans listening to FM radio stations in the '70s, "Truckin'" was the song that came to represent the Grateful Dead, what they sounded like, and who they were. *What a long, strange trip it's been...Living on reds, vitamin C, and cocaine...Busted down on Bourbon Street.* And the easy shuffle of the song gave listeners the feel that this was a soft rock group that probably didn't jam like Hendrix, The Who, or Led Zeppelin. "Casey Jones," "Friend of the Devil," "Ripple," "Uncle John's Band," and the other Dead tunes that received limited FM airplay furthered a narrative of the Grateful Dead as being a band with a clever collection of tunes that unraveled a unique American experience. But as we know, live "Truckin'" is a different animal with climactic and fierce jamming that makes it a bona fide jam anthem.

"Truckin'" debuted on August 18, 1970, in the Fillmore West. This was the first of five acoustic performances of the song. Since the band recorded *American Beauty* around this time, it makes sense that "Truckin'," the iconic last track of the album, doesn't have the spiraling jam following the last verse. Besides, it wouldn't have matched the folksy flavor of *American Beauty*.

The Dead played their first electric "Truckin'" in the Winterland on 10-4-70. From its outset, electric "Truckin'" featured a powerful jam after the last chorus. As with other revered tunes, "Truckin'" exploded when overseas on the Europe '72 tour. In its early years, "Truckin'" vacillated between being a first- or second-set song and it occasionally opened a show, as it did on 4-28-71, the next-to-last show at the Fillmore East. Between '71 and '72, "Truckin'" was played 129 times.

By 1973, the Dead dropped the chorus reprise of "Truckin'" and made it a second-set gateway song. Its most common destination was "The Other One," but "Truckin'" segued into a variety of songs and free-form jams. As the Dead bid farewell to performing for a while, they played "Truckin'" in the Winterland on 10-19-74 (*Grateful Dead* movie version). They played it a year later in Golden Gate Park on 9-28-75 and then put "Truckin'" on the shelf for all of 1976, the only year it wasn't performed.

"Truckin'" made a grand return in front of 150,000 fans in Englishtown Raceway on 9-3-77. This performance and the ensuing '77 versions feature combustible jams. As the years rolled on, "Truckin'" primarily settled into an early post-Drums slot in the rotation. The compressed crescendo jam after the last verse was always thrilling, but somewhat predictable. However, on inspired nights, the jam took off; you could never tell. In the '80s, Weir changed a verse by singing, "Ever since she went and had her sex changed, all a friend could say is ain't it a shame," instead of the iconic, *Living on reds, vitamin C, and cocaine* line. On occasion, Weir signaled the start of "Truckin'" by blowing a whistle to indicate that the circus was back in town. The Grateful Dead's autobiographical anthem persevered through the years. "Truckin'" was performed 531 times.

7-18-72 Roosevelt Stadium, Jersey City, NJ: In the thick of a historic three-set performance, the Dead pair Truckin' > Dark Star for the first time. After a tipsy "Tennessee Jed" that gave Jersey City a taste of Old Weird America, Weir and company deliver "Truckin'" with attitude. Fresh off their European tour, the band flaunts their musical might. Following the last "Get back trucking on," chant, Weir howls, "Whewww!" Look out.

Roosevelt Stadium's reelin' and rockin' in the ragin' "Truckin'" jam as Keith and Jerry mess around with some call-and-response. Garcia's fixated on the simple pleasures of guitar playing, sinking his teeth into certain riffs and building them into powerful sequences using his repetitive lick-with-slight-variations motif against the band's jackhammer groove. Simultaneously, Garcia's conversing with himself, his bandmates, and the audience. Nobody could milk a hot lead like Jerry. After the chorus reprise, a bull-rush crescendo extends the madness. Suddenly, the energy disperses as the jam pivots towards "Dark Star." The energy and creativity of this "Truckin'" is unreal, the perfect jam to ignite an extraordinary "Dark Star."

9-3-77 Raceway Park, Englishtown, NJ: Out comes the whistle, and Weir gives it a blow to signify the first "Truckin'" in three years. For some of us tour veterans who saw "Truckin'" once every three gigs for ten years straight, it's hard to imagine the exhilaration of the "Truckin'" breakout, the first once since 9-28-75. Old-school Deadheads fondly embraced "Truckin'" as a gateway song to long, mind-bending jams, and the new wave of fans embraced this as the quintessential song from *Skeletons in the Closet*. And for historical purposes, the return of "Truckin'" was another notch of distinction for a show that was an instant classic. Weir's in all his glory as he sings the chorus in a falsetto voice, much to the delight of the roaring faithful. The instrumental fanfare is spine-tingling, and after a bellowing hiccup from Phil's bass, it seems like there may be another song. But the return of "Truckin'" in front of 150,000 fans is a smashing success. The Dead improvise a brief, bone-crunching landing before leaving the stage. The fans hoot and holler for an encore and the band obliges with "Terrapin Station."

11-6-77 Broome County Arena, Binghamton, NY: The Dead had a glorious spring tour in April and May of 1977, and their last three shows in upstate New York in November finished their final tour of the year in grand fashion. A spectacular "Truckin'" to end the second set in Binghamton on 11-6-77 was a fitting exclamation point to this storied chapter of Grateful Dead history.

"Truckin'" emerges from a "St. Stephen" handoff. The post "Truckin'" jam spirals to its usual crescendo and mysteriously dissolves. The music slowly rises and the band stops, and then they only play in short bursts to accentuate Garcia's soloing, which takes on a Jimmy Page-like tone. It's a very cool and abnormal Grateful Dead moment. Pretty soon, Lesh and the drummers are hammering away as the "Truckin'" monster revs up for one last thrashing—an amalgamation of blues, acid rock, and heavy metal to end the last East Coast set of '77.

5-19-74 Portland Memorial Coliseum, OR: Nine days after this show, Bill Walton was drafted by the Portland Trailblazers with the first pick of the NBA draft. One would have to assume that Walton, a major Deadhead and college basketball stud for UCLA, was in the coliseum for this sensational night of music. After a soothing, second-set "Peggy-O," cute tuning gives way to "Truckin'."

It always comes down to the jam with "Truckin'." This is an overwhelming display; soundwaves ripple beautifully through the Wall of Sound. As the crescendo spirals, Jerry, Keith, and Phil peak. The music rolls on as the band surfs a jam with no name. There's enough "Truckin'" in there to tie it to the mother song. Billy's cruising; his intricate drumming leads these beautiful music minds into a creative jazz exploration. This is a rogue outfit exploring their own universe in a timeless manner. The improv flows into Mind Left Body Jam > Not Fade Away > Goin' Down the Road Feelin' Bad to end the set.

8-31-80 Capital Centre, Landover, MD: Following a flawless Sailor > Saint, Comes a Time > Truckin' precedes Drums. The brilliance of "Comes a Time" and the unusual placement for "Truckin'" helps fuel this performance. The night before in Philly (8-30-80), and the next show in Rochester (9-2-80), feature several miraculous performances. Maybe the band received a special shipment of performance-enhancing goodies while on the East Coast. Anyway, this tour is underrated, and it should be properly celebrated and praised.

Phil's thundering bass fortifies the spiraling instrumental climax after the last verse. The power of the music is stunning. Jerry carries on with some nice leads as if he's taking the dog out for a simple stroll. Suddenly, he bends some devastating notes. The Dead funnel the jam into the microwave and the whole thing explodes into another jaw-dropping crescendo. The band romps as Garcia hits searing leads that melt the mind. There are hints of "The Other One" in this stampede. This instrumental may be the best one ever played in "Truckin'." The length is ample. There's no need to noodle on. Phil bombs the Cap Center one more time. A booming roar of approval fills the arena. And then Billy and Mickey take over.

7-21-84 Ventura County Fairgrounds, CA: Here's another ripping "Truckin'" arriving in an uncustomary slot. The second set kicks off with my favorite "Cold Rain and Snow." Jerry's vocals are groggy early on, but he makes up for it by passionately belting out four extra rounds of the final chorus. Brent's "Far from Me" follows before Bobby breaks out the whistle to ignite "Truckin'." The group singing is heartfelt as it sounds like the band is celebrating being back in California in between tours. Weir slightly alters an iconic line, "Living on reds, vitamin C, and propane."

In the third slot of the set, the band attacks the spiraling jam with a fresh sense of purpose. Jerry's locked in as his lyrical lines dance off Phil's bass thumping. It's a sweet trip. Nobody in Ventura knows where this is headed as Garcia flows in the zone. As his creative surge winds down, the band organically dips into an easygoing "Eyes." This is a gorgeous four-song segment with "Truckin'" serving as the nucleus.

10-19-74 Winterland Arena, San Francisco, CA: If you crave a long "Truckin'" tease, then this is your favorite version. Following a smoking Sugar Magnolia > He's Gone, the band launches into the signature opening for "Truckin'." Instead of diving in, they play around with the theme for almost two minutes before sliding into a Caution Jam > Drums > Jam segment. The last jam features another tantalizing "Truckin'" tease. When the band finally sings "Truckin', got my chips cashed in," the ballroom is full of bliss.

A defining characteristic of this performance is that the "Get back truckin' on" refrain is only sung once. It seems appropriate being that the Grateful touring hiatus was at hand. The band fires into the crescendo and delivers the goods one more time. This isn't one of the top outro jams, but the pre-"Truckin'" teasing and the weight of the moment makes this an essential version.

NOT FADE AWAY > GOIN' DOWN THE ROAD FEELIN' BAD > NOT FADE AWAY

The most popular Grateful Dead sandwich of all time consists of a cover of a Buddy Holly tune surrounding a remake of a traditional folk song. Before Scarlet > Fire, this was the regular combo that sparked the most compelling forays into segue paradise. The negotiation leading into and out of "GDTRFB" always created drama that never resolved itself the same way. These cover songs lyrically embodied the Grateful Dead experience in a unique way. Not Fade Away > Goin' Down the Road was officially released on *Grateful Dead* (1971), which became known as *Skulls and Roses*. This iconic album version from the Hammerstein Ballroom on 4-6-71 turned many music lovers on to the elusive magic of the Grateful Dead in an easily digestible chunk of rock and roll.

"Goin' Down the Road Feelin' Bad" was born in the middle of "Not Fade Away" on 10-10-70 in Colden Auditorium, Queens College, NYC. It may not have been done consciously, but this new combo replaced Alligator > Caution in the rotation. In Port Chester's Capitol Theatre on 11-6-70, "Alligator" and "Caution" were played in the same show for the last time. Symbolically, they were split apart by the new kids on the block at the start of set two: Alligator > Drums > Not Fade Away > Goin' Down the Road Feelin' Bad > NFA Jam > Caution. The other link between these combos is that the

"GDTRFB" outro was adopted from a segment of the "Alligator" jam.

As the Dead introduced the songs that would make up *Workingman's Dead* and *American Beauty* into their live rotation, NFA > GDTRFB > NFA was a better fit, but old-school Deadheads hungered for "Alligator" (played for the last time on 4-29-71) and "Caution" (played for the final time on 5-11-72). There were five "Caution" jams after Pigpen's passing. NFA > GDTRFB > NFA was played eighty-one times. It was only played twice in 1973; the band opted to play NFA > GDTRFB without a reprise on most occasions. The science of navigating the transitions in this segue took serious focus and group collaboration. The final version came in the Winterland on 2-24-74. Ironically, "It's All Over Now Baby Blue" was the encore on 2-24-74, and that Dylan classic wasn't played again for seven years.

"Goin Down the Road Feelin' Bad" and "Not Fade Away" remained vital pieces in Dead shows through the years. Of the two, "Not Fade Away" has the most compelling history. Like "GDTRFB", "Not Fade Away" was born inside a sandwich when it arrived in the middle of "Turn on Your Lovelight" on 6-19-68 in the Carousel Ballroom. Pigpen handled lead vocals on that brief experiment. "NFA" was next played in December of '69, and Bobby was the primary lead vocalist. Early versions had a tribal feeling, extended jamming, and the upbeat tempo was close to the Buddy Holly original. By the time "GDTRFB" was in the picture and Keith Godchaux joined the band, the driving rock rhythms of "NFA" were expanded by advanced Grateful Dead musical experimentation.

When the band resumed touring in 1976, a revered tune came out of hibernation. "St. Stephen" returned to the lineup, and this led to the St. Stephen > NFA reunion. In 1977, "Not Fade Away" reached new jamming heights as it shined in whatever package it was delivered. In a year that was a coming-out party for songs like "Sugaree," "Mississippi Half-Step," and "Music Never Stopped," folks tend to overlook the extraordinary prowess of '77 "Not Fade Aways." At this point, the "Not Fade Away" saga takes an unfortunate turn.

By 1980, "Not Fade Away" usually materialized out of Space. These versions were solid, but far from epic. In the fall of '82, the band debuted "Throwing Stones," and the fourth time they played it, on 9-21-82, in Madison Square Garden, they paired it with "Not Fade Away." However, it didn't end the show on that occasion. "Throwing Stones" bounced around with a few different partners until it locked onto "Not Fade Away" and found its spot as a second-set closer on 4-17-83 in the Brendan Byrne Arena. "Throwing Stones" was a quality new tune, but it was detrimental to the health of "Not Fade Away." The Throwing Stones > Not Fade Away connection left no room for a major "NFA" instrumental. The song was now locked into two concise solos (by Dead standards) and the "You know our love will not fade away" call-and-response chant with the audience. "Ah umm, bop bop bop bop." This was a great success with the masses, but for those of us who desired unbridled improvisation, this became an all too predictable cookie-cutter cop-out. On the other hand, "Goin' Down the Road Feelin' Bad" kept its independence and continued to be an enticing option that could electrify a show, usually after Drums. Since these songs have rich histories on their own, I've included some standout stand-alone versions of these tunes.

10-31-71 Ohio Theatre, Columbus, OH: This is part of a short but perfect second set featured on *Dick's Picks Vol. 2*, the only single CD release in the series. The Dead finish a hot "St. Stephen" with a little Q and A: "Can you answer? Yes I can, but what would be the answer to the answer man?"

The answer was a common but thrilling transition into "Not Fade Away." There's an infectious bounce to the beat. The song advances with uncanny bravado, and you can sense that Garcia and company are going to tear this up. Describing listening to this "NFA" jam, Dick Latvala said, "I have to put myself in a seat belt. I start shaking, it's so exciting."

I don't like to restrain myself when I listen to this "NFA." I just remove all sharp objects and breakable items in the room before cuing this up. Garcia's fingers bend and pick in a blur, and what he does with this jam is silly. It's his best guitar work within the Not Fade Away > Goin' Down the Road > Not Fade Away framework. Every time I listen to a different version of this combo, I pray it approaches what Garcia does in Columbus. Jerry's out in front of the band, guitar tirades surging to the pulsing rhythm as he refuses to consider the transition into "GDTRFB." Inexplicably, the jam rotates hotter and hotter, and Jerry makes it seem as easy as unspooling yarn.

"Goin' Down the Road Feelin' Bad" feeds off the swirling momentum. This is a vibrant version with two powerful jams, but it's only better than about 75 percent of the versions out there. However, the GDTRFB > NFA transition is in the elite stratosphere of the Scarlet > Fire transition from Cornell. Out of the "GDTRFB" outro, a wondrous jam emerges. The band is conflicted, yet united. Half of the band steps towards "NFA," while the other half tinkers with "GDTRFB." Garcia's in full tease mode, alternating soft, controlled playing with rebellious outbursts, and somehow, the rest of the band rides the wave. How do they know what Garcia's thinking? It's amazing how they instinctively respond when they've never improvised a segue like this before. Maybe these are the rewards of passing the Acid Tests. This type of spontaneous group synergy is unique to the Grateful Dead.

The return explosion into "Not Fade Away" disrupts physics and gravity in Columbus, Ohio. Garcia's voice bubbles as he chants the reprise with Weir. As Weir shrieks falsetto screams, Garcia unleashes frenzied riffs. The climactic crescendo is worthy of The Who and an equipment-bashing tantrum. This is the definitive Grateful Dead rock and roll extravaganza.

11-24-72 Memorial Auditorium, Dallas, TX: A knowledgeable friend insisted that this was a sensational NFA > GDTRFB >NFA. I never focused on this one before. Boy, was he right. Garcia steps out after the second verse with immediate jamming as intense as you'll hear in any "Not Fade Away." After peaking, Jerry steps off and Phil picks up the initiative—sinewy bass leads as the band soft-tosses the beat for a few minutes. Jerry jumps back in the fray with a series of sharp runs leading into "Goin' Down the Road Feelin' Bad." This "GDTRFB" has a lovely instrumental intro and the Boys ramp up a twisted second solo. Garcia's frying-pan licks sizzle, and Donna and Bobby croon the chorus enthusiastically with Señor Sizzle.

The "NFA" reprise is obscene. Garcia rolls with bluesy licks that multiply as the band rocks on. Mysteriously, they wind the beat down to a point of silence, then blast off in unison, "I want to tell you how it's gonna be! Whew! You gonna give your love to me." As Bobby repeatedly howls, "You know our love will not fade away!" Jerry peels off more rolling blues licks that gives Bobby reason to scream on. The smashing instrumental finish is satisfying but not overstated. Jerry chimes in with a taunting, playful lick to close this gem. Like the Columbus version, 11-24-72 is loaded with nuance and pizzazz.

9-3-72 Folsom Field, Boulder, CO: Preceded by a riveting version of "Rockin' Pneumonia and the Boogie Woogie Flu," this Not Fade Away > Goin' Down the Road Feelin' Bad > Not Fade Away is a symmetrically balanced treat. Each segment is slightly over seven minutes in length. The intro is charming as the band toys with the intensity and volume before slamming into, "I wanna tell you how it's gonna be." I love the way Jerry's vocally engaged in this "NFA" and others from this era. The Boogie Woogie Flu pulses through the band's blood as they lay down an unusually funky "NFA," shades of the *Skull and Roses* rendition, but much longer. This fuse is lit, and this "GDTRFB" explodes. As usual, the second solo thrills. Garcia's running stop signs and burning rubber. Rolling through the Rockies, the band plays on for four minutes before the vocal fadeaway of the reprise begins. This is a delectable balance of styles laid out in a clean stream—seemingly easy mastery of the complex performance at hand.

11-15-71 Austin Municipal Auditorium, TX: "Not Fade Away" takes off and thirteen minutes pass by before there's a transition into "GDTRFB." This top-heavy "NFA" has typical hot licks early on. As they impressively scoot along, a brief "China Cat" jam arises. The "NFA" from 11-20-71 has a longer "Cat" foray, but Austin overall is hotter.

The band veers off into an unusually spacey jam for "NFA" before they pick up steam. They've stretched the "NFA" framework and now the intense playing eases towards "GDTRFB." Garcia's festive guitar shredding illuminates the second solo. The return to "NFA" is authoritative without the coy transition foreplay I so admire. Regardless, this is one of the longest performances of this extraordinary combo, and the final instrumental thrashing provides an exclamation point. Fall '71 features the most creative NFA > GDTRFB > NFAs. You'll want to check out 10-30-71 Taft Auditorium and 11-7-71 Harding Theatre as well.

NOT FADE AWAY

9-18-70 Fillmore East, New York, NY: Officially this is a stand-alone "NFA," but it has a trial instrumental run of "GDTRFB" inside. After a scorching "St. Stephen," the Dead slam into "Not Fade Away," Buddy Holly style on steroids, a blues-driven rock and roll buzz saw. The band moves towards the chord riffs of "GDTRFB," which doesn't exist yet. But it's coming soon, and the band puts a lot of feeling into what will be that song's signature outro solo. Charging into the "NFA" finale, Pigpen and Bobby exchange the final lines like heavyweights trading blows in the final round. In three weeks, "Not Fade Away" gives birth to the first "Goin' Down the Road Feelin' Bad."

5-8-77 Barton Hall, Cornell University, Ithaca, NY: The second set of this renowned show gives us a series of incredible performances. After the legendary Scarlet > Fire and "Estimated Prophet," Cornell is blessed with "St. Stephen." As the music progresses, the rigidness of "St. Stephen" juts into the openness of "Not Fade Away." Some clever "Not Fade Away" call-and-response between Jerry and Bob evolves into a freewheeling rampage from Garcia. Squealing this way and screeching that way, Garcia's got the Right Stuff. Yet, this music is so danceable—Barton Hall had to be a sweaty sauna as snow feathered the roof of Barton Hall. On and on they play, each round bringing more aural pleasure. The jam struts into extraordinary terrain as the band teases a few songs, including "Truckin'," before the drummers take over. There are many outstanding "NFAs" from this year. Try out 3-18-77 Winterland, 9-3-77 Englishtown, and 10-11-77 Norman, Oklahoma.

GOIN' DOWN THE ROAD FEELIN' BAD

10-12-81 Olympia Halle, Munich, Germany: If ever there was a performance where you could believe that Garcia consciously entered it with the goal of making it a best-ever version, it would have to be the 10-12-81 "Goin' Down the Road Feelin' Bad" that materializes out of "Estimated Prophet." Europe brought the best out of "GDTRFB." There are several smoking Europe '72 renditions, and there's a standout version from 10-16-81 Amsterdam. "GDTRFB" usually contains three verses and two solos. Garcia repeats a bonus verse in Munich, and doubles listening pleasure with four steaming solos.

After the transition from "Estimated," Brent establishes a pleasant lead-in. Garcia turns up the volume on his guitar and unleashes a concise tirade. After the third solo, it's an elite "GDTRFB." Instead of fading out the performance with their seductive signature ending, the band blasts one more rocking jam, the longest of the four, which erases any doubt—Munich is king. This is the version with the most jamming, although some may prefer the style and substance of a different "GDTRFB."

SHAKEDOWN STREET

By the time their tenth studio album, *Shakedown Street*, was released on November 15, 1978, the Grateful Dead had only played the title track live three times. The album, produced by Little Feat's Lowell George, quickly garnered the epitaph "Disco Dead." "Shakedown Street" and a few other tracks from this album are as close to disco as anything from the Dead's oeuvre. This album unfortunately tarnished the reputation of its title track early on. Those hearing "Shakedown" live in its formative years quickly learned that this was a major song, one that instantly inspired the crowd into a dancing frenzy. It was a unique composition that encompassed several genres; funk, R & B, rock, and jazz. It was a superb piece of pop music with an infectious groove and space for freewheeling improvisation. In reality, "Shakedown Street" embodied everything that Deadheads loved about the band.

"Shakedown Street" was debuted at the start of the second set in Red Rocks on August 31, 1978. This performance has a solid groove but no jamming or "Well, well, well, you can never tell" backing vocals. Yet, it's a much better version than the studio track. If there's a Dead song that best exemplifies Jerry's predilection for the Mu-Tron filter, "Shakedown" is that tune.

Several early versions of "Shakedown" feature stunning intros based on segues from songs such as "The Wheel," or the sensational I Need a Miracle > Shakedown from Springfield on 1-15-79. "Shakedown" landed in the encore slot a few times before settling into its customary position as show opener or the festive tune that ignites the second set. "Shakedown" instantly lifted any crowd's collective spirit and set them in motion, but the alpha ending jam could be hit or miss, and the length of the instrumental varied. The jam never really developed a predictable motif. Sometimes they would riff on a danceable groove and Garcia would work off that. On inspired nights, Garcia might take charge from the beginning, or the inspiration might strike in the middle. And there were nights when they were content to just toss around ideas, almost delighting in the fact that the jam was going nowhere.

In '81 and '82, Jerry and Brent improvised some tasty call-and-response exchanges at the start of the alpha jam. "Shakedown" created space for Brent to display his keyboard wizardry. And of course, Phil took great delight in launching this beloved anthem with bass bombs. The golden years for "Shakedown Street" were between 1978 and 1985.

12-31-81 Winterland Ballroom, San Francisco, CA: "Shakedown Street" opens the last show of another hectic year (officially, the show starts with Joan Baez performing a short set with the band). Jerry dazzles the crowd with his wide smile as the music slides down a funky path. The band's not going through the motions; they're savoring the wonder of their distinct creation. The "Shakedown" jam has a fleeting quality that's similar to "Feel Like a Stranger." Even when the "Shakedown" jam isn't popping, the groove keeps Deadheads dancing.

As the New Year's Eve instrumental develops, there's a compelling cat and mouse exchange between Brent and Jerry. And then Garcia imposes domination. The beloved bearded guru is on a mission as he strings together a series of beautiful ideas in an elegant musical passage—a splendid blend of emotion and execution. The band creates a vacuum that draws everyone into Jerry's universe. The escalating intensity comes off like a stellar "Hard to Handle" jam. This is one of the most engaging "Shakedowns," and a helluva way to kick off another New Year's Eve extravaganza.

6-30-85 Merriweather Post Pavilion, Colombia, MD: Immortal performances sometimes take flight in the tuning. When the band hits the stage for set two, you can hear nonsensical words and sounds from the band as they're tuning up. Garcia's hypnotic tuning is intoxicating ear candy—a countdown to ecstasy.

The band slams the opening chord as one. Thunderous reverberations shoot through the audience until the musicians pound the next jarring chord. In baseball, when a great hitter swings at a pitch and connects squarely, sending the ball into orbit, every fan (rooting for that team) in the stadium rises in admiration knowing the ball is bound for homerun heaven before it gets there. After two thunder chords, everyone in Merriweather was in motion, and experienced Dead connoisseurs could instantly sense that this "Shakedown" was bound for glory.

The tempo is perfect, and the funky groove is absolute. Garcia flubs a word or two, but happiness flows from his eager voice. Bobby and Brent's backing vocals rise to the occasion as the music fuses. Garcia breaks into a between-verse solo that burns and yearns against a grinding groove—wonderful spacing, texture, and poignancy. The singing of the third verse is improbably more compelling than the first two. As the "Nothing shaking on Shakedown Street" chorus rolls on, the musical momentum eases into a comfortable valley.

As the big jam evolves, the pavilion and surrounding fields are crammed with shuffling feet, flailing arms, and pounding hearts. This goes on for several minutes, and it's wonderful for the part of the brain that controls bodily movement; but it's not all that mentally stimulating. That will change—a few notes here and there turn into a decent run. The vacuum of funky restraint opens the gates for a thrilling finale. Riding the band's wave, Jerry's blistering runs unfold hotter and faster, and come together logically—an advanced algebraic equation. Like a great boxer, Garcia knows how to close a jam and impress critics. Even the final chorus and instrumental walk off is special. This may not be the hottest "Shakedown" jam ever, but it's undoubtedly an elite version. And it's probably the most popular "Shakedown" of all time.

9-16-78 Son Et Lumiere Theater, Giza, Egypt: With the Grateful Dead playing at the Great Pyramid of Giza, mystical music was inevitable, or so you'd believe. It was an immense experience for those involved, but the performance brilliance was sparse. The second-ever version of "Shakedown Street" (before Drums) is the shining star of this Egyptian rendezvous. In addition to being one of the best "Shakedowns," it's the most distinctive.

The *well, well, well you can never tell* backing vocals are still missing as Jerry sings the opening verses. The band steps into what would be the between-verse instrumental, but they never return for the final verse. The pull of the Great Pyramid set the band off on another course, yet they still play within the "Shakedown" framework. Garcia spearheads two sturdy rounds and then the jam slithers on, Bobby and Jerry weaving a trippy tapestry that flows like an ancient river. The stream eases and Weir strikes a moody slide guitar segment as Jerry percolates anew. The creativity juices into a one-time-only segment—Cradle of Mankind > Mind Leaves Civilization. We have ourselves an amazing, twelve-minute instrumental prior to Drums. The first "Shakedown" had no jam, and the second version contains the longest "Shakedown" jam ever. Only the Grateful Dead!

4-6-82 The Spectrum, Philadelphia, PA: There was eighteen inches of snow in Nanuet, New York, when I awoke on the morning of April 6,1982. As long as the show wasn't canceled, my insane friends and I were driving through the treacherous conditions to get there. And the rewards were golden. This was my first road trip and third Grateful Dead show. It changed my life.

A resounding bass bomb ignites "Shakedown Street" and the second set of 4-6-82. A funky whirl through the verses of "Shakedown" leads to a crisp opening solo. The band is amped, playing it extra pretty for their obsessed fans in Philly. "Just gotta poke around" morphs into a call-and-response exchange between Jerry and Brent, every bit as engaging as the one from

12-31-81. Phil's negotiating the blues exchange with blasts that make the Spectrum feel like it's melting. Garcia's poking, pecking, and picking against layers of explosive Grateful Dead funk. The Boys can do no wrong as they ride this jam through the heavens. It's unusual that a "Shakedown" jam rockets with this type of sustained energy and concludes with such authority.

2-17-79 Oakland Auditorium, CA: "The Wheel" spins out of Drums > Space, and Chez Garcia dishes out some sizzling butter-hits-frying-pan licks as "The Wheel" rotates to a half-second pause. The band reloads and ignites the funkiest stroll down "Shakedown Street." The thunderous opening is a mix of collective improvisational genius and execution. The 2-17-79 "Shakedown" also features rich group vocals and a charged between-verse solo from Jerry. The lengthy Shakedown > Playin' reprise transition transcends and travels through multiple dimensions of time and space. This was Keith and Donna's last show. The Godchaux Dynasty concluded in grand fashion.

12-31-84 San Francisco Civic Auditorium, CA: It's 12-31-84, and this time the Grateful Dead are closing out the year in San Francisco. Garcia weighs at least fifty pounds more than he did three years earlier, his demeaner is sullen, and his hair is long, frizzy, and unkempt, yet the song remains the same, as the catalyst for the show is a killer "Shakedown" opener. The '81 "Shakedown" jam is a balanced and rapturous free-flowing musical paragraph. The longer '84 "Shakedown" jam bursts out of the gate and splits off in many directions. The musicians are creating thrilling music and the ride is bumpy. At one point, Garcia starts a blues riff like something you might hear in "Get Out of My Life Woman." This eighteen-minute version remains gripping all the way through, and it was deemed impressive enough to be included on the *So Many Roads* box set.

6-30-84 Market Square Arena, Indianapolis, IN: June 30 equals glorious strolls down every Deadhead's favorite street. The Indianapolis "Shakedown" isn't as dramatic or as masterfully crafted as the one from Merriweather but it has an aggressive pace that never backs off. Garcia pokes around on top of the steady groove. There's no trickery or intricate scheme—Jerry and the Boys are turned up full blast. After a substantial run, the band's lost and can no longer return for the "Just got a poke around" finale. Jerry suggests "Playin'." As the band collects themselves Weir sings, "Some folks trust to reason, others trust to might. I don't trust to nothing, but I know it comes out right."

6-24-83 Dane County Coliseum, Madison, WI: The 6-24-83 "Shakedown Street" has the distinction of being one of the best to open a show. The body of the song is performed flawlessly, and Jerry's slashing and dealing from the get-go in the big jam. There's no cute interplay or groove establishment—Garcia's ripping as the audience roars its approval. After a lengthy and impressive surge, the band settles into a relaxed groove and plays fiddle-faddle for a while before landing back in the final chorus.

Jerry Garcia, Egypt 1978 © Adrian Boot

Power of the pyramids, Egypt 1978 © Adrian Boot

Winterland Ballroom 12-27-77 © Ben Upham
www.magicalmomentphotos.com

Bobby's reelin' and rockin', Nassau Coliseum 1-10-79
©Rock n' Roll Joel Levy

Dark Star, 1-10-79 Nassau Coliseum ©Rock n' Roll Joel Levy

Radio City acoustics, 10-30-80 ©Rock n' Roll Joel Levy

Legendary first set, 4-4-85 Providence © Robbi Cohn
www.deadimages.com

7-14-85 Ventura County Fairgrounds © Robbi Cohn

3-30-87 The Spectrum, Philadelphia © Robbi Cohn

Jerry, Bobby, Brent, 8-12-87 Red Rocks © Robbi Cohn

FEEL LIKE A STRANGER

Arriving on *Go to Heaven*, the album after *Shakedown Street*, "Feel Like a Stranger" comes off like Bob Weir's attempt to create his own "Shakedown Street." And that's a good thing. The live evolution of "Stranger" is similar to "Shakedown" in many ways. "Feel Like a Stranger" was born nineteen months after "Shakedown," in the middle of the first set on 3-31-80 in Passaic's Capitol Theatre. It was a clean debut featuring a crisp jam with mellifluous interplay between Brent and Jerry. The architectural design of "Stranger" was efficiently laid out. As in "Shakedown," Jerry's Mu-Tron sound dominates the musical terrain, start to finish.

You know it's gonna get stranger. So let's get on with the show. The lyrics seemed to dictate that "Stranger" was destined to be a show opener, but it didn't find its rightful place in the scheme of things until it opened the festivities in the Philly Spectrum on 8-30-80. "Stranger" bounced around in different spots the first twenty-five times it was performed prior to settling down as an opener. It kicked off my first Dead show in Madison Square Garden on 3-9-81. I never heard the song before, but as I made my way to my seat, I was intrigued and enchanted with the exotic vibe of the jam. It felt like I was joining in on a Hawaiian adventure.

Like "Shakedown," there were few structural changes to the composition, and the ending instrumentals were usually hit or miss. The between-verse "Shakedown" instrumental gave the band a chance to loosen up for the big jam. The between-verse instrumental breaks in "Stranger" are too brief to be called solos or jams. Besides entering this jam cold, the Dead had to stick a perfect instrumental landing without the cushion of a vocal reprise. When the Dead smoked the jam and then nailed a perfect exclamation point, it was pure magic. "Stranger" rarely transitioned into other songs, with the exception of "Franklin's Tower." In that instance, there's really no segue; "Franklin's" just bounces off the ending of "Stranger" without pause. Sometimes "Stranger" fell flat, but the audience was rarely disappointed, and it was a great tune to warm up with. There are many outstanding versions of this tune during its first two years when it was played often. But a hot "Stranger" could materialize when you'd least expect it, so let's get on with the show.

11-10-85 Brendan Byrne Arena, East Rutherford, NJ: The first set of this show was explosive. Energy crackled through the arena and within the music. I was thrilled to hear the noodling for "Stranger" after seven songs in the opening set. When they broke into "Stranger," the excitement was unbearable. I never felt that way about seeing "Stranger" before, but based on the way Garcia shredded "Cassidy," and being that this was final tune of the set, a thrilling jam appeared imminent. Jerry wore a red t-shirt on this evening.

As the band rolled into "Stranger," Garcia was stepping on various pedals in search of the perfect twang. The band bull-rushes the first two verses of "Stranger." Weir's whacking the whammy bar as he proclaims, "You know it's gonna get stranger, so let's get on with the show…Let's go. YO!" Moving into the improvised round robin chorus, Garcia jumps the gun by heartily singing "Feel like a stranger" too early, but that's the loveable mole on this version.

The first thirty seconds of this jam are more compelling than the previous ten "Strangers" combined. Garcia's searing leads snake over the odd chord phrasing of Brent and Bobby. Phil's bass is a frantic nail gun keeping it all together as Bill and Mickey flail away as if their whacking a piñata they can't quite bust open. And it all goes down with flawless synchronicity.

The next phase features frenzied chord riffs bouncing around the Brendan Byrne Arena. At the 6:10 mark, Garcia turns up the volume and goes on a shrill-sounding rampage that could have knocked the walls of Jericho down. The Grateful Dead have fully spread their wings and the stage is set for a dramatic ending.

A well-executed "Stranger" takes succinct timing. What happens in the Byrne is miraculous. Weir leads the band through a perfect, profound, and thunderous refrain as Jerry is there every step of the way hitting climactic notes that never existed in this song before. As "Stranger" lands perfectly, Brendan Byrne Arena goes berserk. Leave it to the Grateful Dead to go beyond a music lover's capacity to dream.

3-9-81 Madison Square Garden, New York City, NY: Garcia's guitar has a distinctive, shrill tone during this "Stranger" opener and throughout the entire show. Bob Weir and mates deliver an attentive and flawless rendition, sailing through the verses as they play "Stranger" in MSG for the first time. It's an album-worthy performance, and then Garcia goes off.

The melody line kicking off the instrumental pierces the listener's brain. The volume's loud and the playing's tasty. Garcia harvests fresh ideas as he takes the jam through several phases. As I mentioned earlier, the music has the vibe of a Hawaiian adventure—Jerry Bond 007 takes on gangsters in Honolulu. Weir's moody rhythms are a substantial part of this journey. Every musical whim from the band aligns as they stick the finale and New York City Deadheads are delirious. It was the start of a night that would get stranger and stranger, and it was this author's first taste of live Dead.

8-30-80 The Spectrum, Philadelphia, PA: A hot "Stranger" opener would often set the tone for the rest of the show, as it did during this brilliant first set that contained ten individual songs without any combinations. This is the first time the Dead opened with "Stranger," and it's an exceptional version. Some venues have magical settings that inspire the band. Deadheads in Madison Square Garden and the Philadelphia Spectrum were the seventh man in the band, inspiring their heroes to new heights. There's a beautiful, clean sound to the 8-30-80 "Stranger." Brent fills the Spectrum with mounds of cushioned organ. The jam has two sublime surges from Jerry. It sounds like the band's going to drift towards the ending after the first surge, but Jerry redirects and establishes a pair of blistering runs. Jerry clearly states it's one of *those* nights. The band delivers exceptionalism during all ten songs of the opening set.

3-2-87 Henry J. Kaiser Convention Center, Oakland, CA: This is the first post-coma "Feel Like a Stranger." Jerry's having a blast reacquainting himself but his timing is off, even on his "Feel like a stranger" background vocals. This is the seventh and last tune of the opening set. When the mojo was rolling, "Stranger" made for a dynamic and surprise set-ender. Garcia steps on the gas and doesn't let up for several minutes. Two things are obvious: He still isn't fully reacquainted with "Stranger," and it doesn't matter because this is the hottest thing he's played since his return. This is a tornado of savage guitar exploration, and despite the sloppiness, it's a standout "Stranger."

4-22-83 Veterans' Memorial Coliseum, New Haven, CT: Big arena East Coast shows brought the beast out of the Dead. Another hotbed for Garcia and mates was the New Haven Coliseum. "Feel Like a Stranger" launches the show, and Weir annunciates an animated rap in perfect cadence and rhyme: "I don't know about you, maybe you feel like a stranger too… (Feel like a stranger). Some nights everything just gets stranger and stranger… (Feel like a stranger). Like a stranger. Sometimes maybe there's just a little element of danger." Everything Jerry, Brent, and Bob throw at the round robin sing-along sounds sweet—improvisational vocal magic. And the funky, layered jam resolves itself with a smooth landing.

4-20-80 Philadelphia Civic Center, PA: Making their annual run in the City of Brotherly Love, the Grateful Dead were feeling like strangers playing in the Civic Center for the first time in ten years. The Spectrum must have been booked solid with basketball and hockey. Weir and company are engaged in spirited singing and Dan Healy turns up the echo during Weir's rap. The instrumental steams as Phil and Jerry are bouncing ideas off each other in unison. The robust sound swarms and regenerates until it morphs into a meaty jam. The Boys strike the ending with scintillating precision. Another long, long, crazy night is launched.

11-3-84 Berkeley Community Theatre, CA: "Feel like a Stranger" starts set two of this outstanding show, which is the last of a six-night residency in the BCT. Brent's quick-handed riffing sets the stage for the jam. Jerry taps into his reservoir of "Stranger" licks. Waves and layers of music bubble below the surface. As Jerry settles down after substantial shredding, Phil takes over and pounds the BCT with a series of booming runs. After ten minutes, the Dead regroup to stick the "Stranger" ending. "Cumberland Blues" bounces out on the other side and is followed by "Gloria" and "Why Don't We Do It in the Road." It doesn't get stranger than that.

DARK STAR

Dark Star" is the song that best embodies the elusive and adventurous improvisational mystique of Grateful Dead music. Researching the best renditions of "Dark Star" was a time-consuming yet rewarding venture. Comparing "Dark Stars" is difficult due to the shifting structure and lengths of the instrumentals from performance to performance. Ironically, a studio track of "Dark Star" was recorded in less than three minutes and released as a single in 1968. "Dark Star" swiftly became an iconic jam anthem when it was released on *Live Dead* the following year.

During the summer of 1967, Robert Hunter joined the Dead in Rio Nido, where he heard them practicing a new instrumental. Trying to capture the essence of the music, Hunter penned the first verse of "Dark Star" and Garcia loved it. "Dark Star" was debuted in the Shrine Exhibition Hall, Los Angeles, on December 13, 1967. Our first chance to hear a live recording of "Dark Star" comes via a soundboard recording from the Carousel Ballroom on 1-17-68. It's an up-tempo, two-verse offering wrapped up in a shade under five minutes—short and sweet, a description rarely applied to this cosmic tune. Although, "Dark Star" still had an intergalactic vibe on this evening. By October '68, versions of "Dark Star" were exceeding ten minutes. Tom Constanten joined the band on keyboards on 11-23-68. His swirling/trippy keyboard riffs enhanced the psychedelic texture of "Dark Star."

Entering a realm of iconic transcendence, "Dark Star" was played sixty-seven times in 1969, more than any other year. It became the Dead's showcase improvisational journey. There are those who consider '69 the peak year for this number, which exceeded twenty minutes on most nights. As the band expanded their repertoire, they played "Dark Star" less frequently in '70 and '71; twenty-one and twelve times, respectively. The structure of the song loosened, and the second verse became optional. Dark Star > St. Stephen > The Eleven; the pride and joy of 1969 was gone. "Dark Star" would never again find itself in a predictable segment. Any song could materialize out of it, and it may return for an unexpected reprise.

With Mickey Hart and Tom Constanten no longer in the band in early 1971, the music was less cluttered, and this space benefitted "Dark Star." As the Grateful Dead embarked on their Europe '72 tour, this brilliant band took a quantum leap forward in musicianship. The Academy of Music run in March '72 was impressive, but the band that landed in London was possessed. Their second show of the tour on April 8 in Empire Pool, Wembley, features an iconic segment, one of the true masterpieces of Dead folklore: Dark Star > Sugar Magnolia > Caution. That "Dark Star" is light-years ahead of anything the band had attempted before. The playing is euphoric, hypnotic, subtle, and violent, all at once—a majestic rhapsody ordained by the gods.

There was no let-up in the brilliance of "Dark Star" between '72 and '74. Every time it was played, history beckoned—masterpiece musical theater. I have a predilection for the thirty-one "Dark Stars" played in 1972. The song was performed nineteen times in '73 and six times in '74. These renditions tended to be even jazzier than the '72 performances. There's nothing quite like a "Dark Star," and when the band returned from their touring hiatus and didn't play it until New Year's Eve 1978, it was obvious that the times had changed. The Dead moved forward with a wonderful batch of new songs and a more concise, yet still satisfying, style of jamming. The era of wild, freestyle improvising was over. For the most part, the intense jamming from the band would come within the boundaries of a bountiful repertoire of originals and covers.

There were two performances of "Dark Sar" in January 1979, and the first "Dark Star" break out of the Brent Mydland era was on New Year's Eve 1981. A grateful audience experienced a "Dark Star" encore on 7-13-84 in the Greek Theatre. After the longest hiatus in the song's history, five years, the Hampton Coliseum went ballistic when the Boys broke out "Dark Star" on October 9, 1989. From that point forward, "Dark Star" was returned to the rotation on a limited basis. The organic and jazzy flow of the jam suited Garcia well later in his career. Whenever "Dark Star" was played, it was a significant event in Grateful Dead history. Amazingly, I saw 152 Dead shows without ever witnessing a "Dark Star."

4-8-72 Empire Pool, Wembley, London: Jerry, Phil, and Billy pounce on the opening of the first European "Dark Star." The music's robust and dense; it emerges like a heavenly symphony—possessed jamming with a séance-like vibe. It sounds as if they're channeling the ancient footsteps and spirits of Europe. The band has more flexibility with the addition of Keith and the subtraction of Mickey, T. C., and the limited role of Pigpen. Sometimes it's what you don't play that helps a jam take off, and Garcia and mates steer this through a cosmic black hole as they turn through the pages of European history: Shakespeare, Plato, Marx, Darwin, Napoleon, and Hitler; it's all there. The mood's mysterious and dark, and the music glows with wisdom. The Dead's last "Dark Star" was two weeks earlier in the Manhattan Center. The London "Dark Star" is in another dimension of existence.

The music radiates for eleven minutes until Garcia sings, "Dark star crashes, pouring its light into ashes." London's casually ripped out of their comfort zone. The band continues their individual forays into the unknown, yet there's an invisible force pulling everything together. There's a seductive flow to this organic opus. Maybe the band needed to leave America to get out of their comfort zone and step their artistry to its highest possible ground.

Jerry's spewing virtuosity towards the end of this version as the band suggests "Sugar Magnolia." Suddenly, they are in segue paradise as they erase the borders between "Dark Star" and "Sugar Magnolia." The negotiation between the two Dead anthems is enthralling. All the uplifting powers of spontaneous improvisation shine brightly. This transition is three of the greatest minutes of music that I've ever heard. "Sugar Magnolia" is the perfect landing tune from a deep "Dark Star" voyage—a blissful rocker extolling the virtues of Southern love and sunshine daydream. This was the second of ten Dark Star > Sugar Magnolias. I believe this combo flowed as naturally as any Dead combo.

7-18-72 Roosevelt Stadium, Jersey City, NJ: This was the Dead's third show after the Europe '72 tour, and they were eager to impress Deadheads in the New York City area with their blossoming virtuosity. Set two begins with a rocking "Truckin'" that spills into a lovely instrumental prelude to "Dark Star."

There's a warm, embryonic flow early on as Garcia strikes with impressive runs that leave just enough open space to create that polished/hypnotic "Dark Star" vibe they established on the European tour. But this is Dark Star Country—an outdoor gig on a hot summer's night in front of zealous East Coast Deadheads. This would have been a sufficient opening jam if Jerry cut to the first verse after nine minutes. However, Garcia raises the stakes and unloads some of the hottest sustained guitar work in any "Dark Star." The energy of the preceding "Truckin'" still burns within this jam.

Eleven excellent minutes pass by before Jerry cranks it up a notch. Garcia locks into five repetitious runs, each one hotter than the last—restless licks that smolder. Kreutzmann's ability to sense Jerry's intentions are essential to this masterpiece. The tension is released with the singing of the first verse after sixteen minutes. Bob Dylan and David Bromberg were in attendance with the 20,000-plus Deadheads. Nobody had ever heard or seen anything like this before.

The second jam evolves into a more typical '72 "Star" structure. Lesh and Jerry frantically manipulate their magic wands as cosmic energy swirls—minds leave bodies in Jersey City. After the psychedelic exorcism, "Dark Star" tumbles into the compassionate calm of "Comes a Time." This four-song second set segment is closed out by the feel-good rush of a surging "Sugar Magnolia." This timeless masterpiece of original compositions is balanced, beginning and ending with Weir's rockers, and the Jerry tunes within go places only the Dead could dream of.

2-13-70 Fillmore East, New York City, NY: This performance, released on *Dick's Picks Vol. 4*, has transcended time and amazed Deadheads for the past fifty years. Garcia's sharp and thoughtful playing dominates the early stages of this journey. It comes off like a virtuosic soliloquy—one man's journey through the galaxy as his comrades remain firmly planted in the Fillmore East. As the first verse seems imminent, Garcia takes a sharp left turn and we are listening to a Tchaikovsky symphony in a Russian theatre. The volume of the music is softer, but the playing sends shivers through the audience. However, we're in the Fillmore East, and the band rolls out the carpet to the first verse, "Dark star crashes, pouring its light into ashes."

The music essentially stops after Jerry sings. Cymbals rattle and crash here and there, but life inside the Fillmore is frozen still. Where do these guys get the balls? And what power! Without prompting, they stopped time and the audience in their tracks. As they carry on, the jam gets loud and takes on an urgent tone. Weir and Phil set the stage for Garcia to bust loose. The epic music shines on as the band suggests several jams within the "Dark Star" orbit without locking into any single trail. Garcia's guitar joyfully shrieks this way and that way. The band crushes it! New York City hustle and bustle. Horns honk as yellow cabs streak down Broadway on a rainy night. The band's got something going on and they're smug about it. The instrumental return to the last verse is ecstatic: "Mirror shatters..." The magic carpet ride continues with "Cryptical." *The other day they waited. The sky was dark and faded.*

12-6-73 Convention Center, Cleveland, OH: Forty-four minutes of "Dark Star" pleasure begins with some relaxed noodling, hypnotic exchanges between Keith and Jerry. One autumn day I had the pleasure of listening to this at the Bronx Botanical Gardens. I was standing by a small waterfall watching colored leaves fall one by one into the river as if it was orchestrated by the universal mind. This led to an orderly parade of leaves heading down the waterfall. The scene was on autopilot; at no point was there a lack of leaves, nor too many. The intoxicating flow of this scene matched the music I was hearing. Nothing was forced.

This "Dark Star" opening flows note by note in perfect harmony. There's no boiling crescendo as layer after layer of aural paradise unfolds until the opening verse. After Jerry sings, Phil bombs this into weird oblivion—extraterrestrial beings are alerted about the strange happenings in Cleveland. This almost takes on the vibe of a Phil and Ned "Seastones" performance. Jerry, Bobby, and Phil regain control of the initiative and ignite a tasty fusion segment before this lengthy excursion rolls into "Eyes of the World."

9-21-72 The Spectrum, Philadelphia, PA: Before their mission of transcendence, the Dead play "Black Peter" and "Mexicali Blues," and out of the between-song silence, they gently glide into "Dark Star." The Spectrum transforms into a flying saucer hurtling through space. Garcia's firing away— dazzling brushstrokes. The band's ensconced in the essence of "Dark Star." Around the ten-minute mark, Garcia's guitar screeches and squawks—the aliens are all ears. The opening verse follows, and one can sense it's going to take a while before this vehicle returns.

Bob and Jerry strike up a groovy riff and suddenly there's a jazz jam on Mars. Kreutzmann steers the ship for a while as Phil and Keith ping-pong leads back and forth. About twenty minutes in, Jerry starts to channel a dark disturbance as Keith slashes electric piano riffs and Phil furiously thumps away. The Dead are sounding like a Miles Davis fusion group as the music spirals round and round like a cyclone tearing far into another universe. They take it to the limit, and then the jam floats around in a vacuum of timelessness—sparse music trying to find a way back home. The Dead rise into a jam that loosely resembles "Feelin' Groovy" and for the next five minutes, they ride an intergalactic trail. This is September 21, 1972, and the show must go on, so they nonchalantly tumble into "Morning Dew."

8-27-72 Old Renaissance Faire Grounds – Veneta, OR: The Grateful Dead launch this second set with thirty-one and a half minutes of consistent "Dark Star" bliss. If I were paid to edit this version down to thirty minutes, I would refuse the assignment. Every second of this performance is engaging. Perhaps a few "Dark Stars" have greater peaks, but few have a never-ending stream of virtuosity that compares to Veneta. This "D Star" takes off with an air of confidence. In the previous set, the band blitzed through what is widely recognized as the greatest version of "Playin' in the Band." Phil's on top of the world in Veneta. His bass blasts create aural astrological charts. The improvisation glows and gleams—a polished musical score that seemingly materializes effortlessly.

After the first verse, the flow and feel of most "Dark Stars" changes. There's usually a stretch of weirdness that develops into a more substantial jam. On 8-27-72, there's little hesitation as the band immediately strikes into a jam as if they're picking up where they left off. After a few minutes, a Phil and Billy duet develops. These guys are on fire! A drums and bass interlude never sounded better. Keith drops into the conversation and Bobby follows with a catchy chord progression. Jerry jumps in with speed-picking sequences. The hottest jazz band in the world is kicking ass and taking names. The amazing sounds spiral on—focus and persistence in the zone. The noodling flawlessly carries into the next song as Weir sings, "Out of the West Texas town of El Paso." What a wonderfully weird selection and segue to stamp the 8-27-72 "Dark Star" as immortal.

5-11-72 Civic Hall, Rotterdam: Snapping strings sing over twinkling keys and rattling percussion as another European "Dark Star" probe ascends. The moody jam surges as Jerry noodles. The band digs deeper and deeper into "Dark Star," yet there's no move towards the opening verse. Fourteen minutes of jazzy mischief leads to a Kreutzmann drum solo. This is a forty-seven-minute "Dark Star," with thirty minutes still left after Billy's exhibition. Phil leads the band back into the fray and Jerry crafts a run of gorgeous melody lines before he sings.

The band moves into a heavy space. The veracity and velocity of Lesh and Garcia's playing is off the charts. How much psychedelic intensity can an audience endure? This was a sonic Acid Test on Rotterdam—an epic adventure with relentless effort—perhaps more notes than Garcia had ever poured into any one song, if there was a way to measure that. Eventually, this needs to resolve into another song. "Truckin'" and "Caution" are teased before they bull-rush into "Sugar Magnolia."

9-16-72 Boston Music Hall, MA: I recall hearing a partial soundboard of this show several years ago, and Garcia's playing after the first verse startled me. I hadn't heard it since. It was a pleasure being reunited with this gem on this journey. It commences tastefully, just like a "Dark Star" should. Billy's playing fills the night sky with stars. Jerry and the Boys flex their muscles and the music is loud and heavy from the eight-minute mark until Jerry sings a touch down the line. The after-verse playing is subdued until Phil and Bobby pick up the pace with a theme that resembles "Mission Impossible."

At this point, Jerry goes off. It's a Tiger > Mind Left Body meltdown. If you pick this up midstream, it sounds like Jimmy Page jamming in "Dazed and Confused." It's a jarring segment in the illustrious history of "Dark Star." And consequently, although this twenty-six-minute rendition doesn't have as much meat as other elite versions, it is indeed noteworthy.

11-2-69 The Family Dog at The Great Highway, San Francisco, CA: I got involved in a Facebook group, 213 Dark Star Project, a celebration of "Dark Stars" as we neared the 50th anniversary of 2-13-70. The group administrator, asked me to review a few "Dark Stars" that I didn't know so well. One of them was this Family Dog "Dark Star," which blew me away.

Garcia's shredding out of the gate during the striking opening jam. The organ/keyboard playing makes for an excellent counterpoint. Pig and T. C. shine throughout. There's a moving escalation to the jam spurred on by Phil. This is an unusually powerful advance for a '69 "Star." Garcia's lyrical playing is fluid—he's a poet/magician with the tenacity of an Olympic athlete. The band's manipulation of space and volume is astounding. I hear a trace of a "Clementine Jam" on the road to Jerry singing the first verse.

Light organ playing sets the stage for the next jam. It's time to board the spaceships as the composer, Phil Lesh, conducts a classical score. From this point forward, there's a touch of just about every theme jam the band could slip into. I hear traces of an "Uncle John's Band" jam, but that official debut would happen six days later on 11-8-69. The main theme is "Tighten Up," and the Boys rip it up. This instrumental becomes action-packed and steps outside the usual "Dark Star" motif—a celestial train of sound rolling down the tracks. After letting it all hang out, there's a stunning return to the "Dark Star" melody—so impressive. Jerry sings! "Mirror shatters / in formless reflections of matter." This is now my favorite '69 "Dark Star."

SAINT STEPHEN/ THE ELEVEN

This is the logical pairing to follow the previous chapter since Dark Star > St. Stephen > The Eleven is the revered combo immortalized during the *Live Dead* era. "The Eleven" was born in the Carousel Ballroom on January 17, 1968, and "St. Stephen" arrived on the scene in the Carousel Ballroom on June 7, 1968. A week later there was an Eleven > St. Stephen combo in the Fillmore East, and the Dead ripped their first Dark Star > St. Stephen > The Eleven trifecta on 8-21-68 in the Fillmore West. All the magic was happening on the coasts (East and West) in 1968. Even though the "William Tell" bridge is the last lyrical component of "St. Stephen," as a listener, I sense that verse seems to serve as a segue between the songs, especially since it was never sung in "St. Stephen" after "The Eleven" was dropped from the rotation.

"St. Stephen" is the lead track on *Aoxomoxoa*, released in June '69. The band jammed an instrumental "Eleven" in the studio. I'd recommend seeking out the expanded and remastered version of *Aoxomoxoa*, which has this version of "The Eleven" along with "Clementine" and "Spoonful" jams— essential listening. "St. Stephen" is a distinctive song that grew in stature as the jam expanded. "The Eleven" will never be remembered as a lovely jingle. "The Eleven" is a monster jam that fits the description Primal Dead better than any other jam. It's outright scary, as if the Dead had tapped into something demonic, some kind of outlawed musical universe. "The Eleven" was an exercise in attempting to control the uncontrollable. Somebody would need to invent the science of sonic fusion to further explain The Beast.

"St. Stephen" is a tremendous composition with lyrics that resonate, but the musical arrangement made it difficult for the band to keep it in the rotation, typical of the tracks from *Aoxomoxoa*. After splitting from "The Eleven," "St. Stephen" found a happy home segueing into "Not Fade Away" most of the time in '70 and '71. Without "William Tell," "Stephen" flourished and more than held its own. The great '71 Halloween show from Columbus, Ohio, immortalized on *Dick's Picks Vol. 2*, was the last time the band played "St. Stephen" for five years. "Hey, Jerry, play St. Stephen!" Deadheads carried on yelling and requesting the song for years, but this was a tune that didn't materialize on a whim.

At their first East Coast show upon resuming their Long Strange Trip, the Dead broke out "St. Stephen" in the Boston Music Hall on June 9, 1976. It was played twelve times that year and was usually linked to "Not Fade Away." On several occasions, the band made a "NFA" sandwich by segueing out of and back into "St. Stephen." The jams in the "Stephens" that weren't sandwiched were longer than before.

The St. Stephen > Not Fade Away > Drums > St. Stephen > Morning Dew segment performed in Barton Hall on 5-8-77 is a treasure, and "St. Stephen" is a key catalyst in that equation. However, the cream of the 1977 "St. Stephen" crop started with a ripping rendition in Moody Coliseum on October 15. The last five "Stephens" of '77 are mandatory listening for those fond of this noble tune. "St. Stephen" was played four times in '78, including on back-to-back nights to end the year. The last "Stephen" of the Keith era was played in the Nassau Coliseum on 1-10-79. The consecrated "Saint" was out of action for more than four years before being resurrected in Madison Square Garden on October 11, 1983. "St. Stephen" was played again four days later in Hartford, and the final performance was on Halloween in Marin County Veterans' Auditorium. "St. Stephen" RIP 10-31-83.

Since "The Eleven" was the stronger jam of the two while they were paired, I'll discuss some of the best versions of that tune before digging into noteworthy "Stephens" not linked to "The Eleven."

2-28-69 Fillmore West, San Francisco, CA: Archivist Dick Latvala proclaimed, "The best and most exciting G. D. show ever is without a doubt 2/28/69 Fillmore West!!!" This is the second show of a four-night Fillmore West stand. There's a remarkable St. Stephen > The Eleven in the middle of set two. The Dead ignite a flammable jam out of "St. Stephen." They delay "The Eleven" blastoff with that wonderful wobbly intro—a warning before the sharks pounce on their prey. Game on! The music swirls as intensity builds in varied increments— a carnival of sound spiraling down a slick slope. Phil and Jerry are balancing impossible musical equations on a floating foundation. This electric barrage transcends time. With an ole-timey feel, "The Eleven" blasts into futuristic dimensions.

After a spirited group sing-along, the band tees off again. Phil's rhythmic pounding leads the way as the drummers frame the impossible beat, and the carnival organ lubricates the path for Jerry's screeching/squawking dashes—controlled cannon blasts The psychedelic electricity bombards the Fillmore West faithful and rolls on like an atomic yo-yo. As the jam approaches madness, the music explodes towards a "Caution"-like jam. After seventeen spiraling minutes inside the beast, "The Eleven" rolls into the familiarity of "Lovelight."

4-22-69 The Ark, Boston, MA: The Boston "Eleven" spans eleven minutes and eleven seconds. It's a dazzling exercise in channeling energy and defying gravity, and a fine example of playing in control and out of control at the same time—giving the illusion of going beyond what's possible. This three-night stand was the Dead's second trip to Boston and they immediately tapped into the East Coast electricity as they had in New York City.

The road to the verse is hot, but after the singing's done, the band creates perverse music. The jam rages loud and strong for several loops before dissolving into a soft, sophisticated swirl. And then "The Eleven" reloads. The sonic regeneration is more alarming and thrilling than before. It's hard to imagine how a small club could endure this without the roof blowing off.

11-8-69 Fillmore Auditorium, San Francisco, CA: During its glorious run, "The Eleven" ran amok in the Fillmores: East, West, and the Auditorium. On 11-8-69 there was a Dark Star > Other One > Dark Star > Uncle John's Band jam before the song loop moved into familiar territory, Dark Star > St. Stephen > The Eleven. Garcia's playing is charming and hypnotic as "The Eleven" takes flight. Jerry and Phil finish each other's sentences and weave a mystical tapestry. Waves crash on shore in unpredictable patterns as the jam keeps listeners engaged. This is one of the smoothest and most lyrical performances of "The Eleven." After thirteen minutes, the band blasts a volatile transition into "Caution."

7-12-69 NY State Pavilion, Flushing Meadow Park – Queens, NY: Five years after the 1964 World's Fair, where attendees were introduced to rudimentary basics of computers for the first time, the Grateful dead played in a venue that would serve as a concert ground for a little while before becoming a vacated wasteland. The Boys made good use of their time with a dazzling set before the headliner, Joe Cocker, followed.

"The Eleven" at this show mirrors the arcane setting. Garcia's laid back on the road to the verse. T. C. and Phil take advantage of their opportunity to lead the dance. It has a jazz/trippy feel, perhaps a road that would have been explored more if "The Eleven" had stayed in the rotation. The jam catches fire on the backend—a raging rollercoaster conjuring up images of The Cyclone in Coney Island—hot fun in the summertime with the Grateful Dead.

10-20-68 Greek Theatre, Berkeley, CA: It's Primal Dead night in the Greek. "Dark Star" takes off like a comet speeding through galaxies. The band's possessed as they bolt into "St. Stephen." The song structure can barely contain the psychedelic strikes, and the release into "The Eleven" is divine. Finally, they've run into a song with ideal tempo and flexibility for their intensity level on this night. Versions of "The Eleven" would grow longer, but the storm surge of this offering is ridiculous. The Dead would play a monumental version of

"Jack Straw" sixteen years later in Syracuse on 10-20-84. It was as if they had a flashback and tapped into the magic of "The Eleven" from Greek '68.

SAINT STEPHEN

1-11-78 Shrine Auditorium, Los Angeles, CA: At the previous two-night stop in San Diego's Golden Hall, only Bob Weir songs were performed as Jerry rested his voice due to laryngitis.

This was the band's second night in the Shrine and Jerry was working his angelic voice back to its natural state. I don't think I had heard this "St. Stephen" until I began research for this project. If I had, I was completely distracted by something else because this is a stunning "St. Stephen."

"St. Stephen" emerges like royalty out of a heavy "Playin'" jam. The flow is steady and confident after a triumphant run of "Stephens" toward the end of '77. Donna and Jerry harmonize the "Lady Finger" bridge beautifully and the instrumentals are extra-crispy. The *One man gathers what another man spills* jam instantly rockets to glory. It hits an amazing peak thanks to incendiary licks from you know who, and appears to be heading toward the final verse. But Mr. Garcia was thinking legacy as he created a pathway to extend the instrumental and set off alarm sirens in the Shrine. It seems like a conscious effort to make this undeniably the hottest "Stephen" jam, just in case anyone in the year 2020 was researching this kind of thing.

"St. Stephen" with the "William Tell" bridge averaged six minutes in length. The Shrine "St. Stephen" stretches out for nine electrifying minutes. As consistently hot as this number was during this era, it's puzzling as to why they would soon dispatch it from the rotation.

10-15-77 Moody Coliseum, SMU, Dallas, TX: The band's inspired as they deliver the third song of the second set, "Terrapin Station." The instrumental refrain of "Terrapin" winds down into a brief pause, and out of the silence, great art is born. The crowd goes nuts as the next tune begins. This was what they were praying for.

"St. Stephen" has returned! Sometimes when a band gives you too much of a good thing, you take it for granted. In fact, the performers can take it for granted. This was the tenth "St. Stephen" of the year, but the first since 6-9-77. On this grand occasion, everybody in the Moody Coliseum is caught in the rapture. The band has a masterful grip on "St. Stephen," and now they are determined to take it to the next level. Each solo burns with the primal promise that this song has always exhibited. After the "One man gathers what another man spills" line is sung, musical paradise breaks loose. The jamming is long and sensational in a way it has never been displayed before. "St. Stephen" has always been mixed up in various assorted affairs. The SMU "St. Stephen" screams I am magnificent! Every twist and turn is glorified as it's performed in its entirety.

11-2-77 Field House, Seneca College, Toronto: This was the Grateful Dead's first show in Canada since they played Vancouver in May '74. An unassuming show was launched to higher ground with a rocking finale to set two: Estimated Prophet > St. Stephen > Truckin' >Around and Around. The smoldering remains of "Estimated" sizzle into "St. Stephen" like butter flicked into a frying pan. Jerry's hotshot picking in the first two brief solos foreshadows the sensational ending jam. The band crushes it in unison, but it's Jerry's lyrical and inventive leads that make this a classic.

6-9-76 Boston Music Hall, MA: The Wall of Sound was gone, along with "Dark Star" and much of the freewheeling improvisation of '74, but when the Dead returned from their touring hiatus, they were performing in intimate venues. On the third stop of their comeback tour in Boston Music Hall, they presented the faithful with the sanctified anthem "St. Stephen." Since "Dark Star" and "Morning Dew" had been rotation regulars, "St. Stephen" was the most coveted and requested song. There were times when the band had to explain to fans shouting: "St. Stephen!" that they no longer played that tune. The band boycott was over when they opened set two of 6-9-76 with "St. Stephen."

This was Donna's "St. Stephen" debut. The song materialized leisurely but tight. The glorious return was celebrated with an unusually long jam. Jerry casually noodled away as the band locked into a groove that sounded like it might head towards "Not Fade Away." Eventually, this landmark eleven-minute version landed for the final verse before bouncing into "Eyes of the World."

10-31-71 Ohio Theatre, Columbus, OH: Out of the ashes of "Sugar Magnolia," the Dead casually ascend the royal stairway to "St. Stephen." Garcia and Lesh pound the pavement on this powerful performance. An engaging conversation between Jerry and Phil leads to a cyclone of cascading chord madness. The band fans and blasts away with heavy artillery. The energy of this "Stephen" regenerates through the ensuing NFA >GDTRFB > NFA, which is simply the best version of that combo. If any Deadheads had come to take "St. Stephen" for granted because it was a staple in the rotation, they would never feel that way again. It would be five years before the holy "Saint" returned to the lineup.

10-11-83 Madison Square Garden, New York, NY: During a gorgeous Space, Jerry picks the strings of his Tiger and I envision Pac-Man gobbling up Pac-Dots and ghosts. There were rumors floating around the scene that the band was going to break out "St. Stephen." I'd heard those rumors consistently for the past six months, and I wasn't going to be fooled again as I absorbed this Space in Madison Square Garden, even though there are hints of "Stephen." There's a hypnotic/dream-like segue as the Dead transition to the holy "Saint" as if the band is sprinkling magic dust in the Garden. The Boys confidently explode into "St. Stephen" as pandemonium breaks out. It's the first "Stephen" in almost five years. Phil's loud and resounding bass matches the emotion of Deadheads howling in disbelief.

This is Brent's first "St. Stephen." His slashing organ runs add a colorful texture to the soundscape. I was so excited at the time it took me a few verses to settle into enjoying the moment. The hot jam is sufficient in length. It was a historic moment, but not yet an elite "St. Stephen." After posing the question,

"What would be the answer to the answer man?" the Dead rip into another jam, similar in feel to the previous one. One could almost believe that "The Eleven" was on deck. But alas, this is 1983, and the crowd would have to embrace "Throwing Stones." The extra solo secured this version in the realm of elite "Saint Stephens."

GREATEST STORY EVER TOLD/ PASSENGER/ CASSIDY

After the intense psychedelic meandering of the last two entries, here's a look at three songs sung by Weir. These tunes were short by Grateful Dead standards, and they gave Garcia an opportunity to tee off on a jam and change the momentum of a show. It was hard for me to omit any of these songs from this project, so I lumped them together. Of the three songs, "Cassidy" is the one that could have stood on its own merit. But in the scheme of things, each of these songs was extraordinary in different periods: "Greatest Story Ever Told" 1972–1974, "Passenger" 1978–1981, "Cassidy" 1981–1995.

"Greatest Story Ever Told" was played for the first time in Port Chester's Capitol Theatre on February 18, 1971. The structure of the song was different from how most have come to know "Greatest Story." During its first two months, this Hunter/Weir composition was a prelude to "Johnny B. Goode." "Greatest Story" was a promising rocker with limited jamming, and the composition was similar to Chuck Berry's iconic tune. "GSET" was placed on the shelf after it was played at the closing of the Fillmore East on 4-29-71.

Outside of Pigpen's health, everything in the Grateful Dead Universe took a glorious turn in '72. Upon its return, a revamped "Greatest Story" suddenly became the most explosive five-minute song in the band's repertoire. It was played eighty-seven times between '72 and '74, and it always had a raging jam that was focused and reliable for two or three minutes. Pinpointing the best versions of this firecracker wasn't easy, but the research was rewarding.

"GSET" was retired for almost five years after being performed in the Winterland on 10-18-74. Were Donna's screams during the blazing instrumental a catalyst or a hinderance? I believe the answer is both, depending on the version. Appropriately, "Greatest Story" re-emerged at Keith and Donna's last show in Oakland on 2-17-79. It's a dynamic return, but the story wasn't so great after that. "Greatest Story Ever Told" went on to become a cookie-cutter song primarily played after "Alabama Getaway." The jam had no expansion or suspense, even though it was still a pleasurable listen. In '87, "Greatest Story" became entangled in a Devil with a Blue Dress > Good Golly Miss Molly > Devil with a Blue Dress medley. Yawn! I guess that was a throwback to the days it was paired with "Johnny B. Goode." "GSET" never came close to regaining its jam anthem status.

"Passenger," a Phil composition sung passionately by Bobby and recorded for *Terrapin Station*, was performed for the first time in St. Louis on 5-15-77. The '77 versions were sharp, but "Passenger" took flight in '78 when a longer second jam was added. Kung Pao! When Brent joined the band, his sweeping/swirling organ progressions greased the rails, and "Passenger" replaced "Greatest Story" as the combustible engine that could ignite any set. It had enough fire to step up to the role as first-set closer in 1979.

Inexplicably, "Passenger" was played for the last time in Oakland on 12-27-81. That was a mistake. It was too good of a tune to kill. "Passenger's" epitaph can be found in the lyrics: *Firefly, can you see me? Shine on, glowing, brief and brightly.*

"Cassidy" was born with "Scarlet Begonias" and the Wall of Sound in the Cow Palace on March 23, 1974. Written by Barlow and Weir, "Cassidy" had an inauspicious live debut. It wasn't attempted again until the band returned from their touring hiatus on June 3, 1976, in the Paramount Theater, Seattle. Since "Cassidy" was released on *Ace* in 1972, it's fortuitous that it was returned at all. The tune was obviously a keeper, and the jam slowly grew year by year.

By 1981,Garcia raised the instrumental intensity, and "Cassidy" began to emerge as a highlight of many opening sets. The jam developed a bridge that led to spine-tingling crescendos. "Cassidy" was often played in the second half of the first set, and on several occasions, it was more powerful than the closing song. "Cassidy" was one of the Dead's hotter songs in their later years as the jam maintained an explosive yet elusive essence.

GREATEST STORY EVER TOLD

5-7-72 Bickershaw Festival, Wigan, England: The Dead launch set two of this majestic Europe '72 show with "Greatest Story Ever Told." Donna's low in the mix and during the jam she cuts loose with two short howls that don't interfere with the raging flow of the instrumental. There's a sharp, restless tone to Jerry's guitar as he slices and dices, and Phil clomps away like a racehorse coming down the stretch. Guitar licks scream and squeal in a steady stream; the mood is rowdy and reckless—the stuff that'll bust your brains out. With this sublime start to one of the great sets of '72, "Greatest Story" was on its way to jam anthem status. I'd also highly recommend the 5-3-72 Paris performance of "GSET."

5-19-74 Portland Memorial Coliseum, OR: Arriving in the third slot of set two, the Portland "Greatest Story" features attentive responses to Bobby's singing from Keith and Jerry. Donna's backing vocals are overly emphatic. She was a better vocalist on Jerry tunes and with the Jerry Garcia Band. "GSET" benefits from the Wall of Sound, as you can clearly hear each band member. Keith's spiraling leads spur a surge from Jerry as he plays in the cozy pocket of Billy's drumming. And then it sounds like Donna's giving birth onstage. After the screaming is over, the band rebuilds. Jerry catches fire again as Weir strums madly. There's crisp execution as the band succinctly touches down for the final chorus. You're also going to want to check out the 6-16-74 "Greatest Story."

2-17-79 Oakland Alameda Coliseum, CA: On the occasion of Keith and Donna's final show with the band, the Grateful Dead opened with "Greatest Story Ever Told," which had not been played since 1974. This thrilling opener establishes the tone for an imaginative show. There are no screaming shrieks from Donna as the house lights remain on and the band rages—Jerry engages his Mu-Tron filter and shreds a shrill run—dramatic and emphatic. The Oakland Coliseum is in heaven. This was the first time "Greatest Story" appeared as an opener, and it was the last extended jam on this tune, as the band chose the path of least resistance on most future renditions. "Greatest Story" would never again rock as hard or as long as it did in the Godchaux era.

PASSENGER

11-10-79 Crisler Arena, University of Michigan, Ann Arbor: The Dead smoked definitive versions of "Feel Like a Stranger" and Cassidy" in the Brendan Byrne Arena on 11-10-85. The Ann Arbor "Passenger" adds to the legacy of superior Weir tunes performed on November 10. "Passenger" didn't have the structure that led to complex jams with shifting phases like "Let it Grow" or "Music Never Stopped." What it did have was raging power, and the band was tapping into that in '79. The second solo of the Ann Arbor "Passenger" wreaks havoc. Bombs away! Phil's all over it as Jerry peels and reels off relentless leads—turbocharged with humor—laugh in amazement as you listen! Brent lubes the tracks with superb organ-grinding. They turn this over six times as Garcia finds a way to keep up his all-out assault using repetition without being repetitive. That may sound impossible, but Jerry's the master of impossibility. Weir and mates are disorientated by the virtuosity as they stumble into the final chorus after this dominant display. A set-ending "Deal" follows.

5-7-79 Alan Kirby Field House, Lafayette, PA: On the heels of a tender "Peggy O," the Boys deliver a "Passenger" blitzkrieg to end the opening set. Brent's organ screeches like a train arriving at its destination. The second solo of Phil's composition is a raging beast as Garcia digs in for several rounds of locomotive fretwork. Two years earlier, when it was born in St. Louis, "Passenger" was a lightweight tune, and now the song has enough presence to justify its place closing the set. **12-5-81 Market Square Arena, Indianapolis, IN**: Romping and stomping all night long in Indianapolis, the Dead played "Passenger" in the eighth slot of a thrilling ten-song set. This version is a shot of pure adrenaline and it's the penultimate version of "Passenger." The interplay between Garcia and Mydland is complex yet flawless, high-tech sonic fusion. Garcia's in quick-picking heaven as the band slams a succinct jam—running through stop signs yet completely in control of the raging beast. It sounds like Jerry is desperately stomping on brakes as Bobby sings the last chorus and "Passenger" come to a grinding/screeching halt. It's a shame this song was dropped from the rotation, but a new tune was stepping up to take its place as a dominant force.

CASSIDY

11-10-85 Brendan Byrne Arena, East Rutherford, NJ: The fourth song of the set is "Cassidy," and the lead singer is the most excited person in the building. As he had done during the 10-20-84 Syracuse "Jack Straw," Weir's forceful vocal phrasing inspires the band and the crowd. Weir's emphatic artistry could lead you to believe that this is the most important song of the twentieth century. There's a sublime musical conversation taking place onstage. Brent's organ riffs gleam like pearls as Jerry's guitar licks race to the scene. *Fare thee well now, let your life proceed by its own design. Nothing to tell now, let the words be yours, I'm done with mine.* This is where Garcia separates himself from any musician who has ever strapped on a guitar.

Garcia draws the jam into a vortex with a run of lower register notes. There's a colorful, glossy sound from the band as Jerry leads them out of the darkness with ascending runs that tingle the senses. Thanks to the early vortex, the band has only reached a plateau where they can regroup and strike again. The music magically swirls, and any experienced Dead listener knows Jerry's about to shift into Beast Mode.

The pinball is launched. Jerry and mates ring all the dramatic bells as the jam surpasses the majesty of any previous version. There's a modest blemish when Weir misses his cue to sing "Flight of the seabirds, scattered like lost words," by one second. It wouldn't be a Dead masterpiece without a taste of imperfection.

7-24-87 Oakland Coliseum Stadium, CA: The Grateful Dead played three sets on this night, two of their own and one with Bob Dylan. "Cassidy" is the next-to-last song of the band's opening set. As the instrumental unfolds, Phil and Bobby set a dark tone as they seemingly dig a crater for the Jerry volcano. Unlike "Greatest Story" or "Passenger," "Cassidy" is moody and suspenseful. Temperatures and passions plunge and rise. In Oakland, the band creates a substantial narrative. There's lots of ladder-climbing for Jerry and he's up to the task. On the extended road to ecstasy, Brent's slashing runs and the forceful drumming thrill the hollering and hooting crowd. Garcia's playing sparkles, and this is a thunderous group triumph.

10-12-83 Madison Square Garden, New York, NY: This smoking "Cassidy" comes in the thick of one of the Dead's hottest tours of the '80s. This is an insane jam, six madmen weaving intense layers of sonic complexity. Phil's a carpet-bombing demon start to finish. Weir's strumming hard and the pulse of this instrumental is molded by his odd chord phrasing. Garcia's shredding scales and he's utilizing a clever assortment of licks within the "Cassidy" framework. The walls and halls of Madison Square Garden could hardly contain this bombastic performance. This is a prime example of slightly sloppy 1983 jam mastery.

CUMBERLAND BLUES/ BIG RAILROAD BLUES

Since I took the liberty of lumping three related Weir numbers together, I decided to pair off Jerry's blues brothers, "Cumberland" and "Big Railroad Blues." I had already selected "Cumberland" as a jam anthem but felt bad about not inviting "Big Railroad" to the party. This is the solution. These are Garcia tunes born around the same time, and they essentially filled the same role in Dead sets during the same eras. And they both share the bond of being played in acoustic and electric sets in 1970.

"Cumberland Blues" was born in the Fillmore West on November 8, 1969. This Hunter/Garcia jingle was recorded in the studio and included on *Workingman's Dead*. Early on, "Cumberland" had a jug band feel to it as it straddled the acoustic/electric line. This is one of those songs that intensified in modest increments, show by show. The "Cumberland" from the Dead's second show of the 1972 European tour from London became the opening track of their triple album release, *Europe '72*. It's in the upper echelon of opening tracks on any official GD release. Few songs better capture Garcia's wizardry. You can hear that Bill Monroe/Earl Scruggs picking influence electrified and intensified. That's what the Acid Trips will make you do.

Despite its uplifting presence, "Cumberland" remained a rarity in the rotation for years. It was played twenty-two times in '72, six times in '73, and seven times in '74. After being performed on the Dead's last Winterland stand before their '74 touring hiatus, "Cumberland Blues" was retired for seven years until it was returned, to the yodeling delight of Deadheads in Long Beach Arena, on 8-27-81. Before the year was over, the Dead whipped "Cumberland" back into shape, playing it eleven times. It was a tune that stayed in the rotation, although it was never overplayed.

"Cumberland" was played every year from '81–'95, with 1987 being the peak year with twelve performances. To keep the streak alive, Jerry played his beloved workingman's tune at his last show in Chicago 7-9-95, the only "Cumberland" of the year. The Grateful Dead played Cumberland County Civic Center in Portland, Maine, eight times without ever playing "Cumberland Blues" there.

The "Big Railroad Blues" dossier is similar to "Cumberland Blues." An acoustic version of "Big RR Blues" opened the 6-24-70 Capitol Theatre show in Port Chester. This was the first complete performance of "Big RR." "Cumberland" was played later in this acoustic set. The next, and last, acoustic "Big RR" was performed during a masterful set in the Fillmore East on 9-20-70. The band's first "Big RR" of 1971, in the Manhattan Center, was captured and released on the double album *Grateful Dead* (Skull Fuck). The lyrics and arrangement of "Railroad" was simpler than "Cumberland," but both up-tempo numbers featured rowdy but tight jams that became longer, especially in the early '80s. After sixty-five performances of "Railroad" between '72 and '73, the tenacious rocker was played only twice in 1974 before being sidelined until Keith and Donna's last show on 2-17-79. It's intriguing that neither "Railroad" nor "Cumberland" were played in 1977, a year that featured powerhouse virtuosity. These songs were a perfect fit for that era, but it never happened.

"Railroad" remained in the rotation and was saved for the right occasions. From '79–'95, it was played every year but 1989 and 1993. And like "Cumberland," "RR Blues" was played at one show in '95, on June 28 in Auburn Hills, Michigan. The Blues Brothers were independent forces usually exploding in the middle of a hot first set, yet their histories are oddly similar and intertwined. Deservedly, they enter legendary jam status side by side.

CUMBERLAND BLUES

10-12-83 Madison Square Garden, New York, NY: If I had to pinpoint one week as the most underrated in Grateful Dead history, it would be the one that started in MSG on 10-11-83 and ended in Portland, Maine, on October 18. There's an abundance of extraordinary performances, and this 10-12-83 "Cumberland Blues" is one of them. It's a ten-minute romp, longer than any other version I'm aware of. After a blazing "Cassidy," which was discussed in the previous chapter, the band digs the groove as they hammer the intro of "Cumberland Blues."

The opening instrumental scoots along, *pickety-packety-a-pickety-packety-pu*. Garcia's fingers scramble as Brent chases. Phil is an animal! Pounding and astounding the Garden with concussive bass strikes. The next solo moves like a high-speed car chase—Beverly Hillbillies meets NASCAR—electrified bluegrass. There's sustained joy as Brent, Bobby, and Jerry sing the next verse. You can visualize the smile on Jerry's face as he croons, "Make good money, five dollars a dayyy!" When Jerry's happy, Madison Square Garden smiles. The third solo is an aural barrage that rolls on and on. Jerry's in the moment, time be damned!

4-8-72 Empire Pool, Wembley, London: We've got ourselves a candidate for best-ever track from an official Grateful Dead album. This "Cumberland" kicks off the first side of *Europe '72*. Lesh leads the charge with that irresistible bouncing bass as Weir chops in with a fetching riff. It's a swirling mix with hints of blues, jazz, and bluegrass—intricate, yet easy to groove to. "Cumberland" is the seventh song of the opening set. The Dead were artistically peaking, and London was experiencing a new direction in sonic exploration.

Solo two wreaks havoc. How can five musicians improvise at such a reckless pace and still make the sound melodically melt in one's mind? "Cumberland" catapults through time and space; it's a streak of aural enlightenment. The Dead dip back into the song and efficiently polish off an essential performance beyond anything that can be created in a studio; a perfect track beyond any producer's dreams.

9-27-72 Stanley Theater, Jersey City, NJ: Towards the end of a thirty-minute "Dark Star," an upbeat tempo arises as the jam wheels on, dizzy with possibilities. It could drift into "Big River" or "Sugar Magnolia." Wait a minute, here comes "Cumberland Blues." It's a strange, one-time connection, but with the right head of steam coming out of "Dark Star," it works. The opening riffs crackle as the Dead dive into the mine.

Zany energy propels this performance. Billy's hands and feet frantically fly in sync as the band plunders. The middle instrumental is furious. When the music can't logically peak any further, Garcia finds screaming notes to extend the rout. The 9-27-72 "Cumberland" is one of the longer and rowdier expeditions of the year.

6-27-84 Merriweather Post Pavilion, Columbia, MD: Cumberland, Maryland, a two-hour drive from Columbia, is located in the thick of coal mining country. This may be the origin of the song title, but I can't definitively confirm that.

The band rolls out "Cumberland Blues" with the fourth song in the first set. There's a unique, casual pace to this version. Jerry's rolling slow as he lays out ideas in the opening solo. There's a distinct workingman's rhythm as the band digs away. And eventually, Jerry steams the rice at the end of solos two and three. This version captures the reluctant joy of toiling for pay as the audience dances away. It's another day of improvisational sweat for the hardest-working band in the land.

3-24-85 Springfield Civic Center, MA: I attended this show, but may not have listened to it since 1985 because I'm a huge devotee of the following night's performance at the same venue. This impressive second set begins with "Samson and Delilah," the perfect springboard for "Cumberland." To borrow the title of an album by The Who, the beat is *Meaty Beaty Big and Bouncy*. Garcia's guitar tone pierces in soothing waves. All three instrumentals are substantial. The audience must have been in spinning/dancing heaven. Jerry's creative picking squeaks and squawks with sharp twists and turns during the second solo. It's a rewarding version that I may have never heard again if it weren't for this research.

BIG RAILROAD BLUES

10-21-83 The Centrum, Worcester, MA: It's Brent's birthday, and the band's ripping through a hot first set as they launch "Big Railroad Blues" in the eighth slot after "Brother Esau." On the Dead's second night in this new arena, they decide to christen it with a stunning eight-minute "Big Railroad." Perhaps they were inspired by history. Providence and Worcester Railway began construction of one of the major East Coast railroad lines in 1844. It was opened three years later. Or maybe this was simply a band on fire that had been performing knockout versions all tour, and now was the time for "BIG RR" to shine.

Phil's bass thumps the Centrum like a train rumblin' down the line. Sparks fly in a first jam that's as long and powerful as most second jams. As solo two unfolds, the intensity is off the charts—a time out of mind power drill that could ignite a barroom brawl or a raucous celebration. Garcia forges ahead round after round, and he can feel the pressure of Phil and Brent on his tail. At the end of this savage jam, the birthday boy pounds a slashing organ round. The Worcester express heads into the "Promised Land" to conclude a powerful set.

10-9-84 The Centrum, Worcester, MA: It's déjà vu all over again as the Boys rev up another "Big Railroad Blues" for Worcester as the next-to-last song of the opening set. Yes, the ghost of "Railroad" past is in the building. The first Jerry solo soars, but it's not as long as the one a year earlier. The next expedition shocks and rocks. Garcia's shredding with attitude as the sound waves crash through the Centrum. Jerry's chopping the ingredients for the stir fry and the band has oil sizzling in the pan. I was at this show in row two, bouncing off the cement floor like a world-class gymnast. After experiencing what it was like to be steamrolled by "Big RR" again, Worcester enjoyed the harvest of "Let it Grow" to close the set.

10-9-83 Greensboro Coliseum, NC: On its own, "Big Railroad Blues" would not have made the cut as one of the thirty-three jam anthems, but these '83 and '84 versions are huge, twice as long as their '70s predecessors. Like the "Railroad" a year later in Worcester, this sets up a "Let it Grow" conclusion to the set. Brent's organ slashing/stabbing at the end of Jerry's lines are a key component of these elongated "Railroads." The band puts their best foot forward in the herky-jerky second instrumental. The tracks are rickety and the brakes are worn but Jerry accelerates to the delight of those in the Greensboro Coliseum. Brent has a standout run, but Garcia won't be outdone as he pushes "Railroad" to an appropriate climax. It's a relatively simple blues tune, but in the early '80s, a steamrolling "Railroad" could catapult an opening set to immortality.

LAZY LIGHTNING > SUPPLICATION

Separated versions of "Lazy Lightning" and "Supplication" are the opening tracks of Bob Weir's *Kingfish*, recorded in 1975. Even though these are studio tracks, the divide between songs is odd, because most of us experience them as a seamless two-part musical piece.

Lazy Lightning > Supplication was debuted at the first show of 1976 in Portland, Oregon's, Paramount Theater on June 3. The combo's odd 7/4 time signature and psychedelic guitar intensity combine to embody that unique Grateful Dead sound that separated them from their peers in popular music. I may be taking a bit of a leap here, but the unbridled energy of this jam reminds me of "The Eleven" more than any other jam in the post-'74 era.

There are three instrumentals in this pairing, the precise between-verse "Lazy Lighting" solo, the meaty ascension to "Supplication," and the fiery closing jam. From the lyrics to the song structure, this was a complex combo that led to many vocal flubs. The band usually found a way to successfully play through instrumental mishaps. Lazy Lightning > Supplication was played at twenty-five of the forty-one shows in 1976, making that by far the busiest year for the Kingfish duo. The power of the cagey "Supplication" jam continued to surge until the song had enough presence to close opening sets in 1978. Lazy Lightning > Supplication was played 111 times, with 7 of those performances coming in the second set.

Whether it was this combo's innate peculiarity or the meticulous execution it demanded, Lazy Lightning >

Supplication was played less and less as the band jammed their way through the early '80s. The miscues were more numerous as the band played it less, but some of their best versions are from this period, as the band was very in the moment with this distinctive duo.

What is it about Halloween that led to last-ever versions? The Dead stopped playing "St. Stephen" for five years after 10-31-71, and the final version was on 10-31-83. The last go-round for Lazy Lightning > Supplication was 10-31-84 in the Berkeley Community Theatre. It was a long version that veered between sloppy and exhilarating. The "Supplication" jam lived on after "Lazy Lightning" was discarded. It was played thirteen times. As someone who had seen several hot Lazy Lightning > Supplications, I was always disappointed by these solo jams. It always sounded like Weir was about to step up to the mic and start singing, but that never happened. These jams are more entertaining in retrospect. However, the truth is that this gem of a combo was replaced by tunes that were easier to play and not as rewarding. Lazy Lightning > Supplication is one of those pieces of music that made the Grateful Dead a band beyond description.

4-14-82 Glens Falls Civic Center, NY: Outside of an early vocal miscue by Bobby, this performance is flawless, a description that is almost never attached to a serving of Lazy Lightning > Supplication. Garcia's tone is razor-sharp as he embarks upon the between-verse "Lightning" solo. Sonic loops of lazy lightning surge through the civic center. Weir's vocals are aggressive and precise as he sings, "My lightning too!" in falsetto, and as Bobby and Jerry howl the last "whew," the band nimbly drops into the delicate beginning of "Supplication." They are like magicians removing the ground beneath your feet.

The ascension of the "Supplication" jam is one of the understated pleasures of listening to the Grateful Dead. Brent's slick organ work sets the stage as Jerry's leads surge in progressively hotter waves. Bobby's in heaven as his sublime strumming is the focal point of the instrumental. And the lid blasts off the pot as Garcia boils until Weir sings, "Whoo! Well, dizzy ain't the word for the way that you're making me feel now." Jerry's mad chord riffing builds the tension as Weir salivates through "Supplication." Garcia applies the final electric brushstrokes on a blazing outro jam that ends precisely on the final "Whooo!" The Dead end the set by launching a surprise "Bertha." This set is loaded with dynamic performances. The 4-14-82 versions of "Little Red Rooster" and Lazy Lightning > Supplication have no equal.

6-8-77 Winterland, San Francisco, CA: This is the middle show of a three-night Winterland stand after one of the Dead's most prodigious touring months. Spirited singing and sexual urgency surge during this set-ending combo. Jerry's bending and squeezing the juice out of notes when appropriate. "Supplication" emerges bold and dreamy, clean execution without being rushed. Rhythms and bass gracefully grind with Garcia's guitar. On this night, they're raising the stakes in "Supplication," playing it with purpose. Bobby's all fired up as he sings the verse and the jam after rages on longer than any other version to that point. Lazy Lightning > Supplication closed the set and entered the realm of jam anthems.

5-22-82 Greek Theatre, Berkeley, CA: This was the Lazy Lightning > Supplication following the Glens Falls tour de force. The Boys brought back loops of psychedelic intensity for the Greek after their East Coast tour. From the get-go this is cocaine crisp—shake, bake, shimmy, and bounce. "Supplication" soars in the fast lane; the music comes across like a strange language that could only be processed by Deadheads. The sounds thunder from the stage and ricochet off the earth's atmosphere and return to the Greek. Phil's bass pumps like velvet thunder. This isn't as clean as Glens Falls, but the energy's on the same level. A rowdy post-"Supplication" romp is followed by a hilarious Ric Flair punctuation courtesy of Weir, "Whooo!"

10-18-83 Cumberland County Civic Center, Portland, ME: One of the problems that plagued this combo in its final years was sloppy execution, which eventually led to its extinction. In Portland, there are blown lyrics and instrumental miscues all over the place. On occasions like this one, it's a blessing. The band is on fire during this first set, and each mistake is an opportunity for the band to atone via extra jamming. The instrumental on the road to "Supplication" verse is long and wild. This "Supplication" barrage is a bountiful feast for Jerry lovers.

3-10-81 Madison Square Garden, New York, NY: I love the sounds from this two-night MSG stand. The artistic intention to make things sound different is obvious on these blessed nights. "Lazy Lightning" is intense and subtle at the same time. Garcia and Mydland playfully harmonize, "My lightning too." Brent leads the way at the start of "Supplication." Jerry's throwing in tasty licks, but he takes a step back to hear what his mates are creating. The texture of the jam is trippy as the drummers and Weir strike a powerful progression leading to the verse. After Weir sings, Jerry goes nuts. Kung Pao! Another weird and wonderful Lazy Lightning > Supplication enters the greatest vault of music known to man.

7-18-76 Orpheum Theatre, San Francisco, CA: There's nothing like the innocence of an exquisitely performed original composition, and that's what we have here in the Orpheum. The band has a handle on this odd yet enticing Kingfish tandem. Donna's backing vocals sound superb, and Keith chops away like Herbie Hancock. The music stews in its strange, newborn glow—instrumentals feathery and cool. This concise performance transitions into "Let it Grow," and it's the gateway to of one of the great musical segments of the Bicentennial year, 1976: Lazy Lightning > Supplication > Let it Grow > Drums > Let it Grow > Wharf Rat > The Other One > St. Stephen > Not Fade Away > St. Stephen > The Wheel > The Other One > Stella Blue.

2-17-79 Winterland Arena, San Francisco, CA: Any time the online topic is hot versions of Lazy Lightning > Supplication, someone always mentions 2-17-79. It's a dynamic version that ends a historic first set (Keith and Donna's last show). The music's gorgeous as Garcia's garrulous guitar gobbles away. Keith opens the road to "Supplication" with swirling piano runs. Garcia's smoking out of the gate; insane pecking. Both jams surrounding the "Supplication" verse come across with urgency. This is a shorter rendition than most of the ones listed above, but 2-17-79 gets an A for quality.

COMES A TIME/ STELLA BLUE

Once Drums became a regular feature in the middle of the second set, the most anticipated post-Drums song became the long, slow Jerry ballad. "Morning Dew" is the undisputed jam champion of songs in that role. Of the other tunes that regularly filled that slot, "Stella Blue," "Comes a Time," "Black Peter," and "Wharf Rat," I chose "Comes a Time" as one of the jam anthems. It was also the rarest of all these Jerry ballads, played only sixty-six times over twenty-three years. Garcia rarely left a "Comes a Time" jam uncooked. But as I started writing this, I couldn't pass on the opportunity to praise "Stella Blue." Even though the outro wasn't as consistent, there's nothing like a "Stella" jam when the water's boiling over the pot.

"Comes a Time" was debuted along with "Jack Straw," "One More Saturday Night," "Mexicali Blues," Tennessee Jed," and "Ramble on Rose," during Keith's first show on 10-19-71 in Northrop Auditorium. It was a spirited debut with two gripping solos and a touch of falsetto singing during the chorus from Jerry. On this version, and a few others from this tour, there's an extra verse that starts with the line, "When the words come out like an angry stream." That verse was scrapped, and "Comes a Time" settled into the most basic of song structures: chorus > verse > chorus > jam > verse > chorus > outro jam. The slow tempo and simple structure of "Comes a Time" allowed Garcia to pour his heart and soul into the spirit of the lyrics, and his guitar solos were emotive forays that restated the sentiment of Hunter's words. This song was a deep emotional undertaking for Jerry, and consequently, that's probably why it remained a rare tune saved for the right moments.

Exactly one year after its birth, "Comes a Time" was played in the Fox Theatre (St. Louis) on 10-19-72, and then it was retired for almost four years. With the abundance of fresh originals at their disposal during this era, it was inevitable that some gems would be stored for later use. Already a slow ballad, "Comes a Time" was slower than molasses when it was returned to the rotation on 6-12-76 in the Boston Music Hall. The new version was recorded in the studio and included as the last track on Garcia's third solo album, *Reflections.* The standstill pace of the tune benefited Jerry's maturing voice, as he was able to dig deep and sing "Comes a Time" with chilling conviction and tenderness. And with the slower version came longer jams. "Comes a Time" went from seven minutes to over eleven minutes by 1977.

Most aficionados would agree that '77 was the finest year for "Comes a Time." All five '77 versions are from May, and if somebody were to rank the all-time best versions, and the top five slots were from 5-77, it would be tough to argue with that assessment. "Comes a Time" was played once each in both '78 and '79. There were six outstanding performances of "Comes a Time" in 1980 before it was dropped from the rotation for five long years. The beloved ballad gained another layer of poignancy as Jerry crooned it by himself without any backing vocals.

Celebrating their twentieth anniversary in the Greek Theatre, the Dead broke out "Comes a Time" on opening night (6-14-85). As Garcia continued to battle the demon of his drug addiction, this number retained its poignancy, even if Jerry's voice had to croak its way through at times. "Comes a Time" was only played seven times after Jerry's 1986 coma.

"All the years combine. They melt into a dream." Hunter's opening lines were sung live by Jerry for the first time in the Hollywood Bowl on June 17, 1972, at Pigpen's last show. "Stella Blue" had a temperature, vibe, and pace similar to "Comes a Time," but there was a bridge and extra verse. "Comes a Time" was performed evenly, while "Stella Blue" had more twists, peaks, and valleys. For the first few years, the stunning vocal performance from Garcia was bigger than the instrumentals. Jerry tapped into the essence of "Stella" quicker than "Comes a Time," and consequently it was a mainstay in the rotation.

The Dead performed "Stella Blue" 326 times. It managed to walk that fine line of staying in the rotation without being overplayed. The longest stretch the band went without playing "Stella" was seventeen shows between late '77 and April '78. The outro jam, which is the reason "Stella Blue" is being examined here, peaked in a seven-year stretch between 1977 and 1984. On many nights, the outro was abrupt as it quickly transitioned into the likes of "Around and Around" or "Good Lovin'." But when the outro cooked, it was so powerful and awesome that "Stella" had to be inducted into the Jam Anthem Hall of Fame.

COMES A TIME

8-31-80 Capital Centre, Landover, MD: Literally and figuratively, this is as close as musicians can come to stopping time in its tracks. The night before, in Philadelphia, the band rocked elite versions of "Althea" and "Jack Straw," and the show after Landover featured a masterpiece presentation of Iko Iko > Morning Dew > Sugar Magnolia.

The Landover "Comes a Time" lifts off with its signature dreamlike, floating intro. The lone voice is gorgeous yet heartbreaking; Jerry's mastered the art of bittersweet. As he finishes singing, "Can't see much difference between dark and light," there's a yearning gurgle in the last word—little nuances mean everything.

The tone of the Tiger is exactly perfect as Garcia bends emotive licks and plays them off the silence. Deep human emotion drips from his guitar, and the listener can feel the meaning of the song viscerally. The sad, perfect landing of the solo gives way to that vulnerable voice that tugs at our hearts. A well-played "Comes a Time" exhibits seemingly effortless perfection easier than any other song I can think of.

Garcia shreds a substantial outro solo that is meaty all the way through. He kind of pounces on these solos in the '80s as opposed to slowly building them as in '76 and '77. The band feeds off the 8-31-80 "Comes a Time," segueing into a "Truckin'" that becomes extra rowdy.

5-9-77 War Memorial Auditorium, Buffalo, NY: The night after Cornell, the Dead pounded out a great first set and then hypnotized Buffalo with "Comes a Time" towards the end of set two. Garcia's poignant crooning fills the War Memorial, and Donna's at her best harmonizing with Jerry. This version has a little extra pizazz separating it from the four other outstanding May '77 versions. The band deliberately unwinds a spiraling outro jam as Jerry bends sorrowful notes followed by quick-picking streams of hope and compassion. With the overall perfection of this performance and the sizzle of the instrumental, it's tough to top the 5-9-77 "Comes a Time."

10-15-76 Shrine Auditorium, Los Angeles, CA: This rendition is served in the thick of a one-time-only gourmet presentation of The Other One > Comes a Time > Franklin's Tower > Sugar Magnolia to end the second set. No encore was necessary, and the Dead didn't play one.

The Shrine "Comes a Time" is another blessed performance. Flawless. Jerry pinches notes that sigh and squeal as the outro unravels. Jerry's leads spiral in time with the aggressive piano playing. The jam reaches a peak. Keith creates a bridge that extends the jam and draws some additional heated fretwork from Jerry before spilling into a surprise "Franklin's Tower." If you're a Keith fanatic, this tape's for you. His playing stands out all night long in the Shrine.

3-23-86 The Spectrum, Philadelphia, PA: This was my 100th Grateful Dead show, and the second time I witnessed "Comes a Time." Jerry's feeling this one, belting it out soulfully. The slight struggle in Jerry's voice helps this performance resonate. This is of a higher vocal quality than most from this era. Healy added the right touch of echo and reverb as Jerry sang, "You can't let go because you're afraid to fall. But the day may come when you can't feel at all." The hippie masses huddled in the Spectrum were soaking in Jerry's essence in awe, syllable by syllable. This was a heavy tune that hit home in Jerry's later years. Perhaps it was too personal, and that's why the Dead only played it seven times after 1986. Smooth, slicing Tiger guitar licks fill both instrumentals. This is heartbreaking and oh so rewarding.

STELLA BLUE

12-9-81 Events Center, University of Colorado, Boulder: My focus on all these "Stellas" will be strictly based on the outro jam. We're all familiar with the immense power of Jerry belting out "Stella." There's a restless feel as Garcia strikes the opening licks—instant messaging that will be memorable. The band senses the mood of their inspired leader as they roll out the velvet carpet. A sparkling series of leads features swift-picking confidence without sacrificing ambiance.

Garcia puts what seems to be the finishing touches on an above-average outro before this gets out of hand. The rest of the band is either indecisive as to the next tune, or they're waiting for Jerry to blow the roof off the Events Center. The Bearded One obliges, inexplicably picking up where he left off. The band comes together to fire off another stunning outro progression—mathematically precise and Chernobyl hot. When Jerry rips a "Stella" solo like this, you wonder why it wasn't like this more often. Now that Boulder's been blitzed, the show may continue. "Well the joint was jumping, going round and round. Hey reelin' and rockin', what a crazy sound!"

10-21-78 Winterland Arena, San Francisco, CA: "Morning Dew" was only played once between 4-15-78 and 11-8-79. "Stella Blue" never consistently shined like "Dew," but in heat index and DNA, "Stella" was the closest thing to the "Dew." There are many noteworthy "Stellas" from this era, and this rendition may be the best.

Garcia's ringing the alarms with thick, piercing notes early on. An intense focus takes hold of the band as Jerry darts through scales. A wonderful soundboard recording cowers in fear of what's to come. In other words, an audience recording is spliced in to capture the searing ending. A chord-fanning frenzy of the highest possible frequency puts this four-minute outro to bed.

10-6-81 Rainbow Theatre, London, England: Instead of "Sunshine Daydream," "Stella Blue" emerges after "Sugar Magnolia." The "Stella" outro creeps quiet as a mouse, but leftover "Sugar Mag" combustion infuses this jam. Jerry's solo shifts from moody and mellow to volatile in seconds. The band is hammering away in unison as the intensity and velocity of Garcia's repetitive scale surges verge on impossible. In fact, the band waves the white flag, but Jerry's still shredding mid-flight. Garcia carries on and when he realizes the band isn't with him, his leads roll into a smashing chord that's triumphant and a touch angry. The show marches on with an upbeat "Good Lovin'."

7-3-78 St. Paul Civic Center, MN: The Dead are in good spirits four days before their debut in Red Rocks. As the "Stella" carousel spins, every note is a pleasure pocket. Jerry bends early, warning signs foretelling the impending rampage. Jerry wraps his leads around Phil's authoritative bass, up, down, and all-round the spine. After working through a series of accelerating scales, the chord fanning ensues. Jerry scratches away, taking this to the highest possible register. This is a master's class in how to squeeze the juice out of the "Stella" lemon.

11-4-77 Cotterrell Gym, Colgate University, Hamilton, NY: Phil introduced himself and his mates as the Jones Gang at the start of an immortal second set. Towards the end of a stunning "Playin'" loop featuring Eyes of the World > Estimated Prophet > The Other One, "Stella" sets sail like a soothing prayer and Jerry's voice hangs onto those final sighs: "Stela Blue-eew, Stella Blue-ewwe-whew." Time to dust off those rusty strings one more time. Jerry's wheeling and peeling, images of ballroom dancing. The outro unfolds in short paragraphs with proper escalation. It's not as combustible as some of the versions that followed, but this outro is played to the hilt, and it's a worthy representation from this show and this year.

7-21-84 Ventura County Fairground, CA: Jerry and mates took the road of least resistance on many "Stellas" during the

'80s. This wasn't one of them. Somehow, the lazy silence at the end of Jerry's last "Stella Blue" sigh suggests mayhem. You can sense the energy before it's unleashed. Garcia starts to slice away. One lick leads to a savage run. Phil and the band have the pulse of this jam—majestic, moody, and bold. Jerry's leaning back, digging in—all human emotion rolled into one. This is a radiant jewel in a minefield of duds from this era.

SAMSON AND DELILAH

The unlikely combination of biblical sermon and rock 'n' roll powder keg fused into one, "Samson and Delilah" delighted the faithful from its debut at the first show of 1976 through the Dead's final show in Chicago. "Samson and Delilah" is a traditional Dead adaption heavily influenced by the version of bluesman Reverend Gary Davis.

In his element, Weir sang with controlled passion throughout as Jerry displayed his knack for creativity within a repetitive framework—a more compressed "Fire on the Mountain." Billy and Mickey enjoyed kicking the song off and establishing tempo. And the coda featured the chorus with a split-second ending followed by a sing-along reprise. This led to several timing mishaps and hilarious moments, but on most occasions, it was pulled off with authority.

After "Samson's" debut in Portland on 6-3-76, the jams fattened as the song maintained a funky feel. "Samson and Delilah" was one of the more potent tracks of *Terrapin Station*. The Dead stepped on the gas in 1977 as "Samson" flexed muscle and fit in nicely alongside originals like "Bertha" and "Terrapin Station." "Samson" sizzled on, rarely easing back to its funkier 1976 form.

Usually, "Samson and Delilah" was a second-set selection, often feeding off a hot Garcia combo like Scarlet > Fire, Help on the Way > Slipknot! > Franklin's Tower, or China Cat > Rider. It also worked well with Estimated > Eyes and "Shakedown Street." Occasionally our biblical couple opened a second set, but its finest quality was its ability to effectively step up after a raucous opener and keep the fire burning. "Estimated Prophet" and "Playin' in the Band" were the other big Weir tunes for this slot. However, those songs felt like a new beginning changing the flow of the show, whereas "Samson" imposed itself as a continuation—lighter fluid to a campfire.

Of all the jam anthems dissected for this endeavor, "Samson" has the fewest variations version to version. On top of their game, the Dead may extend any of the jams half a minute more than usual. The temperature and time in the oven varied, but "Samson" was "Samson," reliable, gritty, and tough. Many classic Dead moments dive headfirst into "Samson." The debut of "Quinn the Eskimo" (12-30-85), the Merriweather "Shakedown" (6-30-85), etc. Without further ado, here's commentary on some of the most volatile "Samsons."

2-5-78 Uni-Dome, University of Northern Iowa, Cedar Falls: Great accidental art takes flight as set two starts with "Samson." After a sharp intro jam, Donna and Jerry sing the chorus and then Weir either forgets the lyrics, or his microphone is not working. When all else fails, the Grateful Dead know exactly what to do. Boy, does Garcia answer the call. The ensuing solo is easily the best of any "Samson." Garcia unloads wave after wave; guitar runs pile on top of each either as they incrementally become faster and hotter for several minutes. Weir hollers: "Whoo-hoo!" indicating his pleasure for Garcia's virtuosity and simultaneously letting Jerry know he's ready move forward.

The opening five minutes of this "Samson" is sensational, and it couldn't have consciously occurred if it weren't for the miscue. If the band had planned to rip the intro jam before the set, it could never have come off as hot as this accidental masterpiece. There's no letup in the two ensuing solos of the beefy 2-5-78 "Samson," which ends after eleven and a half minutes. The rowdy opener helps propel the rest of the set as the Dead go on to crush sublime versions of Scarlet > Fire and "The Other One."

6-7-77 Winterland, San Francisco, CA: A smoking opening solo that goes on for more than two minutes will just about ensure the elite status of any "Samson." Coming out of Drums, Garcia and mates wheel, deal, slice, and dice a rousing, three-minute "Samson" intro. The energy crackles through the next two solos. The band's channeling the spirit of Samson, the strongest man that ever lived on earth. Performances of "Samson" from this year exude a raw, metallic grind, indicative of the Dead at their rocking '77 peak.

A hot "Samson and Delilah" was an effective prelude to a great segment. It was a workout of a tune that got the juices flowing. On this night in the Winterland, the Dead followed "Samson" with Terrapin Station > Morning Dew. "The Dew" is a monster. Two nights later in the Winterland, "Samson" opened the second set of 6-9-77. The opening solo isn't in the same league as 6-7-77, but the rest of the song rocks and sets the tone for one of the legendary sets of the year: "Funiculi Funicula" tuning, Help on the Way > Slipknot! > Franklin's Tower, Estimated Prophet > St. Stephen > Not Fade Away > Drums > St. Stephen > Terrapin Station > Sugar Magnolia.

11-7-85 War Memorial Auditorium, Rochester, NY: From the summer of '85 through the end of the year, the Grateful Dead displayed a 20th Anniversary banner at all their shows. On the first of two nights in Rochester, the banner was lowered behind the band during the first song of the second set as they neared the end of "Touch of Grey." Everybody was singing, "We will get bye-eye-eye, we will survive." The building was shaking from thunderous crowd noise as Billy and Mickey pounded into "Samson and Delilah."

The opening jams from this period tended to be brief, but an inspired Garcia took a few extra spins around the block in Rochester. Brent slashed exotic organ riffs to play off Bobby's spirited vocals. The band locked in tight in the fast lane. This "Samson" finishes in a shade under seven minutes, but it's a compressed and urgent attack.

Towards the end of the third jam, Garcia kicks into overdrive. As the band triumphantly returns for the final sing-off, Jerry hangs onto the final word of, "Tear this old building dow-ow-own!" Everyone in the band is laughing too hard for the next line. Good times rule after all these years. After the energetic opening combo, Jerry settles Rochester into the most poignant "High Time" you will ever hear.

7-18-82 Ventura County Fairgrounds, CA: Set two is launched and turbocharged with "Samson and Delilah." Brent's slick organ sounds form the powdery slope for the band's downhill slalom skiing. The playing is graceful as Garcia races pole to pole. It's the middle of summer and they're playing by the shore, but these are the images that come to mind. And while powdery slopes come to mind, it's not much of a stretch to imagine that members of the band may have indulged in some nose powder during intermission.

During solo two, Weir's slide-playing spurs Garcia like a bullfighter enticing a bull. The jams are tight and action-packed. Listening to solo three, one could get the idea that "Samson" was a sprinter—the swiftest man alive. Everything comes off as it should. All vocal contributions resonate. This slick "Samson" creates the perfect launch into "Franklin's Tower," the only time these tunes were hitched. Later in the set, the Dead break out a touching "Crazy Fingers," the first time it was played in six years. A set-opening "Samson" successfully strikes again!

12-31-76 Cow Palace, Daly City, CA: In the thick of a super-long set, after the third performance of "Good Lovin'" since 1972, the band bobs and weaves its way into a funky "Samson" with a compelling segue. As opposed to the usually powerful opening, this transition is a hypnotic massage. Jerry's adding tasty licks as Bobby emphatically belts out the final syllable of each line. Keith and Phil are active in the open space in this arrangement. Garcia's licks shriek as the jam grinds and turns gracefully. It's a presentation that's powerful and playful at the same time. It's a unique "Samson" that stands out from others before or after it.

10-17-83 Olympic Center, Lake Placid, NY: Deadheads and the band were inspired by the venue. One of the greatest sports moments of the twentieth century, the Americans beating the Russians in hockey, had taken place in this venue less than three years earlier, and the thrill was still tangible. The Dead let it all hang out with legendary versions of "Sugaree" and "Deal" in the opening set. Since a song called "David and Goliath" wasn't in the band's repertoire, they played the next closest thing, "Samson and Delilah," on the heels of a "Touch of Grey" second-set opener.

Garcia jumps the drummer's intro with a substantial solo. There's extra effort in every jam—the Lake Placid motif—and a sense of jocularity fills the music. The aggressive second jam seems to tap into the biblical magic of the Miracle on Ice. The power of the third jam takes on a comical tone. The band gives it their all as if effort and enthusiasm are the only criteria. This beast of a "Samson" is a nine-minute thriller.

3-31-88 Brendan Byrne Arena, East Rutherford, NJ: Feeding off the flow of a smoking "Fire on the Mountain," the Boys pounce on "Samson and Delilah." Garcia's licks are razor-sharp and purposeful. The jams aren't as long as the ones from Lake Placid, but they don't need to be. This is an active volcano—a romp and stomp, exactly what the situation called for in front of a hungry East Coast crowd. After scrappy singing during the chorus, Weir declares, "That's right," and Jerry strikes the golden opening chords of "Terrapin Station."

DANCIN' IN THE STREET

Although they are both cover songs that ended up on the album *Terrapin Station*, the history and evolution of "Samson and Delilah" and "Dancin' in the Street" could not be more different. "Samson" joined the band's repertoire in '76, and it remained the same, a reliable staple delivered without structural changes. It was played 364 times. The Grateful Dead debuted "Dancin' in the Street" in the Fillmore Auditorium during the summer of 1966. They would go on to play it 117 times over the next twenty-one years. "Samson and Delilah" gave off the illusion of being a Dead original, since most people, including myself, had never heard it anywhere else before. On the other hand, "Dancin' in the Street" was a 1964 hit for Martha Reeves and the Vandellas, and it was successfully covered by many major artists through the years. When the Dead played "Dancin'," everybody knew the tune. It took a ton of creativity for the Dead to transform this into a unique jam anthem.

The musical beat rejoices, "Hop-skip-and-a-jump now," and Pigpen's keyboard chimes loud. Weir sings, "Calling out around the world, are you ready for a brand new beat? Summer's here and the time is right for dancin' in the street."

We're in the Fillmore Auditorium on July 3, 1966, and the Grateful Dead are opening the show with "Dancin' in the Street." It's a brilliant choice, as if the band's asking this audience, and future audiences, if they're ready for the revolutionary new sound that the Grateful Dead will be laying on them. At the same time, these musical crusaders are giving the audience a taste of a commercial song they're bound to know, yet the Dead are about to transform this beloved Motown tune into an eight-minute rock/funk swirl with a prolonged instrumental break. It might be the only song that people seeing the band for first time know as they learn to love the Grateful Dead.

From its debut through April '69, "Dancin'" was an occasional guest in the band's live repertoire. With their evolving canon of psychedelic jam tunes, the Dead couldn't find a slot for "Dancin'" in the scheme of things. Was it a feel-good crowd-pleaser or a vehicle for heavy jamming? From May '69 through 1970, "Dancin' in the Street" was performed thirty-one times. The correct answer became B: vehicle for heavy jamming. Weir's vocals and the group harmonies on "Dancin'" improved during this period, and the jams were extremely rowdy and flexible. As the flow of instrumental veered in different directions, the intensity and length of the jam remained intact. You could always count on at least seven minutes of high-intensity improvisation.

The authors of "Dancin' in the Street," Marvin Gaye, William Stevenson, and Ivy Jo Hunter, never intended this to be more than a party song, but when inner-city riots broke out across America in 1966, some protest leaders used the song as an anthem while organizing demonstrations. I don't believe the Grateful Dead were consciously using this as a protest song in 1970. Sometimes the events of the times can change the feelings and meanings of the songs in a way that the creators or performers never intended. The Dead played many college campuses in 1970 around the time of the slaughter of four students by National Guardsmen on the campus of Kent State. With all the antiwar protests and student strikes, "Dancin' in the Street" tapped into the something in the air. And the powerhouse performances from the Dead had a revolutionary vibe. It was a soundtrack of the times.

With the abundance of new Hunter tunes being worked into the lineup, "Dancin'" was one of the longer jam tunes cut from the rotation. After 1970 it was played on 12-31-71, and then put into hibernation until the first show of 1976 on June 3 in Portland. The revamped version was focused and funky, with excellent group harmonizing. I don't think it's fair to categorize anything the Dead ever played as disco, but these '76 and '77 versions tapped into the times again. Disco was king, and "Dancin' in the Street" struck a disco vibe as much as any song until "Shakedown Street" was debuted in 1978. "Dancin'" was performed at twenty-six of the band's forty-one shows in 1976.

As with other jam anthems, '77 was a peak performance year for "Dancin'" (thirteen performances). Steaming, compressed versions of "Dancin'" surfaced twenty-one times over the next two years before she faded away again. "Dancin'" returned in Kansas City on 7-7-81, and then was sidelined until 6-24-84 Saratoga Springs. The new arrangement resembled a tighter and shorter version of "Dancin'," circa 1970. The later-day renditions made for thrilling show openers, but they weren't as substantial as their predecessors. The last dance for "Dancin'" went down on 4-6-87 in the Brendan Byrne Arena. It was a subpar ending for a glorious jam anthem.

5-15-77 St. Louis Arena, MO: In the middle of one of their most revered tours, the Dead tear it up for St. Louis, City of Blues. Ms. Donna Jean Godchaux is the most dominant vocalist on this version. This performance would shine on a best of Donna Jean compilation. The group singing is gorgeous and the jam is steady, resolute, and rapid. If you love Garcia's garrulous Mu-Tron ramblings, this is your ticket. The dance party is on! Garcia's digging the groove and dominating the jam as he rages down a river of madness and the band dives headfirst into the funkiness, à la Sly & The Family Stone. Jerry bounces an assortment of riffs off the solid rock foundation: piercing squeals > rapid-fire fretwork > bass bombardment and chord fanning.

After a long jam, the band nails the shuffling funk transition back to the chorus. That passage is exhilarating, almost up there with the funky riffing at the end of '73 and '74 "Eyes." Donna, Bob, and Jerry stagger the "Dancin' in the Street" chant—lots of giggling, yelping, and yodeling as the pounding percussions egg them on—a Grateful Dead Motown revival. The band's passion for the music they are playing and their respect for the people that are digging it are irrefutable. After the longest "Dancin'" chant simmers down, Weir says, "We're gonna take a short break," and then the band shakes the St. Louis Arena with a thunderous finale flourish, a unique gesture that separates this from any other rendition.

4-12-70 Fillmore West, San Francisco, CA: This was the last show of a four-night stand that featured Miles Davis opening for the Grateful Dead. Miles mesmerized the audience and the Dead with groundbreaking music from his recently released double album *Bitches Brew*. His intense fusion improv probably inspired this scintillating performance of "Dancin'."

The Fillmore West is hopping as the Dead push forth a funky groove. Weir sings with authority and Garcia's letting it all hang out as he belts out the backing vocals. The band has made serious vocal strides in the last year or so. The "Dancin'" jam takes off briskly, and Garcia steams towards an early peak. Phil's bubbling bass redirects the flow of the jam against the continuity of Pigpen's organ, which is turned up louder than usual. The crisp tempo never wanes as Lesh and Garcia take turns rebuilding and deconstructing. Garcia's guitar sears as the band races along cohesively. At times, the jam sounds as if it's veering back and forth from "Dancin'" to "Hard to Handle." Just as it seems they've milked this for all it's worth, Phil and Bobby bounce into a "Feelin' Groovy" jam, thereby luring Garcia into one more rampage. The 4-12-70 "Dancin'" is special, and it was immortalized on the 1997 CD release *Fallout from the Phil Zone*.

5-2-70 Harpur College, Binghamton, NY: The Harpur College affair is a remarkable show in the thick of chaotic times on college campuses. This isn't as finely crafted or harmonized as the 4-12-70 rendition, but that's the way the Grateful Dead roll, and this "Dancin'" rolls on for almost sixteen minutes.

There's an organic flow to the first stage of the jam. Led by Weir's rhythm and Phil's bold bass, the band creates a stir-fry of sound. Chez Garcia's chopping and slicing away, tossing in a unique blend of riffs and leads. A "Tighten Up" jam develops, and Jerry peppers away on the fringes. This is the longest and rowdiest advance into this motif. "Tighten Up" slips into some cosmic noodling; "Dark Star" flashbacks. And then the band blasts back into "Dancin'." Binghamton challenges 4-12-70 for best "Dancin'" of the year, although it's not as possessed or urgent as that gem from the Fillmore West. **10-11-77 Lloyd Noble Center, Oklahoma University, Norman**: This is one of three shows that archivist Dick Latvala labeled as Primal Dead. I hear it in this raging "Dancin'." Although, I'm surprised he blessed this show with that prestigious stamp. It's irrefutable that the Dead played with raging energy on this tour. The drummers are locked in and pounding—runaway freight trains. "Dancin'" gracefully launches set two. Before stepping into the instrumental, Bobby, Donna, and Jerry have a "Dancing, dancing, dancing in the street" sing-off, hanging onto that phrase for several minutes.

Garcia's conversing in Chinese via his Mu-Tron filter. Phil's burping and bouncing bass off Jerry's eccentric phrasing. Weir and the drummers relentlessly push the pace. When it sounds like they may head into the funky transition riff, Jerry peels off a series off runs, pecking away east, west, north, south, up, down, and around Highway 61 and back again. The beast is loose yet the band's controlling it like a puppet on strings. The high-tech funk transition storms the senses. The Norman "Dancin'" forced the faithful into seventeen minutes of unholy pleasure. Samuel Lloyd Noble, oilman and philanthropist, would have been proud.

10-9-84 The Centrum, Worcester, MA: *Hop-skip-and-a-jump now...*It's an old-school arrangement of "Dancin' in the Street" to open the festivities. These '84 and '85 versions aren't as long or powerful as the '70 and '77 jam fests, but they're awesome in their own way. The 10-18-84 Brendan Byrne Arena "Dancin'" has a hotter jam than this one. But I prefer the construction of the Worcester jam. It's the first song of the night and you can hear Jerry's fingers actively snap and bend those rusty strings. It's a robust journey. Garcia takes it logically A–Z. It sounds like Jerry is ready to turn back the clock and take this into overdrive, but Bobby cuts back to the final verse. His singing is controlled on this night, no superfluous falsetto. If only the Dead could have recorded a studio version that sounded like this.

11-9-79 War Memorial Auditorium, Buffalo, NY: This is the third "Dancin'" of the Brent era. Earlier this tour, the Dead wowed Cape Cod Coliseum with a powerful Dancin' > Franklin's Tower to open set two on 10-27-79. The Buffalo Dancin' > Franklin's is a few degrees hotter.

Brent's voice worked better than Donna's in the scheme of things, but not in "Dancin'." However, Brent's organ pushed the instrumental pace of "Dancin'" into the excessive speeding lane. Bobby's chord strumming is exceptional throughout, the backbone that Jerry and Phil weave their magic upon—scales up and down in the key of life. The drummers hammer away at an improbable pace. The jam careens out of control, too hot to handle. Somehow, they find their way back to the funky chord riff and the final chorus. It's not as long as its '77 predecessors, but the mission was more dangerous. A few weeks earlier in Cape Cod, the Dancin' > Franklin's transition is clean. This one's dirty. Half the band doesn't want to let go of "Dancin'" as they trickle into "Franklin's." It sounds like they had something magical going here, but the Dead didn't play "Dancin'" again until 1981 in Kansas City.

4-22-77 The Spectrum, Philadelphia, PA: In the middle of the second set during the first East Coast show of the year, the Dead play a one-time-only combo: Dancin' in the Street > Got My Mojo Working > Dancin' in the Street. They were really dancing in Philadelphia, PA. The upbeat strut of "Dancin'" comes off with more kick than usual on the heels of "It Must Have Been the Roses." Garcia noodles and doodles over a relentless rhythm that shares the tenacious nature of South Philly.

In the middle of this instrumental workout, there's a subtle shift in the chord sequence and Weir sings a few verses of "Got My Mojo Working," the first of three Dead versions of Howlin' Wolf's classic. It's as if the band never left the "Dancin'" framework so they would have a simple transition back to the jam. Garcia whittles away as the band rams into the fetching, funky finale. After the final sing-off, there's a clever segue into

"The Wheel" and the show ends with "Terrapin Station." That's a powerful way to say goodnight.

ESTIMATED PROPHET

This is the third Bob Weir/Jerry loves Mu-Tron number from *Terrapin Station*. Like Lazy Lightning > Supplication, "Estimated Prophet" has that unique 7/4 time signature. The jazzy/reggae feel of the music adds to the composition's allure. "Estimated Prophet" was debuted in the Swing Auditorium on February 26, 1977, the first show of the year. The first performance of "Terrapin Station" kicked off the festivities, and "Estimated" was delivered in the fourth spot of the opening set. Although it would go on to be a signature second set transition song, the initial eighteen performances of "Estimated Prophet" were stand-alone versions. Out of the sixty Grateful Dead shows in 1977, Weir's pride and joy was played fifty times.

The first "Estimated" segue took place the night after the legendary Cornell show in Buffalo on 5-9-77. On that evening, the Dead played Estimated Prophet > The Other One during the second set. The first Estimated > Eyes of the World was consummated on 5-15-77 in St. Louis. This was a perfect fit, as "Eyes" went on be the most popular landing destination for "Estimated." As in Scarlet > Fire, there was transition magic in Estimated > Eyes. When the "Estimated" noodling started to suggest "Eyes," the audience would salivate in anticipation of "Eyes." However, the band never locked into Estimated > Eyes as they did with Scarlet > Fire, especially during '77.

During the 6-9-77 Winterland show, the Dead smoked Estimated > St. Stephen, and this combo was revisited in Toronto on 11-2-77. The songs seemed to speak to each other musically and lyrically. The tales of a false prophet and a saint worked well side by side. In Colgate on 11-4-77, the Dead reversed the natural flow with an Eyes of the World > Estimated Prophet > Other One.

The Dead returned to the Eyes > Estimated combo several times in 1990. "Terrapin Station," "Uncle John's Band," and "He's Gone" emerged as landing songs for "Estimated," but Weir's pride and joy shined best when it was paired with "Eyes," even if the combo was rushed at times during the '80s. It took me an amazing twenty-two shows before I saw my first "Eyes of the World." I caught Estimated > Uncle John's, Estimated > He's Gone, and Estimated > Drums, before catching my first Estimated > Eyes in Providence on 4-20-83.

Throughout 1977, "Estimated" had a concise explosion of a between-verse jam that was always equal in length until they doubled down on the length in the Winterland on 12-27-77. The frontier was crossed and there was no turning back. In 1978 and beyond, the between-verse jam expanded to four rounds or more on a regular basis. The extended instrumental gave "Estimated" a peaking solo with a crescendo that ensured its place as a jam anthem. The spicy noodling in the substantial outro made for memorable jazz moments, but rarely created stunning climaxes. The "Estimated" outro purposefully built anticipation for whatever may come next.

During its eighteen-year run, "Estimated" was always in the Dead's rotation. The longest stretch of shows without a "Prophet" was thirteen. As Weir came into his own as a rock star in the '80s, no song captured that rise to glory better than "Estimated." During this decade, Weir turned it up a notch, thrilling a healthy percentage of the crowd with his scaling falsetto howls prior to the outro: "A no-no-no-no-a-haaaa! No-no-nah-nah-nah-ah-hiiiiii! Na-na-ah-haaaaa! Ah-hah-hah-hiiiiiiiiiiii!" Spit flew and girls screamed as the estimated prophet did his thing in his purple Lacoste polo. It was good, clean fun for all.

There weren't many changes to the structure of "Estimated" outside of the length. In the spring of '82, there was brief flirtation with a refrain to the middle jam at the end of the outro. This experiment was well received but left in the dust after the tour during which it was conceived. These versions had me thinking that the band could have possibly done some long loops that returned to an "Estimated" reprise, but that never happened. However, "Estimated" remained a pathway to paradise in the Grateful Dead universe through the years.

7-8-78 Red Rocks Amphitheater, Morrison, CO: This was the Dead's second and final night of their first appearance in the wondrous Red Rocks Amphitheater. After opening set two with "Samson" and "Ship of Fools," the Dead rise to glory on the wings of "Estimated Prophet." Weir says, "I'm moving to Australia," before "Estimated" begins. This tape was among the first dozen of my bootleg collection, and when I initially heard it, I was amazed at how alive this rendition was compared to the album version. I would have moved to Australia to hear more versions like this.

Weir's expressive singing leads to beautiful exchanges with Donna and Jerry during the double-decker bridge. The four-round between-verse instrumental is astonishing—a vacuum of awesomeness. The length of this jam would continue to expand, but the aural ascension of the Red Rocks rendition cannot be topped. The outro is more than substantial. This is a perfect performance that will stop you in your tracks. In Red Rocks it was a launching pad for one of the best sets of year.

4-19-82 Baltimore Civic Center, MD: On the last show of this East Coast tour, Weir's calling down thunder: "California, knock-knock-knocking on the golden door." Bob is hyped and the band's feeding off it. Bob and Jerry are singing and laughing as they approach the final bridge to the jam. Weir goes off: "And might and glory gonna be my name, Ah-HIIIIIIIII!" Weir's frisky strumming is mirrored by Brent as the band launches into orbit. Garcia's en fuego—Roman candles with a trail of string cheese. Explosive and attentive, the jam morphs into a chord stampede. You can envision Weir charging to the front of the stage before retracing his steps and repeating.

When the jam's finished, Weir wanders into escalating falsetto ecstasy. Baltimore's loving Bobby. The outro jam sets sail. As the band noodles along looking for its next dance partner, they dramatically charge back to the motif of the previous jam. It's a powerful and stunning moment. The Dead pulled this maneuver a week earlier in the Nassau Coliseum on April 12, but the Baltimore reprise has more edge. After some more noodling, this evocative "Estimated" drifts into "Terrapin." *Let my inspiration flow.*

9-2-78 Giants Stadium, East Rutherford, NJ: Donna and the Boys were reeling and rocking in the industrial/swamp wastelands of New Jersey. After a bountiful Scarlet > Fire, the jam abundance flows with Estimated > Eyes. With a touch of hubris, the Dead hammer "Estimated." They played in front of 150,000 folks in Englishtown a year before. Entertaining 80,000 in Giants Stadium is a piece of cake.

Two months after Red Rocks, the Dead ravage a between-verse solo that's the longest to date. The fierce playing throws Bob off as he jumps in with "My time coming" too soon. After a quick override from his mates, Bobby's steps back to the mic. Jerry puts his head down and just blisters round after round of "Estimated" runs. After fifteen minutes, this mega version segues into "Eyes" and earns its place in jam anthem history.

3-29-90 Nassau Coliseum, Uniondale, NY: Branford Marsalis joined the band at the start of set two for an "Eyes of the World" that is one of the legendary individual performances in Grateful Dead history. The enormity of this "Eyes" messed with my ability to appreciate the ensuing "Estimated Prophet" because I repeatedly listened to the *Without a Net* "Eyes" instead of just going to the tapes of 3-29-90. Following a transcendent performance isn't easy, but the Nassau "Estimated Prophet" is a subdued treasure.

Branford can't blow a bad note. His elegant licks imbue "Estimated" with the blues in between Bobby's singing. Brent plays off Branford's riffing. Weir's performance is tastefully laid-back. He understands the magic brewing around him. Jerry takes charge with a powerful between-verse solo. As Bobby heads into his signature "Ah-hahs," Branford's riffing, so

Bobby defers to Mr. Marsalis. Branford leads the way as the outro develops. Are we on 52nd Street or in the Nassau Coliseum? "Estimated" is a natural fit for his sound as blues and jazz flow from his horn. In "Eyes," Branford built his incredible solo off Jerry's lead-in. This time, Jerry's following the muse. His inspired fretwork rolls from what Branford created; it flows with similar texture and tone. After fifteen minutes of "Estimated," the outro rolls into "Dark Star." And to quote Mr. Marsalis, "The crowd went apeshit!"

12-26-79 Oakland Auditorium Arena, CA: The time has come to bid farewell to the '70s. On the first night of the Dead's New Year's residency, they open set two with a ripping Uncle John's Band > Estimated Prophet. Brent's accentuating "Estimated" with colorful brushstrokes as the song progresses. The first Garcia solo is substantial and meaty. Weir mistimes "My time coming" as the band plays through. And when the band finishes, Weir meekly sings, "My time coming," as he almost misses his cue again.

Brent leads the band into outro noodling. The music swirls all over the place. In late '79, the Dead got into some serious improvisation before Drums on an almost nightly basis. Jerry flirts with speed-picking suggesting "Eyes of the World." Phil drops bombs that seem to negate that notion. Garcia continues to fiddle with the "Eyes" motif. And to the delight of those in Oakland—and future listening audiences—the jam roars on. This is now a jam of its own volition, but if you choose to give credit to "Estimated," that would make this a nineteen-minute rendition. Weir and Garcia skittle-skattle chords as the drummers accelerate the pace. There's a touch of "Caution" in there, and Phil takes charge. His playing rocks the arena as he toys with "A Love Supreme." And then this episode of Grateful Dead mischief resolves itself with a He's Gone > The Other One before Drums.

6-9-77 Winterland Arena, San Francisco, CA: After a festive Help on the Way > Slipknot! > Franklin's Tower, the final segment of set two launches with "Estimated Prophet." The Dead have played "Estimated" at every show up to this point in '77, and no boredom has set in. All aspects of this group effort are attentive. Garcia's in Mu-Tron heaven as he scuba-dives through the Rasta/jazz outro. Although it's different in structure and key than "Slipknot!," the resolute flow of the music is similar, as if "Slip" and "Estimated" are cousins. As the "Estimated" solo winds down, sparks fly and sizzle into the opening notes of "St. Stephen." This is the first Estimated > St. Stephen. The future shakes hands with the past. This was a great combo that was only played once more, on 11-2-77.

4-20-83 Providence Civic Center, RI: Outside of the fact that the band was playing well, could there be a more inauspicious start to a second set than the first two numbers on this night, "My Brother Esau" and "Maybe You Know"? The band and audience were amped for song three, "Bertha." It's a standout version that ignites "Estimated Prophet." Weir's singing fills the sky with flames—passion and precision. The band steamrolls the between-verse jam as powerfully as any I've ever heard. Garcia runs wild in measured increments. Weir emphatically delivers his scat-singing howls. The outro shines without overstaying its welcome. They had important matters to attend to. After twenty-two shows, I was on the verge of seeing my first "Eyes of the World." The Estimated > Eyes transition peaked on the highest mountaintop.

ALL ALONG THE WATCHTOWER

Except for "It's All Over Now, Baby Blue," and one-time performances of "It Takes a Lot to Laugh, It Takes a Train to Cry" and "She Belongs to Me," the Grateful Dead didn't cover Dylan tunes until 1985. Interpreting Dylan was a Jerry Garcia Band specialty. Once the Dead started covering Dylan it became addictive, especially after touring with Dylan in the summers of '86 and '87. And Dylan liked what he heard. In a 1991 interview with *Rolling Stone*, Dylan said, "The Dead did a lot of my songs, and we'd just take the whole arrangement, because they did it better than me. Jerry Garcia could hear the song in all my bad recordings, the song that was buried there. So if I want to bring out something different, I just bring out one of them Dead records and see which one I wanna do. I never do that with my records."

Jimmy Hendrix also had a knack for successfully transforming Dylan songs. Jimmy's version of "All Along the Watchtower" from *Electric Ladyland* (1968) went on to become one of the undisputed jam anthems of FM radio. It was only a matter of time until the Grateful Dead took a poke at "Watchtower." But throughout the '70s, the Dead were building their legacy on the great compositions of Hunter/Garcia and Barlow/Weir. When that abundant well of songwriting genius dried up a bit, the band broke out some Dylan classics in 1985: "Desolation Row," "Just Like Tom Thumb's Blues," "The Mighty Quinn," and "She Belongs to Me." Although it's part of a set list from 1-7-66, there's no existing recording of "She Belongs to Me" until 4-4-85 Providence.

In preparation for their 1987 tour with Dylan, the Dead played "Watchtower" three times. The first performance was in the Greek Theatre on 6-20-87. "All Along the Watchtower" was played during all six Dylan/Dead shows, usually as the last number of Dylan's set. It was one of the highlights every night, and it was enthusiastically received in large sports stadiums filled with mostly Deadheads. There was no way the Dead were going to leave this number behind.

With three opportunities for Garcia to unleash lightning solos, "Watchtower" became an essential post-Drums jam anthem. The first Watchtower > Morning Dew in Madison Square Garden on 9-18-87 was the highlight of a storied year in the band's history. Even as the Dead's playing became sluggish in later years, Watchtower > Dew had the power to salvage any show. "Watchtower" remained a staple in the rotation. It was played 123 times. The only Dylan song played more often by the Dead was "It's All Over Now, Baby Blue."

3-26-88 Hampton Coliseum, VA: The Hampton "Watchtower" was one of the most electrifying live experiences of my Deadhead career, and it still astounds and confounds every time I listen to it. This was an average show through Drums. You can find a solid video of this set on YouTube. After Space, a lively "Gimme Some Lovin'" was followed by "The Wheel." Smiling Jerry's stoked as he uncharacteristically pumps his fist in a circular motion as he sings with Bobby and Brent, "Small wheel turn by the fire and rod. Big wheel turn by the grace of God." Garcia's outro licks slash as "The Wheel" spins to a near-stop before Weir strums the "Watchtower" chord progression. Garcia digs in with sparkling licks. Game on.

Weir's singing is excitedly sloppy on the first verse. There are times when he sings "Watchtower" brilliantly. Sometimes he tried too hard. The falsetto didn't always work. After a brief outburst of a solo, Weir checks in: "No reason to get excited."

As the verse goes along, it sounds as if Weir has just sucked in nitrous oxide.

It's possible the silly treatment of Dylan's song fired up Jerry. He dials up his guitar volume and digs in. His fretwork is gnarly tough as he brings it to a plateau that's really more of a launching pad. Garcia shreds again. This time, he's in Hendrix Heaven. I was part of the general Admission faithful on the floor. But I spent the last two jams of this "Watchtower" airborne. The sonic rush was overwhelming. All the power this band could unleash was present and accounted for in these rampaging solos.

Weir sings the last chorus with the proper balance of excitement and respect for the lyrics. Garcia's an agitated bull out of the gate—nostrils flaring. The impact of the music is immense. Garcia's in his basic stage stance, but he's applying total physicality to his guitar playing; bending his knees, the strings, and seemingly, the guitar itself. This solo is more direct and impressive than the previous one.

Once again, Garcia reaches a temporary plateau. The finale is filled with the brightest and loudest fireworks in his "Watchtower" arsenal. This is a stunning piece of music cut from the same cloth as the 10-20-84 "Jack Straw" from Syracuse. "Morning Dew" hadn't been played on this tour yet, but Jerry eased into "Black Peter." It was a fetching "Black Peter," and probably the right choice because it would have been almost impossible to recreate that guitar magic in the "Dew." After seeing this and some of the heroics of 1987, I dreamed that Garcia and the Dead were on the verge of a new golden age. The Fall 1988 East Coast tour shot those notions down.

8-20-87 Park West Ski Resort, Salt Lake City, UT: The post-Drums lead into this "Watchtower" is The Wheel > Gimme Some Lovin', the reverse of 3-26-88 Hampton. These tunes seemed to efficiently prepare the band for "Watchtower." As "Gimme Some Lovin'" fades out, Garcia and Weir agree upon "Watchtower." As the band ignites an organic rhythm, Jerry retreats to dial up the perfect tone. Solo one is concise, hot, and a perfect stepping-stone.

Weir's singing's awesome without any superfluous embellishments. Jerry picks up where he left off with clean leads that please. At this point Jerry changes direction, as he opens a can of whoop-ass on this unsuspecting ski resort. The band creates a vortex that Garcia scurries out of. This leads to a repetitive scale dash that defies physics. The sonic benefits of this run on mental health should be studied. It invigorates my soul every time I hear it. However, Garcia's not finished. On a roll, our hero changes guitar position and fires off two more rounds. Weir powerfully exclaims, "All along the watchtower princes kept the view." Garcia knocks out a hot but concise final solo. This Utah "Tower" doesn't have the power or wildness of the Hampton version, but it's still got the Right Stuff.

7-12-87 Giants Stadium, East Rutherford, NJ: In my book *Dylan and the Grateful Dead: A Tale of Twisted Fate*, I elaborate on the impact of this show on Bob Dylan and how this performance, and his experience touring with the Dead, helped ignite the next stage of his career: The Never Ending tour. "All Along the Watchtower" is the penultimate number of this landmark Dylan/Dead set. Dylan's vocals here are powerful yet choppy. You can sense the excitement of a performer being reborn onstage as he rediscovers the joy of singing a beloved anthem.

Garcia had a superb night on guitar, perhaps his finest and most consistent performance of the year. All three solos burn without being overstated. At the conclusion of "Watchtower," Dylan howls, "Thank you, Grateful Dead!" And then he strums his guitar and sings, "Come gather round, people, wherever you roam." Finishing the set with "The Times They Are a-Changin'" was a huge emotional rush for those in Giants Stadium. I was there, and yes, I was weeping.

7-4-89 Rich Stadium, Buffalo, NY: This was another quality performance from the Dead's summer '89 tour, and the July 4 fireworks display peaked with "All Along the Watchtower." After Brent's "I Will Take You Home" lullaby, Garcia's ripping on the "Tower" intro before Bobby sings. There's a gruff tone to the opening solo. Jam two begins with an excellent organ solo from Brent. In most cases I could pass on any interruption of Garcia's flow in "Watchtower," but this segment is beautiful. Garcia shreds tenacious repetitive licks on the heels of Brent. This is one of the elite "Tower" jams, almost as hot as Hampton.

Jerry follows with a final solo that has intensity and length. The transition to "Morning Dew" thrilled Buffalo Deadheads, but "Watchtower" was the star on this evening.

9-18-87 Madison Square Garden, New York, NY: Did the "Watchtower" ignite the moment, or did the moment inspire the "Watchtower?" It was an emotion-packed night with pre-Drums "Terrapin Station" magic, but the crowd buzz exceeded the results. That changed as the "Goin' Down the Road Feelin' Bad" coda segued into "All Along the Watchtower." This was the eighth time the Dead played "Watchtower" without Dylan, and the first time it was unleashed in Madison Square Garden. A giddy roar filled the arena in anticipation of this beloved rock classic. I was among those in attendance on September 18, 1987, which was also the seventeenth anniversary of the death of Jimi Hendrix.

The Garden bounces as Weir sings. As the band cuts to jam, Garcia is a man possessed. Feeding off the equally possessed audience, Jerry rips a series of climactic shrieking runs that nearly blow the roof off Madison Square Garden—very uncharacteristic for the first solo. The crowd goes nuts, and Weir cuts loose with a falsetto shriek, "No reason to get excited!!!" In this moment, Weir's vocals frame the pandemonium. There's no way Jerry could top that opening solo.

The band digs in for two more ample jams. "Watchtower" winds down, and you can sense that the audience is praying for the "Dew." The segue is gorgeous and royal and then comes one of the loudest roars in the history of the World's Most Famous Arena as Jerry strikes the golden chord for "Morning Dew." This is not the hottest "Watchtower" of all time, but it was the catalyst for the greatest musical segment of 1987.

8-23-87 Calaveras County Fairgrounds, Angel's Camp, CA: Three days after the blazing Utah "Watchtower," Carlos

Santana joined the Dead onstage towards the end of the opening set. After firing away on "Iko Iko," the musical brothers thrilled Angel's Camp with "All Along the Watchtower" to end the set. As in Utah, Weir's singing was excellent all the way through. Jerry ripped a curt opening solo. Carlos kicked off the second jam with Hendrix-style shredding and handed off to Jerry. These two legends communicated effortlessly as Jerry turned up the heat. They repeated the same Santana > Garcia motif on the last jam. These jams aren't overstated. It's a thrilling version with a vibe similar to the legendary Hendrix rendition.

As the band heads for break, Weir addresses the crowd, "Say thank you, Carlos." And the grateful crowd had no problem with compliance.

9-15-90 Madison Square Garden, New York, NY: In search of one more standout "Watchtower" for this project, I listened to at least twenty renditions I wasn't familiar with, and 9-15-90 was the easy winner. I only saw the Grateful Dead four times in the '90s. I missed this excellent six-night MSG run, the first one featuring Bruce Hornsby and Vince Welnick, two months after Brent's passing. Garcia was psyched to play with Hornsby, and for New York City. His inspired performances from this six-night stand were some of the best of the Dead's final decade.

Jerry must have been thinking, "Hey, let's show these new guys how we like to cook 'Watchtower.'" Jerry shreds an amazing and lengthy intro solo before Weir steps up to sing, "There must be some kind of way out of here." Weir belts out the lyrics with controlled reverence. The band clicks on all cylinders, and Jerry delivers two more solos that are action-packed and substantial. If they had dug in for a final outro assault, this could have challenged Hampton for the greatest "Tower" of them all. The last solo didn't fall flat as much as the band called it off so they could lead the new keyboardists towards "Stella Blue."

LOST SAILOR > SAINT OF CIRCUMSTANCE

A bsence makes the heart—and ear—grow fonder. When I saw Lost Sailor > Saint of Circumstance on 3-24-86 in the Philadelphia Spectrum, I couldn't have imagined that it would be the last time "Lost Sailor" would be played. As the Dead carried on with stand-alone performances of "Saint of Circumstance," it seemed odd not having "Lost Sailor" setting it up. I saw many pairings of Sailor > Saint between 1982 and 1986, but I don't think I ever fully appreciated the magnitude of this Weir/Barlow composition until my touring days were over.

"Lost Sailor" was debuted on 8-4-79 in the Oakland Auditorium Arena. The first "Saint of Circumstance" segued out of "Lost Sailor" on 8-31-79 in Glens Falls. The initial performance of "Saint" was a bit ragged, and the lyrics were still a work in progress. However, this couple became inseparable. There were 137 consecutive Sailor > Saints until the streak was interrupted by Sailor > Drums > Space > Saint in Richmond on 11-1-85. This was followed by three additional Sailor > Saints until "Lost Sailor" was permanently and unceremoniously dumped from the rotation, like "Lazy Lightning" was two years earlier.

"Saint of Circumstance" continued to be a Weir favorite. It was played 233 times, with the final performance coming at the next-to-last Dead show in Chicago on 7-8-95. However, it was never as rewarding as when it materialized out of "Lost Sailor." The hypnotic opening of "Sailor" was an enchanting delight. If music can capture what it's like to fire up a bowl of weed or knock back your first cocktail after a long day's work, the beginning of "Sailor" has that effect. "Sailor" always came off as a soothing shift of direction without hindering the flow of a show. It also has that vibe of ascension, matching the title of its studio album, *Go to Heaven*.

Other *Go to Heaven* tunes, like "Althea," "Alabama Getaway," and "Feel Like a Stranger," gelled quicker than Sailor > Saint in concert. With practice, Sailor >Saint became a polished piece placed towards the end of set one, or early in set two, by the summer of 1980. Sailor > Saint was my final selection for jam anthem status, but it should have been a no-brainer due to all the jamming nooks and crannies within. "Sailor" has a between-verse solo and lots of noodling in the coda as Weir sings. Sparks fly during the transition. Saint has two jams, the last being a master blaster. At the end of a quality "Saint," Garcia usually finishes with a mad flurry. Sailor > Saint's a minor masterpiece, underappreciated in its heyday.

10-19-81 Sports Palace, Barcelona, Spain: The embers of the blazing Barcelona "Fire" are extinguished by the chill opening of "Lost Sailor." When you hear this on CD or tape it sounds like a perfect album side, as you might hear on either side of *Who's Next*, *Abbey Road*, or *Highway 61 Revisited*. "Sailor" is enchanting as it sets sail. Garcia's solo gracefully slices through the seas. It's a precise rendition, extremely pleasurable. As storm clouds gather, the band busts into "Saint of Circumstance."

This was Garcia's first and only performance in the land of his ancestors and he was intent on making it transcendent. As Bobby and Brent alternately chant, "Rain falling down," Garcia's a tiger in a trance, sharpening the sound of his guitar. Led by Phil, the band pounds out a trench from which Jerry can unload. Phil digs deeper and deeper as Jerry's ornery, quick-picking barrages pile on top of each other. The jam explodes as the band furiously keeps the crescendo flowing. Lava flows from Jerry's guitar and Weir jumps in at the apex: "Well I never know! Ah-hi!" After the "Sure don't know what I'm going for" sing-off, Garcia goes nuclear—a brilliant twenty-second meltdown. And is if Jerry had it planned all along, he plays on, a guitar soliloquy as the band sparsely backs him before Drums. I've named this five-minute segment "Barcelona Jam." After Drums, Barcelona gets a brief "Spanish Jam."

4-6-82 The Spectrum, Philadelphia, PA: The band's smoking on autopilot after "Shakedown" dazzles to open set two. All the licks are touching down in all the right places. Brent and Jerry continue their conversational motif from "Shakedown." Weir's singing is crisp and witty. "Maybe going on a dream. Whatever moves you." Garcia fluidly pecks away as the turnover to "Saint" beckons.

Garcia's guitar sings in unison with Weir throughout "Saint." If only they could have created like this in the studio for *Go to Heaven*. Garcia's cutting loose with intensity as the jam boils early. The rest of the band races to support Jerry. As Weir returns to sing the coda, Garcia's exploding notes are loud exclamation points. Weir improvs a rhyming rap: "(Sure don't know what I'm going for.) Maybe crazy, maybe out of line now. (But I'm gonna go for it for sure.) I'm on the road and I'm feeling fine now." Garcia's post-coda riff gently cascades into "Terrapin Station." Sailor > Saint is rarely the extraordinary highlight of the night, but it often is an essential portion of a greater segment, as it was on this night, amply filling the gap between "Shakedown" and "Terrapin."

4-4-85 Providence Civic Center, RI: In this circumstance, Sailor > Saint ignites a fiery, set-ending LSD punch, Lost Sailor > Saint of Circumstance > Deal. Before this segment, this set was on its way to glory, and the LSD factor assured its place as the opening set of the year. This was the first Sailor > Saint since 11-2-84. The band now seemed to be saving it for special occasions. "Sailor" is a breath of exhilaration in this spot, the promise of extended jamming, and a Jerry cooker to end the set hangs in the balance. "Sailor" floats on a bit rockier and raw than usual. Garcia's drifting and dreaming and slicing and dicing. Weir signals it's time for "Saint," but Jerry shoots that down. *You ain't breaking up my party!* The band recalculates to create a dramatic ending. Weir's falsetto chants add to the pageantry as another minute is tacked onto this standout "Sailor."

Deadheads bounce as one as the Dead plunder and pillage on the way to the "Tiger in a trance" jam. Phil's bass astounds, like a Clydesdale pounding down a dirt track. Garcia's inspired. He's happier than anybody in Providence about this breakout. Raging guitar steams down to the core and screams up to the heavens—a sonic whirlwind of sound. Weir reins the band back in for the final sing-along. As "Saint" reaches its destination, Jerry's final barrage sizzles, rivaling the great afterburn of 10-19-81 Barcelona. The band catapults into "Deal" at excessive speeds. Gonzo Dead!

3-10-81 Madison Square Garden, New York, NY: This show and the night before have wonderful offbeat versions of jam anthems, and this Sailor > Saint is as deliciously strange as the rest. Following a sizzling/eccentric Scarlet > Fire, Weir calls on the muse of the seas, "Ah-whooo, where's the Dog Star? Ah-whooo, where is the moon?"

This version has that unique Garcia guitar tone all the way through. The band was determined to reinvent music they knew, and the audience knew, inside out. The "Saint" jam smokes. A content Weir cuts to the final chorus, perhaps a little quicker than usual. His bearded brother, Señor Garcia is enraged as he plays a furious stream of notes as if he's attempting to drown out Weir. If the version seems botched, Garcia and mates salvage it after Weir sings the final chorus. Garcia strikes up the "Tiger in a Trance" jam again, and the band resurrects it briefly. And then the Dead continue to poke around—fragments and streams of "Circumstance" go this way and that way before giving way to Drums.

8-31-80 Capital Centre, Landover, MD: The Dead celebrate the anniversary of the first Sailor > Saint with a gripping and flawless performance in Landover. This time, Weir's duo is sandwiched by other combos. Here's the alluring pre-Drums lineup to start set two: Greatest Story Ever Told > Uncle John's Band > Lost Sailor > Saint of Circumstance > Comes a Time > Truckin'. One of the most underrated Dead tours is this late-summer 1980 East Coast rendezvous.

"Sailor" is delivered with a drifting/dreaming feel. Garcia's guitar licks ascend to a fiery peak as "Sailor" closes in on "Saint." The band channels their rock and roll desires into a perfectly constructed "Saint" jam. The Dead push the boundaries of Sailor > Saint, yet the performance is delightfully smooth—album-worthy. The mojo generated here spills over into an elite pairing of Comes a Time > Truckin'.

9-27-81 Capital Centre, Landover, MD: Let's call this the second birthday bash for Sailor > Saint at The Cap. This time Sailor > Saint closes the first set, and it is the star of the show. It's a quality version all the way through, but oh my, that "Saint" jam boils and explodes! Phil and Jerry square off and create a rolling crescendo of fire. It's a stunning example of how the band can improbably extend a peaking jam when it doesn't seem logical. Even though Sailor > Saint was bound for regular pre-Drum duty in set two, it proved that it had the gravitas to close out a set.

9-15-82 Capital Centre, Landover, MD: After writing the first draft of this book, I decided I needed one more Sailor > Saint. Without considering that I already had two versions from the Cap Centre, I sampled several new renditions and came across this show that I had attended. Is this merely a coincidence, or is the "Seems like I've been here before" theory back in effect? Is it possible that the band recalled their past "Saint" accomplishments in this building, or were the ghosts of hot "Saint" jams swirling and influencing the proceedings on 9-15-82?

This show opened with "Playin' in the Band." Although the "Playin'" loop was never closed, "Playin'" noodling popped up here and there throughout both sets. After set two opens with "Shakedown Street," the band messes with "Playin'" space before settling into Sailor > Saint. The band loses their mind during the "Saint" jam. The drummers spike the instrumental early with hyped pacing. Jerry explodes. Patience be damned! Garcia locks into fiery repetition to keep Weir at bay and keep the jam alive. The band improbably rides the crescendo. This may have been the hottest "Saint" jam of the three from the Cap Centre. Bobby's a rhyming maven down

222 | Lost Sailor > Saint of Circumstance

the homestretch. Before they transition to Drums, Garcia leaves burn marks with his final "Saint" licks.

SPANISH JAM/ CAUTION (DO NOT STOP ON THE TRACKS)

After playing "He's Gone" in the Nassau Coliseum on May 6, 1981, the Grateful Dead segued into a historical musical segment: Caution Jam > Spanish Jam. It was the first time these essential jams from the band's formative years were paired, and it was the last performance of "Caution Jam." Looking at it from the perspective of thirty years of live Dead, these were rare tunes. "Caution" was played sixty-two times, "Caution Jam" was played thirteen times, and "Spanish Jam" was played fifty-three times. These powerful jam numbers emerged from the same golden era, but that's where the similarities cease.

"Caution (Do Not Stop on the Tracks)" is the band's second original tune, and Pigpen is credited as the lyricist. An early demo of the song appears on the *So Many Roads* box set. It's a concise version with a raunchy Pigpen harp solo that teases the explosive potential of the composition. If ever the title of a song matches the sound, this is it. This jam is a sonic locomotive raging down the tracks. With all due respect to Pigpen and his fine vocal performances during "Caution," the power of the instrumentation overwhelms the song. This is a step-on-the-gas-full-blast-ahead jam that became one the Dead's early showstoppers alongside "Viola Lee Blues" and "Turn on Your Lovelight."

"Caution" was played live for the first time on January 8, 1966, in the Fillmore Auditorium. There are eight known live performances of "Caution" over the next two years before it was recorded for *Anthem of the Sun* (1968). When "Alligator" was added to the band's rotation in '67, Alligator > Caution were linked almost exclusively through 1969. With performances often surpassing fifteen minutes, "Caution" was a raging blues blitzkrieg. It wasn't sophisticated, subtle, or very psychedelic. However, "Caution" is an idiosyncratic sampling of Primal Dead.

As the band's live repertoire became swamped with an abundance of great songs written by Hunter, "Caution" was eased out of the rotation. It was only played five times in '70 and once in '71. "Caution" re-emerged for a final hoorah in Europe '72, where it was played five times. These versions are sublime. The song was retired after Pigpen's death, but thirteen "Caution Jams" popped up over the next nine years. And there were several brief flirtations with the raging theme that didn't warrant "Caution Jam" sanctioning.

According to several sources, "Spanish Jam" was lifted from a segment of "Solea," the last track of the landmark Miles Davis album *Sketches of Spain*. As a huge Miles fan, I disagree with the "Solea" assessment. I don't hear it. I believe "Spanish Jam" is a basic flamenco chord progression influenced by *Sketches of Spain*. Either way, Bob Weir introduced this melody to the rest of the band during the *Anthem of the Sun* sessions. Eager to test out this new instrumental piece, the Dead performed a stellar "Spanish Jam" after "Born Cross-Eyed" in the Carousel Ballroom on 1-17-68. The haunting jam lingered for eight shows in '68 before disappearing until the 2-11-70 performance with the Allman Brothers in the Fillmore East. There was a brief "Spanish Jam" tuning in the Fillmore East" on 4-25-71, but the next legitimate version was performed in the Philly Spectrum on 3-24-73. As if they couldn't escape it, "Spanish Jam" was played a week later in Buffalo. Gorgeous, moody, and haunting, "Spanish Jam" is a tune that sticks like glue. Whenever I hear it, it continues to play in my head for hours, sometimes days, and it could even infiltrate my dreams. It may have had the same effect on the band. "Spanish Jam" was often played in clusters before it would disappear for a while.

The greatest "Spanish Jam" cluster occurred in '74, when it was played eight times between 6-23-74 (Miami) and 10-17-74 (Winterland). These versions were moody voyages that materialized organically out of extended second-set jams. The instrumentals unfolded patiently with a haunting vibe, as if they were waiting for precisely the right moment to pop out of the Wall of Sound. These 1974 versions convey that feeling that the music was playing the band.

"Spanish Jam" returned for one show in the Orpheum Theatre on 7-16-76. After five years on the shelf, the mystical Caution Jam > Spanish Jam in the Nassau Coliseum on 5-6-81 led to a new cluster. "Spanish Jam" was played eight times that year, with the final performance fittingly taking place in Barcelona, Spain, on 10-19-81. The final resurgence for "Spanish Jam" was during '83–'84, when it was played ten times. But "Spanish Jam" refused to die, making nine more appearances. The final "Spanish Jam" came on 6-18-95 in Giants Stadium.

SPANISH JAM

6-26-74 Providence Civic Center, RI: Creeping out of an "Other One" jam, Billy strikes up the marching beat of "Spanish Jam." Keith creates Spanish ambiance with the sounds of his Fender Rhodes as Weir precisely measures the haunting chord progression. Jerry lets the jam resonate before he adds to the canvas. Bright colors drip as he splashes paint on the aural masterpiece. Guitar velocity intensifies as Garcia maintains the integrity of the melody—sizzling whirlpool runs. A woozy feeling takes over. A dazed boxer is bravely battling back. This is a wonderful segment as the band effortlessly meshes emotion and virtuosity. Six additional minutes of noodling give way to "Wharf Rat." This playing straddles in and out of "Spanish Jam" consciousness. This fourteen-minute "Spanish Jam" is a mind-blowing bridge, the salsa that transforms a meal into a gourmet feast.
7-19-74 Selland Arena, Fresno, CA: "Let it Grow" segues into improvisation. Phil pounds bass lines through the Wall of

Sound that shake Fresno and indicate an impending trip to Spain. As the band shifts into "Spanish Jam," Garcia's leads snake in under Keith's licks. The band proceeds assuredly. This is a celebration, a victorious soccer outing for Madrid. The consistency of this version is amazing. The band's speaking with one voice. Phil's playing as if this will be the last song of the night and he's ready to roll with this theme for another hour. Jerry suggests "Eyes of the World" and nobody bites until the band comes back to the realization of who they are and where they are. They have this brilliant new song to unload on San Francisco, so they roll into "Eyes." Bits of "Spanish Jam" regenerate through the early part of "Eyes." Let it Grow > Jam > Spanish Jam > Eyes > China Doll. What a segment!

4-23-84 Veterans' Memorial Coliseum, New Haven, CT: This was my 50th Grateful Dead show, and I don't recall this "Spanish Jam." I didn't have many tapes with "Spanish Jam" at the time, therefore, this passed by like a puff of wind. I was shocked to hear how good this was thirty-six years later.

The opening chords are powerful, dark, and chilling. The audio mix and sound of the instruments adds to the urgency of this version. After a few minutes it sounds like the jam recedes, but Bobby and Phil bang out the urgent beat and Jerry rips stinging notes from his Tiger. After four minutes there's a "Truckin'" tease followed by "Other One" noodling without leaving the "Spanish" framework. After seven minutes, the negotiations lead to "Truckin'." This is the most satisfying "SJ" of the '80s.

6-23-74 Jai-Alai Fronton, Miami, FL: "Spanish Jam" arises out of "Dark Star" at exactly the right time. It hadn't been played in a year, and the band embraces it enthusiastically. Garcia's steaming; his emotive playing is punctuated by Phil's bass. Billy leads the band into battle as Garcia whittles away to the bombardment of Commander Lesh. "Spanish Jam" doesn't get hotter than this! We're only looking at three minutes of "Spanish Jam" here, but the fever burns on as the Dead move towards "U.S. Blues." It's the grandest intro Uncle Sam ever received—the band rejoices in the longest "U.S. Blues" opening. This is a powerhouse "Spanish Jam" on its own, but as with other versions from 1974, it serves the greater musical purpose of the segment it's in.

2-11-70 Fillmore East, New York, NY: If you like bang for the buck, nothing tops this "Spanish Jam" with the Allman Brothers Band joining the Grateful Dead on stage. After a "Dark Star" that didn't flow with typical grace, the musicians busted into "Spanish Jam." This proved to be an inspired choice, even though the Dead hadn't played it in two years.

The Dead sets the stage with up-tempo playing and the Allmans slammed it to the next level. Some tenderness is lost, but miles and miles of "Spanish Jam" unravel. With an abundance of talented musicians improvising in an intimate venue for a hip audience, execution gives way to the moment. How awesome is this for those there, and those listening in the future? Every "Spanish Jam" is one of a kind. This was a workshop of dreams never seen.

7-16-76 Orpheum Theater, San Francisco, CA: Here's another fascinating outlier "Spanish Jam." The band's in the thick of their legendary Orpheum run when Jerry's tuning noodling takes on a Spanish tone after "Samson." There's a fetching flamenco flavor to Jerry's picking as the band settles into "Spanish Jam." With Keith's piano playing, this version comes closest to invoking *Sketches of Spain*. The band subtly locks in as Garcia boils—wave after wave in even-keeled increments, but moody as hell. After seven healthy minutes of Spanish exuberance, the drummers take over.

1-17-68 Carousel Ballroom, San Francisco, CA: Oh, to be young again! After debuting a new tune, "Born Cross-Eyed," the Dead segue into that new tune that Weir's been teaching them, "Spanish Jam." Garcia's guitar speaks the language fluently. The flow is Miles Davis cool. Jerry's guitar sings sharply over the steady drive of the band. This is an extraordinary fifteen-minute performance. The is the cleanest, and one of the most exhilarating, instrumentals of a fabulous show. "Spanish Jam" was here to stay, and here to haunt the band and the faithful straight through 1995.

CAUTION (DO NOT STOP ON THE TRACKS)

4-8-72 Empire Pool, Wembley, London: This show concludes with an epic segment: Dark Star > Sugar Magnolia > Caution. "Sunshine Daydream" rams into "Caution." It's a perfect springboard as the band instantly soars. There's a polished gleam to the sound; the band has taken a quantum step forward during the second show of Europe '72. This "Caution" has frantic energy equal to the '68 and '69 versions, but the ride is smoother. You might need a seat belt for some of the earlier performances. The 4-8-72 ride thrills without turbulence. The resurgence of "Caution" in Europe was timely with Pigpen's passing early the next year. One could only imagine how great a Europe '72 "Hard to Handle" might have been.

After the opening stampede, Pigpen's voice howls through the Empire Pool, "All you need, all you need!" Smooth keyboard playing mingles with Jerry's noodling to the next segment. After a brief stop, Ron's at the mic again and he's firing up England: "Do you feel all right? I can't hear you. Do you feel all right? Just a little bit louder. LOUUUDERRRR!" Phil blasts the rhythmic pattern again and Jerry's on the move. Pig grabs a harmonica and starts to blow and Jerry pokes and pecks with him. Phil revs up the theme again and the band moves to what appears to be Feedback, but persistent Phil hits the signature "Caution" line again and Jerry goes bananas. The band unloads as they take this seventeen-minute monster down the homestretch. After the final blow, manager Sam Cutler grabs a mic and says, "Grateful Dead!" The other Europe "Cautions" were awesome. This one beat them by a hair.

10-20-68 Greek Theatre, Berkeley, CA: "Caution" anchors this presentation of Primal Dead. The band's on fire when Phil lays down the tracks as "The Eleven" segues into "Caution." The music's deliciously out of control. Improbably, the band's pumping away in unison, heading down the waterfall in the same barrel. There's spooky, multi-layered singing before the music erupts again—ten minutes of pure steam. The Boys pull the brake and the music screeches into four additional minutes of Feedback. Greek Theater indeed!

2-14-70 Fillmore East, New York, NY: Pigpen delivers his Valentine's Day present for New York City. "Caution" arrives via a pleasing transition from "Mason's Children." Ron's powerful voice belts out the blues as Jerry shreds under Pig's "Mojo hand." The arrangement is more advanced than the straight-ahead rumbling force of '68 versions. Bob and Jerry's chord riffing plays off the pumping pulse of Phil's bass. Ron's back for another verse and Bob and Jerry join him for a fiery "All you need" round robin sing-off. And then, lookout! The gloves come off as the Dead dive into a wild jamming binge. The sledgehammer chords return and then Weir incites the final mad dash. Don't think about stopping at the tracks, you'd be foolish! After fourteen furious minutes, "Caution" screeches into Feedback. "And We Bid You Goodnight" concludes this iconic show that was immortalized with the previous night's Fillmore East performance on *Dick's Picks Vol. 4*.

5-6-81 Nassau Coliseum, Uniondale, NY: A compelling, eleven-song first set kicks off another evening with the Grateful Dead in Nassau. Set two started well, but no one could have imagined what was to come after a "He's Gone" that was dedicated to Bobby Sands, a member of the Irish Republican Army who died of a hunger strike the day before.

This jam begins with quick-picking runs from Jerry. Phil's "Caution" runs aren't as prevalent as in the old days—the feel and flow is different—but this unique improvisation is a blessing. Jerry and Brent steam on, run for run. Mt. Fuji erupts on Long Island. "Caution" makes sense after "He's Gone." *Like a steam locomotive rolling down the tracks.* The intensity of the music begins to cool but Garcia's still crafting a lovely melody that gradually nears "The Other One." It was time for the rarely played "Caution Jam" to shake hands with "Spanish Jam," which hadn't been played in five years. Bobby, Phil, and Jerry lock into inspired riffing—"Spanish Jam" on mescaline. The bull is provoked—surreal dreams. This Caution Jam > Spanish Jam is a futuristic fifteen-minute flashback. A cluster of "Spanish Jams" would ensue. This was the final "Caution" of any note.

VIOLA LEE BLUES

There are forty-four known performances of "Viola Lee Blues" from 1966–1970. Approximately thirty of these performances were captured on tape. As a rule for jam anthem consideration, I should have excluded this song due to lack of longevity. However, rules are made to be broken. "Viola Lee Blues" is the original Grateful jam anthem. It's the rebellious last track of the band's eponymous debut album, standing out from other songs in length (ten minutes) and raw power. Performed live, "Viola Lee" was an epic jam exceeding twenty minutes on occasion.

As the band expanded their minds with LSD, "Viola Lee Blues" became an incredible musical workout that helped shape the flow of future jams in other songs. The structure of the "Viola" jam is basic and repetitive. What goes on inside is an exercise in group execution as they adjust the speed and intensity to give the jam a timeless feel. The band creates a sense of anticipation and exhilaration from the start, and then they find different routes, motifs, and tempos as they push the instrumental along. And when they eventually hit the climactic peak, they go to work on the melody that leads to the final verse, playfully regenerating leads. When Garcia finds those notes that never existed before in other revered tunes and the band pushes the jam beyond the realm of imagination, the seeds of those moments were sewn in these epic "Viola" explorations. I've selected six outstanding "Violas," including the first and last version, and arranged them chronologically to tell the tale of the Dead's first jam anthem.

3-19-66 Pico Acid Test, Carthay Studios, Los Angeles: To reinvent a famous lyric, the Grateful Dead were living on "Milk, meat, and LSD," and living in a pink house in Los Angeles courtesy of their patron, Owsley Stanley. Amazingly, there's a decent soundboard recording of this extravaganza.

The show begins with the debut of "Viola Lee Blues." The Grateful Dead mind flourishes as the band harmonizes these odd Noah Lewis lyrics confidently. A steady, funky beat pulses forward. Jerry's opening solo is fluid and rings out like an electrified banjo. The man was already an extraordinary musician with a fresh sound in 1966.

Those digging the music at this Acid Test must have been awestruck by the long, freewheeling jam that followed. Phil thumps away—a consistent pitter-patter pulse as Garcia's leads spiral round and round. The rest of the band fills the musical landscape behind this intriguing Lesh/Garcia conversation. The music sounds ideal for some kind of arcane religious ritual—or an Acid Test with Neal Cassidy and friends.

Garcia's guitar strikes explode. He likes what he's hearing so he digs in and repeats the motif by placing it under the magnifying glass. This incredible "Viola" debut is eleven minutes long. A new genre of music was busy being born in Los Angeles.

9-3-67 Dance Hall, Rio Nido, CA: "Viola Lee Blues" was played twenty-two times in 1967, and Rio Nido was treated to the best version ever on this Labor Day weekend. This show commences with the legendary thirty-one-minute "Midnight Hour" that was released on *Fallout from the Phil Zone*. "Viola Lee" is the sixth tune of this eight-song affair, and the first minute or two of "Viola" is missing from the soundboard recording. The good news is that the following 22:50 is rip-roaring Primal Dead, the kind of stuff that will make your head spin.

The band's in fearless mode as the jam wobbles and swirls in a jet stream. Phil's deep bass forays are tapping into unknown musical realms. Garcia gets tangled up in some jarring repetition and Billy accelerates to higher ground. Garcia's reeling and raging as Pig's striking organ riffs illuminate the sonic deluge.

Garcia goes wild around the nine-minute mark. The music dissolves to a split second of a stop. Pigpen's controlling the flow. When the jamming picks up again, Garcia dashes into a ballsy "When the Saints Come Marching In" jam. We can really appreciate Pigpen's musicianship as his swooshing organ spurs Jerry on.

Just when it seems like the band has left "Viola" terrain, they sprint through a side door and into a whirling crescendo. It sounds like a high-stakes game of musical chairs when the peak is reached.

On the other side of the crescendo, the Boys rage on—a "China Cat"-like jam fills the Dance Hall. It would be a few months before the Dead debuted "Cat," but this is the precursor. Rio Nido is in *Aoxomoxoa* heaven two years before the album becomes reality. Eventually, the band nimbly transitions back to "Viola Lee Blues." The Summer of Love, Drugs, and Improvisation never sounded so psychedelic/sweet.

11-10-67 Shrine Exhibition Hall, Los Angeles, CA: This concert was billed as "Amazing Electric Wonders," and it also featured Buffalo Springfield and Blue Cheer. The Dead lived up to the Amazing Electric Wonders moniker by opening with "Viola Lee Blues." The band's rolling smooth and playing with attitude before they reach the first verse. Mickey Hart recently joined the group, and this is his first "Viola." Garcia's licks unfold like a Q and A session during the between-verse instrumental. This version's not as long as the one from Rio Nido, but this fifteen-minute beast unfolds logically with immense might.

As the epic jam takes flight, a spinning, spiraling kaleidoscope of sound overwhelms the Shrine. A psychedelic groove balances the furious attack. Phil's bass clears the way as Jerry strikes all over the fret board and cymbal crashes set the pace. Intensity rises as the music remains mellifluous. A jazzy feel is mixed into the blues pounding. You can hear the birth of "Caution" in these '67 "Violas." After spiraling and swirling to a peak, a stunning regeneration jam leads back to the final verse. This is a resounding performance by a band maturing in leaps and bounds.

4-6-69 Avalon Ballroom, San Francisco, CA: After performing "Viola" on March 3, 1968, the Dead didn't play it for 114 shows until this evening in the Avalon. With the first batch of Hunter tunes taking flight in the Dead's live repertoire, the band rested "Viola Lee" for a while. On 4-6-69, the band played "It's All Over Now, Baby Blue" for the first time in three years. After this riveting rendition, Garcia said, "What else do you want to hear that we used to do?" Some Deadheads must have been howling for "Viola."

After a lengthy "Lovelight" smackdown, the show comes to an end with a stunning "Viola Lee." The band jumps into it with fierce confidence, and the percussionists stand out here. As the jam develops, some sizzling organ-grinding kicks this into gear. And then Lesh pumps out foreboding bass runs.

It's time for Jerry to dig in. And holy moly! The jam shifts into a state of supersonic sound—a breakaway iceberg that will obliterate anything in its path. Group synergy rages at impossible speeds. It's one of the more breathtaking moments in any "Viola."

Right after they hit the apex, the plug is pulled—literally. The electricity onstage is cut off and Weir says, "I think somebody's trying to tell us something." We are deprived of the jam that leads back to the lyrics, but the drummers carry on as the Boys defiantly sing the last verse. It's a fitting ending to a memorable performance. "Viola" was played two more times in April, and then retired for the remainder of the year.

5-2-70 Harpur College, Binghamton, NY: "Viola Lee Blues" was returned to the Dead's repertoire on a limited basis in Port Chester's Capitol Theatre on March 20, 1970. Of the seven "Violas" of 1970, the undisputed champ is from 5-2-70. The third set of this remarkable show begins with "Morning Dew," and ends with Viola Lee Blues > And We Bid You Goodnight.

There was major unrest and protests against the Vietnam War on college campuses across America. This show takes place two days before the Kent State massacre. There's revolution in the air and the Harpur College "Viola Lee Blues" taps into that rebellious vibe. The band storms through the verses. The power and control of the musicians is scary. Weir's growth as rhythm guitarist is noticeable as he strikes the right chords and rhythms while Lesh and Garcia exchange savage volleys. There's magical pauses and notes that are not played to increase the tension. This bawdy jam will make you smile and laugh at times. It ranks up there with the best versions of 1967.

After scaling the "Viola" peak, the regeneration jam back to the verse is heavy, a slow train back to Bluesville. The Grateful Dead let it all hang down in Binghamton.

10-31-70 Gym, SUNY Stonybrook: The Dead played an early and late show on this Halloween Eve in Stonybrook. The early show ends with this triplet: Viola Lee Blues > Cumberland Blues > Uncle John's Band. This is the final "Viola," the third jam anthem that was put to rest on Halloween. "St. Stephen" and Lazy Lightning > Supplication are the others.

The final outing for "Viola" scoots along impressively. Garcia approaches the first solo in understated manner and finishes it with a knockout blow. The band lyrically flows into the big jam. Around seven minutes in, an impressive "Cumberland Blues" riff arises. For a few minutes, the jam encompasses both "Viola" and "Cumberland" before bidding farewell to "Viola" forever. The original jam anthem had served its purpose. The time had come for the harvest of Hunter/Garcia tunes to carry the torch.

PLAYIN' IN THE BAND

As the Grateful Dead soared to new artistic heights seemingly every time they hit the stage in 1972, "Playin' in the Band" is the tune that best documents the journey. "Playin'" was adopted from "The Main Ten," a Mickey Hart riff played in a 10/4 time signature. With lyrics by Hunter and arrangement by Weir, "Playin' in the Band" was debuted on 2-18-71 in the Capitol Theatre in Port Chester. A tight performance of "Playin'" from the Hammerstein Ballroom on 4-6-71 was included on *Skulls and Roses*. A terrific studio version of "Playin'" was recorded by members of the Grateful Dead in early '72 for Bob Weir's solo album *Ace*. Lively improvisation imbues the studio "Playin'," making it one of the best tracks ever recorded by the band.

"Playin' in the Band" was performed 582 times, the fourth-most of any song. It was played seventy-nine times in 1972, making it the most frequently played song of arguably the Dead's greatest year. The first version of the year on January 2 in the Winterland barely reached six minutes. By the end of the year, several versions of "Playin'" were approaching twenty-five minutes. The intense jamming expanded the improvisational possibilities for rock bands as the Dead had done before with "Dark Star." During this era, "Playin' in the Band" often found a home near the end of the opening set.

"Playin'" is a legendary stand-alone jam anthem, but perhaps its greatest contribution in the scheme of things is as a gateway tune, the ultimate segue to some of the wildest song loops known to man. The first "Playin'" loop occurred in the

Fox Theatre on 10-18-72: Playin' > Drums > Dark Star > Morning Dew > Playin'. It's a loop that was as ambitious as it was brilliant. As if it never happened, the Dead went an entire year without splitting up "PITB" again until 10-21-73 in Omaha, when it was successfully parted by Mississippi Half-Step > Big River. The possibilities were now endless, and "Uncle John's Band" quickly emerged as a favored transition partner. On 5-21-74, in Washington University's Edmunson Pavilion, "Playin' in the Band" opened set two and carried on, uninterrupted, for almost forty-seven minutes. They stretched it to the max.

Rarely performed as a stand-alone tune again, "Playin' in the Band" became the ultimate anything-could-happen Grateful Dead number. There were two thirteen-show stretches when "Playin'" didn't make an appearance: once between '86 and '87, and once in '92. "Playin'" became a vehicle of imagination, usually leading to a major Jerry tune, such as "UJB," "Terrapin Station," "Crazy Fingers," or "China Doll." The segue would usually return for a "Playin'" reprise after Drums, but sometimes the loop was never completed. The song had an uncanny flexibility that made it thrive. Other monumental jam anthems had to appear on the right night in the right slot. "Playin'" could arrive at any time and add to a budding masterpiece or change the flow of a subpar show.

8-27-72 Old Renaissance Faire Grounds, Veneta, OR: I remember hearing a tape of this show for the first time and without warning, I was blown away by the "Playin' in the Band" that opened set two. My first batch of boots were '77 gems, but the 8-27-72 "Playin'" was a different kind of awesome from the Cornell Scarlet > Fire or the Englishtown "Mississippi Half-Step." The Veneta "Playin'" jam burns and yearns from the start. Garcia's relentless leads were hotter than the Oregon sun which scorched the band and Deadheads with triple digit heat.

The music seems to mirror the disorientating euphoria of a peak acid trip. The band is locked in tight—free-flowing psychedelic energy crackling through amps and into human minds—a preview of the future in a distant millennium. The music is heavy and dark around the ten-minute mark as the mood and texture of the jam shifts. Garcia launches another atomic pinball as Bill and Phil fuel the cosmic journey. Keith lays down some gorgeous piano riffs as if he's Thelonious Monk. The musical flow shifts again and Garcia steps on the gas—here comes another shooting star—glorious aural debris.

Garcia wisely steers this back towards the return of the final chorus—everything's just exactly perfect. Even Donna's wailing screams sound good. The band efficiently wraps this masterpiece up. Two more hours of mind-bending music beckons on this blessed evening in Veneta.

11-24-72 Memorial Auditorium, Dallas, TX: The Dead are cooking Veneta-style for this "Playin'" that closes the opening set. The band reels with supreme confidence as Jerry's washing windows and squeezing lemons at the same time—playful virtuosity—repetitive licks, deep string bending. Phil's hammering away, influenced by the possibilities of quantum physics. Keith's in a mad jazz zone, more Bud Powell than Monk. The theme and overall structure isn't as well-designed as 8-27-72 but the raging musicianship is overwhelming, and this version is a few minutes longer than Veneta. Sparks fly as the Grateful Dead blitz the cosmic highway at the speed of sound. The Dallas "Playin'" stands out as it streaks through time and space, yet it's only a notch or two above most "Playin' in the Bands" from the latter part of 1972.

8-6-74 Roosevelt Stadium, Jersey City, NJ: Prior to this endeavor, I probably wouldn't have considered this show as one of the greatest ever. That might be because I often listened to *Dick's Pick's Vol.31*, which contains segments from this show along with portions of the previous two nights in Philadelphia. And that means I rarely listened to 8-6-74 start to finish. The opening set features the best "Eyes of the World" and ends with Playin in the Band > Scarlet Begonias > Playin'. This is a meaty sandwich that was only played one time. "Begonias" benefits from this configuration, but let's focus on "Playin'."

It's a good thing the "PITBs" from this period are long. It gives the listener time to recover from Donna's primal screams. They are brain-rattling on this rendition. The jam lifts off in explosive fashion as Jerry's spiraling leads take this out of the realm of musical theory. The jam hits a jazzy plateau as Phil, Keith, and Billy guide this towards something that sounds Coltrane-influenced. You can hear traces throughout of "Mind Left Body." Like most 1974 "Playin's," the flow becomes odd and experimental, but it's not at all long-winded. Keith gets into a groove on electric piano as the jam shifts into a funky motif prior to the "Scarlet Begonias" handoff, which occurs twenty minutes in. The "Playin'" reprise is not as long as others from this era. The Dead make up for the brevity with an authoritative finish. This is the most focused "Playin'" of the year.

10-19-73 Fairgrounds Arena, Oklahoma City: An elastic exploration of "Playin' in the Band" ends the opening set in OKC. The Dead roll out the canvas and Jerry takes off in all directions, yet the music still rolls in logical and linear fashion. As the jam seethes, the band unloads a dump truck of ideas— sinewy metallic runs cascade like spiderwebs across the aural landscape. It's a symphonic rhapsody, a blastoff into the subterranean abyss—bright, colorful sounds that send your mind out of time. There's a clever move back into the final chorus and the band rocks the finale hard.

11-17-73 Pauley Pavilion, UCLA: At the start of the second set, the Dead produced one of their most revered song loops: Playin' in the Band >Uncle John's Band > Morning Dew > Uncle John's Band > Playin' in the Band. This "PITB" jam has a different feel and pace than the relentless scorcher from Veneta, but it has that same jaw-dropping effect. Garcia dominates Veneta. The UCLA version is sophisticated, and there's more space for Phil and Billy to go off early. Once Garcia starts to unload, he weaves a tapestry of unique riffs and bubbling leads into a spellbinding symphony.

After the epic UJB > Dew > UJB, the sandwich inside the loop is completed with a "Playin'" reprise. This is a substantial and gripping journey brightened by fusion fireballs. If you splice together the start and finish of the UCLA "Playin' in the Band," you have one of the best versions ever.

5-26-72 The Strand Lyceum, London, England: This was the Grateful Dead's last show of Europe '72. After a draining tour, during which their musicianship took a quantum leap forward, it would be understandable if the band were tired and they simply delivered an average performance. Forget about it. This was a peaking band on a holy mission. They dazzled London with a nineteen-song opening set. "Playin' in the band" was the tenth song of a set that ended with these cherished combinations: China Cat > Rider and Not Fade Away > GDTRFB > Not Fade Away.

Keeping with the extra-effort theme of the set, "Playin' in the Band" was eighteen minutes, at least five minutes longer than any previous version. The jam's firing on all cylinders early. Phil, Keith, and Billy direct the middle section. Keith shines throughout. It's almost like his bandmates are putting the spotlight on him. Let's see what you got, rookie. And Keith responds. His runs are colorful, tasty, and he's inspiring the rest of the group. After thirteen minutes, it sounds like they're ready to wrap this up, but it ain't over until the great Garcia unloads those fusion fireballs. The music burns and blisters, and Donna's primal screams lead to a thunderous finale. This was a turning point in "Playin'" history. It would never be a neat, ten-minute song again. And why stop at eighteen minutes when you could stretch out to forty-seven?

8-7-82 Alpine Valley Music Theatre, East Troy, WI: "Playin'" is the fifth song of a terrific second set. And as it would happen at many shows in the '80s and '90s, Jerry led the band into a noodling extravaganza that crashed into Drums. The jamming is above-average, but the star here is the reprise. On the other side of Drums, Space spins into "The Wheel." The Wheel > Playin' transition is dreamy and mesmerizing. Weir emphatically preaches the virtues of being a rock star as the band rams this home. Jerry's wailing and Weir's popping as the drummers race past all normal reprise barriers. The only "Playin'" reprise I would rate ahead of this one is 10-12-84 Augusta. But on that night, there was just a "Playin'" reprise inside an "Uncle John's" loop. The beginning of "Playin'" never took place. Back in Alpine Valley, the fiery reprise leads to the holy grail, "Morning Dew."

9-21-82 Madison Square Garden, New York, NY: Six days earlier, Playin > Crazy Fingers opened the show in Landover, Maryland. I was there for that indelible experience. As the set progressed there were two "Playin'" instrumentals, and a third one in set two, although the "PITB" reprise never materialized. In Madison Square Garden, the Dead opened with Playin' > Fingers again. There were no instrumental reprises, but the "Playin' in the Band" was superior to the Landover version.

After individually introducing the members of the band, John Scher exclaims, "Would you please welcome back to New York, the GRATEFUL DEAD!" Rapturous Madison Square Garden applause fills the arena as a four-beat count-off explodes into "Playin' in the Band." The excitement of the sung portion of "Playin'" in front of an electrified New York audience is unreal. Weir croons like a conquering hero as the band slams the chord progressions. Garcia's noodling rushes through the audience as Billy and Mickey push the pace—hotter and hotter—on par with a '72 version. This type of psychedelic purge is just about unprecedented at the start of any show. They're on fire, and nothing's slowing this train down until they weave a gorgeous transition into "Crazy Fingers." One song in and Madison Square Garden has landed on Pluto.

TURN ON YOUR LOVE LIGHT

I f you think of a 1969 "Turn on Your Love Light," the first association that should pop into your mind is Pigpen. This was Ron McKernan's signature showstopper, a song embedded with his essence. Garcia had that knack as well. He infused cover songs with a spirit that made them come alive in a distinctive manner. Even if you were familiar with the original artist and other versions of the song, Garcia could put it across in a way that made it seem like a new creation. Pigpen had that same gift when it came to performing his favorite blues numbers.

"Turn on Your Lovelight" was first recorded by Bobby "Blue" Bland in 1961. The Dead debuted "Lovelight" on July18, 1967, at the Masonic Temple in Portland, Oregon. The first known Dead tape with "Lovelight" is from Toronto on August 5, 1967. Pigpen discovered his inspiration for this number when he saw James Cotton play "Turn on Your Lovelight" when Cotton opened for the Dead in 1966.

With Pig's raunchy vocals and the band's desire to endlessly improvise, the simple musical arrangement of "Turn on Your Lovelight" gave the Grateful Dead an instant jam anthem. When I was listing contenders for this project, this tune was a no-brainer. But comparing "Lovelights" and deciding on which ones to honor here was a more difficult task. The earlier versions were usually around ten minutes long. And then "Lovelight" branched off and mutated every which way, with versions going on for more than forty minutes.

Within the simple structure, improvisational anarchy ruled. Jams and Pigpen raps could arise at any time. Sometimes the raps were accompanied by sparse backing instrumentation. On other verses, the band created intricate backing support as Pig encouraged the audience to get to know each other better. The rap could deflate, pause, or accelerate the momentum of the jam. It was an entity unto itself, different from anything in any other jam anthem, thrilling for us to hear on tape and even more exhilarating for those who experienced it in the moment. However, in picking out the hottest "Lovelights," I focused more on the jamming, and there is no scarcity of that.

For many Pigpen loyalists, it was sacrilegious to hear Bobby Weir take over lead vocals when the band brought "Lovelight" back in the '80s. With rented equipment, the band thrilled Amsterdam with the first post-Pigpen "Lovelight" in Amsterdam on 10-16-81. The next "Lovelight" in Alpine Valley on 7-7-84 signified a new era for the song as a second-set closer, although on that night, "Lovelight" was sandwiched within "Not Fade Away." For good or ill, "Lovelight" was here to stay.

Although it was a cleaner and tighter entity, some of these versions were pure smoke. When the band was having *one of those nights*, a hot "Lovelight" could burn the house down and touch the hearts and souls of snobbish fans. I'm especially fond of several versions from the '84–'85 era. However, on too many nights it was a weak impersonation of what was once a mighty jam anthem. In that regard, it went through the same sad cookie-cutter regression that "Not Fade Away" did in later years.

Regardless of the criticism from tour veterans like myself, football stadiums full of fans danced and cheered for "Lovelight" finales every time.

5-7-70 Dupont Gymnasium, Massachusetts Institute of Technology, Cambridge, MA: If you like bang for your buck, this thirty-minute MIT "Lovelight" is loaded. No soundboard exists from this show. The audience recording is decent by 1970 standards. It excels at capturing the raw excitement of the performance in conjunction with the titillated mindset of the audience. Some have labeled and tracked this epic segment of music as: Turn on Your Lovelight > St. Stephen Jam > Jam > Darkness Jam > Jam > China Cat Sunflower Jam > Turn on Your Lovelight. In my view this is simply "Turn on Your Lovelight," forget all the thematic jams. These jams exist within this "Lovelight" the way other thematic jams pop up in "Dark Star." Other "Lovelights" from 1970 also contain some of these elements. Whenever I hear this connected jam segment in the 5-7-70 "Lovelight," it reminds me of the "Overture" from a famous 1969 rock opera. *Tommy, can you hear me?*

"Not Fade Away" segues into the final number of the show, "Turn on Your Love Light." The band's flying and flexing muscle. Garcia rips a vibrant between-verse solo. Pigpen has the audience on lockdown with soulful singing and focused vocal improv. Jerry and Bobby aggressively sing the backing vocals. The band's bobbing and weaving with Ron. Weir's chopping funky riffs as Jerry noodles and Phil hammers. Pig responds to Jerry by mimicking the sharp bending twang of his leads. They go back and forth for a while before the jam storms down the tracks.

There's a blues-infused charge into a "St. Stephen" theme for a few minutes. The train ride continues until Phil blasts his way to the brief "Darkness" jam. The mood of the jam shifts from bluesy to psychedelic and eventually spills into a "China Cat" jam. The handoff back to Pigpen and the final sing-off is sophisticated. Ron's voice hits the high notes and his soul's on fire. Weir provides his excited backing vocals to counter. The music spins and spins—a little bit higher! There's the chorus reprise, massive howling from the singers, and a bone-crunching ending—not a wasted moment or gesture in this multi-faceted musical marathon.

5-7-72 Bickershaw Festival, Wigan, England: In a span of four years, the Dead played three outstanding versions of "Turn on Your Lovelight" on May 7, Billy Kreutzmann's birthday. The "Lovelight" not discussed here is from 5-7-69 Golden Gate Park. Bickershaw is a completely different listening experience compared to MIT. The recording is a pristine soundboard mix, and the performance is thirteen compressed minutes. Towards the end of a sprawling show that featured some of the band's most audacious experimental jams, the Dead rocked the socks off Bickershaw with a Sugar Magnolia > Turn on Your Lovelight > Goin' Down the Road Feelin' Bad > Not Fade Away finale.

There's an audio hiccup as they break into "Lovelight." The band quickly pauses and restarts. Lookout! After Pig knocks down a verse, Garcia, Lesh, and Kreutzmann unload. It's scary how phenomenal they are individually—and together—by this point in their career. This rowdy yet brilliant blues assault must have sent mud flying from the frantic dancing of fans. Earlier in the show the band blew out their minds, and now the Dead turned this into a physical affair.

The impossibly tenacious solo by Jerry is stunning. Billy stirs this beast forward in unflinching fashion. Pigpen's voice sounded strong, but he was ill and physically weakened. His rap took flight briefly but the band dominates here, crushing it all the way through. You can't pack more punch into a thirteen-minute version.

After the last verse, they storm ahead as if they're going into "Caution," but there's a sudden detour to "Goin' Down the Road Feelin' Bad."

2-13-70 Fillmore East, New York, NY: A thirty-minute "Turn on Your Love Light" burns the house down, concluding the hottest third set the band ever played: Dark Star > That's It for the Other One > Lovelight. The pistons are poppin' and the Pig is a-rockin'. Singing instrumental exclamation points accent every sung verse. The band steams an instrumental and hands it back to the master of ceremonies. There's an easy flow to Pigpen's rap and his cagey cadence is irresistible. The preacher engages the eager audience in an "All you need" call-and-response, and then yells, "Play your guitar!" A subtle blues jam emerges as Phil and Bobby interact with Jerry's tasty leads. More rap leads back to the signature melody. The Dead are masterfully in control as they rev up the finale. Ron and Bobby sing and howl as the band plays on and on. Garcia improvises an astonishing fanfare finish and Pigpen unleashes a macho howl. It's a milestone moment for the Grateful Dead and the Fillmore East.

2-28-69 Fillmore West, San Francisco, CA: Dick Latvala heralded this show as an example of Primal Dead, and his appraisal is perfect. "Turn on Your Lovelight" ends the opening set of 2-28-69. It's odd that nothing from this night made it onto *Live Dead*. Maybe these performances were too hot for vinyl.

There's a tribal feel as Pigpen howls through the opening verse and the band savors the groove. The opening jam is filled with intense playing that rolls on and on like the Bickershaw version. After stepping on the gas for several minutes, the band breaks the jam down and explores various pathways. Jerry and Phil bounce ideas off each other as the seven-minute jam leads back to Pigpen. After a healthy rap, the band ramps up the intensity full blast down the homestretch. The Fillmore West trembles as the music thunders. I prefer this version to the one that ended up on *Live Dead*, 1-26-69 Avalon Ballroom, although that version is a rocker that also captures the essence of "Lovelight."

10-22-1967 Winterland Arena, San Francisco, CA: This was the Dead's fourth performance of "Turn on Your Lovelight." It's a simple musical arrangement, but the way the band confidently romps through this version is scary. Pigpen's voice brings the macho swagger out of "Lovelight" as the band swings free and easy. The drummers push the pace as Garcia peels off lyrical guitar—organic, psychedelic energy. There's a sweet, steady rush of sound that flows like a Coltrane solo. Garcia's heading down the slope and managing the turns as Pigpen riffs swirl underneath the surface. Hippies must have been airborne in the Winterland. If you ever have a Dead dance party, this is a must for the playlist. This joyful adventure would have been ideal for a royal celebration like the end of Prohibition. I continue to be amazed at how masterful the band was back in 1967.

10-16-81 Club Melkweg, Amsterdam, Netherlands: With a 500-person capacity, Club Melkweg was the most intimate venue the band had played in many years, and they would never play a gig like this again. Towards the end of the underrated

Europe '81 tour, a pair of shows in France were rained out. Instead of taking a few days off, the band rented equipment and arranged to play those shows in Amsterdam on October 15 and 16. These performances became known as the "Ooops" concerts. Bob Weir celebrated his 34th birthday on 10-16-81. It was a surreal performance—unfathomable, if it weren't for the tapes.

The first set was acoustic, and the second electric set featured the band's first live performances of "Hully Gully" and "Gloria." As a raunchy jam roars out of "Gloria," Weir fixes his sights on the first "Turn on Your Lovelight" without Pigpen. The transition is subdued as Weir starts the first verse, and the song takes hold as Phil pumps the signature lick. The group's output is scrappy and impossibly exhilarating. Garcia shreds two solos as the band fearlessly motors down the highway. Weir comes back for a "Shine on me" refrain as Garcia sets off the Roman candles. This is a gutsy six-minute performance. Surprisingly, Weir waits three years before breaking out "Lovelight" again.

4-8-85 The Spectrum, Philadelphia, PA: Around and Around > Turn On Your Lovelight closes the show. On most nights, I loathed seeing that combo. "Around and Around" had become a complete cookie-cutter segue primarily used as an intro for "Good Lovin'" or "Lovelight." When Weir brought back "Lovelight" there were several hot versions, but eventually, the rest of the band seemed to be going through the motions as Weir had his showcase rave. This was the last show of the tour, and the band had already made 4-8-85 a memorable affair.

As they transition into "Lovelight," there's an explosion of energy. The zesty tempo couldn't be refused. The infectious groove swallows the Spectrum and puts everybody in motion. Garcia sparkles early and often as the band exercises supernatural control over the tempo. Weir leads the band as they weave through a pair of high-octane jams. There's a sudden de-escalation of tempo as Weir steps to the mic for his moment of glory. His controlled falsetto singing builds a bridge for the band to stage a climactic finale. Weirs shrieks: "Shine on me!" one last time and Garcia hits the sweetest "Lovelight" licks as his mates stick a dramatic conclusion. A sustained euphoric roar fills the Spectrum as the greatest band in the land pulls off another distinctive musical extravaganza.

THE OTHER ONE

This quintessential jam anthem from the band's most experimental studio album is deservedly the last entry of *Deadology Volume 2*. "The Other One" is tucked in the middle of the opening track of *Anthem of the Sun*, "That's It for the Other One." The Grateful Dead played "The Other One" 583 times, making it their third-most played song, trailing only "Me and My Uncle" and "Sugar Magnolia." "Playin' in the Band" was performed 582 times.

The evocative lyrics of "The Other One" capture a time and place in the band's history with the Merry Pranksters. And the swirling psychedelic vibe of the musical arrangement matches the spirit of the song. Any time the Dead broke into "The Other One," the audience was receiving an essential dose of the Grateful Dead experience. It was a jam tune that was easily adoptable for any year, or era, during its twenty-eight-year run. With all the variations in style, approach, and length, "The Other One" was a fascinating and time-consuming song to study for this project.

Cryptical Envelopments > The Other One > Cryptical Envelopments was performed for the first time on October 22, 1967, in the Winterland Arena. The standout jam in many of these early versions usually occurred during the "Cryptical" reprise. "The Other One" emerged into a raging force by 1969. Long jams forcefully swirled and surged around the verses. Cosmic energy burst from the instrumentals. "The Other One" seemed to share that same mysterious propulsion present in "The Eleven." This is Primal Dead.

"The Other One" developed an independent streak from "Cryptical" as it appeared on its own, and sometimes only with the opening of "Cryptical. In 1972, "Cryptical Envelopments" was only played once, on September 23 in the Palace Theater, Waterbury, Connecticut. "Cryptical" returned to the lineup during the Dead's Twentieth Anniversary Tour in the summer of 1985 and was played for the last time on September 3 in Kansas City. That leaves us a plethora of stand-alone "Other Ones" to consider.

"The Other One" instrumental loosened up and became more explorative after 1969. Instead of unfolding as spiraling jams wrapped around the nucleuses of the two verses, "Other One" forays veered into territory unknown. On occasion, it formed a sandwich around an unexpecting tune like "Me and My Uncle."

When the Dead steamrolled Europe in '72, several songs exploded to new artistic heights, and one of those numbers was "The Other One." It emerged as a major masterpiece timing in as long as many "Dark Stars." On 4-26-72 in Frankfurt, Germany, the band improvised more than thirty-six minutes during "The Other One." There's no denying 1972 was the banner year for "The Other One."

There was a wonderful mix of old-school psychedelic power with cosmic drifting that really got *out there*. During '73 and '74, the Dead continued to push the boundaries of "The Other One" as they split and segued their pride and joy as part of larger presentations. In '74, "The Other One" transitioned in and out of instrumentals like "Spanish Jam," "Nobody's Fault but Mine," "It's a Sin," and "Mind Left Body."

Tighter renditions of "The Other One" materialized when the band resumed touring. In 1977, the Dead flexed their muscles, teeing off on fierce "Other One" jams. From this point forward, "The Other One" usually emerged after Drums, segueing from Space, "Truckin'," or "The Wheel" on most occasions.

Coming out of Space added a new dimension to the intro. The band would seemingly weave in and out of consciousness until Phil stepped up and hit his signature blastoff. It was disappointing when Weir sang "Spanish Lady" too quickly. But when the band let Space > Other One marinate and they played a substantial pre-verse solo, the results were sublime.

In the '80s and '90s, "The Other One" was noticeably shorter than before. However, it never sunk to the cookie-cutter status of other formerly magnificent jam numbers like "Not Fade Away," "Around and Around," or "Turn on Your Love Light." There were many worthwhile "Other Ones" over the Dead's last fifteen years. With Jerry's psychedelic noodling, Weir's inspired vocals, and Phil's thunder, there was always reason to get excited when the Grateful Dead broke into "The Other One."

2-13-70 Fillmore East, New York, NY: This is an astounding thirty-minute "That's It for the Other One," seven minutes longer than the legendary version from the Fillmore East on 3-1-69. The New York performance flows out of an epic "Dark Star." After Jerry croons a gorgeous "Cryptical," there's a meaty drum duet. As the drummers take off, you can hear Bobby briefly mess around with a "Not Fade Away" chord progression. "The Other One" blastoff from Jerry, Phil, and Bob stuns the senses. Everything on this night must be epic, and the sonic power throttles the Fillmore East. Jerry sears and soars against crunching chord progressions from Weir. The playing's furious but the band's got it mapped out—a series of twisters touching down. When the storm clouds clear, Weir pounces on the lyrics without the signature instrumental lead-in—gotta keep it fresh.

The second instrumental arises from the ashes. It takes a minute for the Boys to hit spin cycle, but boy, do they unload. Garcia and Lesh shift into crazed mode like squirrels chasing each other up, down, and around oak trees. This has all the frenzy of a 1969 version, but the craftsmanship is more sophisticated.

Jerry boils, hitting a shrill string of notes. Everything must be epic. The band finds a way to regenerate the jam for another high-flying run that leads back to verse two. Both instrumentals are substantial, without any superfluous waste. To top off the magnus opus, the Dead shred the "Cryptical" reprise. These were Renaissance men breaking through to the other side in the Fillmore East on 2-13-70.

9-17-72 Baltimore Civic Center, MD: The epic, thirty-nine-minute Baltimore "Other One" checks all the boxes; it has everything you could expect from an essential jam anthem and more. A curt "He's Gone" instrumental eagerly gives way to "The Other One." A few fierce minutes of jamming leads to a Billy drum solo. This doubles our pleasure because after Billy gets his licks, Phil must kick it off again. The sonic onslaught is breathtaking. Garcia tweets piercing notes off impressive electric piano from Keith. "The Other One" really gets *out there* in '72, and this version exemplifies that. After the swirling, spiraling charge, the jam flows into jazzy terrain. Phil and Billy alter the direction by laying down heavy funk. After seventeen minutes, Weir finally breaks into the "Spanish Lady" verse.

That was the short instrumental. Jam two veers straight into the avant-garde abyss—moody, new age vibrations—Lesh in his glory. Garcia strikes and bends an anguished note that stops time in its tracks. The Dead march forward, disregarding audience expectation. The group mind has one focus: inspired improvisation.

Jerry moves towards some "Tiger"-influenced leads. As the journey expands, there are hints of several thematic jams, but the band doesn't lock into any one motif. Only Miles Davis had a band that could do this kind of thing in 1972. A cool Billy/Keith segment emerges and then Phil takes Keith's place. Weir intensifies the groove as Jerry's leads layer and sizzle like bacon on a grill. As if they had discussed the meeting point earlier, the band hops back into "The Other One" on a dime with conviction. When Weir's done with verse two, almost a full side of a ninety-minute cassette tape has been filled. If you like this version, make a point of checking out the 9-9-72 "Other One" from the Hollywood Palladium.

5-7-72 Bickershaw Festival, Wigan, England: Oh, to be young, and to be a Deadhead at the Bickershaw Festival on the muddy Sunday afternoon of May 7, 1972. After four crisp, stand-alone songs to start set two, the Dead launch a one-verse

"Dark Star" voyage that segues into a drum solo. Billy was celebrating his twenty-sixth birthday. Instead of returning to "Dark Star," the band launches "The Other One." It comes off like an atomic slingshot after the hypnotic playing that preceded it. This is the only time "D Star" and "Other One" were played in the same show during their European rendezvous.

After the massive initial surge, the jam redirects into subtle exploration. The band cherishes every second as they rebuild towards another resounding surge and "Spanish Lady." Keith and Jerry exchange sparkling leads between Weir's vocal lines. Phil leads the band into abstract exploration with a serene vibe. Sounds stream through a black hole into another dimension as Garcia dives into quick-picking "Tiger" territory. Phil pounds out a rich musical canvas, one backbone-rattling bass note at a time. At the twenty-four-minute mark, Garcia starts to construct a bridge that leads the band back to the "Other One" zone. These next five minutes may be the most incredible of any "Other One." The band pounces on the signature chord progression, yet they leave room for Jerry to embark on a euphoric rampage. Although it's eight and a half minutes shorter than the 9-17-72 Baltimore version, the Bickershaw bus to never-ever land is every bit as impressive.

9-3-72 Folsom Field, Boulder, CO: We have ourselves another 1972 three-set extravaganza. The Boulder bonanza features He's Gone > Other One towards the end of set two. The charge into "The Other One" is a glorious gallop, a force to be reckoned with. Phil thrusts levers as Jerry steers the ship through the eternal night. Billy's fluid drumming keeps the advance on point, and Keith's piano twinkling lights up the sky. Lesh works up a nifty bass riff around ten minutes in, and Jerry plucks a repetitive melody line to match. This heroic instrumental gives way to the first verse after fourteen blazing minutes.

The next movement's a blast of improvised fusion that comes off like a predetermined score. It doesn't move into the strange terrain like other "Other Ones" from this period. This entire presentation is fluid, like a spinning top that can't be slowed down or altered. It could cure the insane or cause insanity. It's time to leave the capsule if you dare. Re-entry into "The Other One" is an upbeat stream of pure heat. Chalk up another remarkable '72 "Other One" masterpiece for the Grateful Dead.

5-18-77 Fox Theatre, Atlanta, GA: After Drums, cascading bass bombs launch "The Other One." There she goes into orbit, the best version of '77. Garcia and mates are super-charged as they recklessly smash forward. This had been a night of many mellow ballads. It's as if Garcia was conserving energy all night so he could kick ass on three predetermined songs: "Music Never Stopped," "Eyes of the World," and "The Other One."

Jerry's leads are savage, swift, and relentless. Listen in awe as the Dead lay down the almighty '77 hammer. Phil and the band magnificently restate the theme several times before Weir belts out, "Spanish lady, come to me, she lays on me this rose."

Part two of the jam rages and screams as it peaks, and peaks, and peaks again, until it finally eases into cosmic weirdness. There is no second verse; it's as if the music actually escapes through the lily fields and comes upon an empty space.

Garcia noodles away, a lovely and seductive soliloquy. "The Other One" slowly dissolves into the gorgeous opening of another ballad, "Stella Blue." This twelve-minute "Other One" demands your attention and delivers more sizzle per minute than any other version.

11-7-71 Harding Theatre, San Francisco, CA: As they would do in Bickershaw a year later, the Dead bless the hometown faithful with Dark Star > Drums > The Other One. As the band catapults into "The Other One," you, the listener, may experience instant whiplash. The band has bad intentions, but it's a short instrumental that leads into the "Spanish Lady" verse.

On the other side of Weir's singing, Phil takes off like a demon. Jerry fills in with space noodling. In my mind, this segment creates the illusion of a dazed fighter valiantly trying to fight back. The woozy playing leads into "Me and My

Uncle." It's a succinct pairing, a bizarre murder ballad emerging from a Prankster anthem.

A crisp "Me and My Uncle" obediently gives way to "The Other One" chord progression.

Once again, instant whiplash gives way to dreamy noodling. Garcia's spacy whirling is backed by a hornet's nest of bass. The dazed boxer's fighting back and his head is clearing. The band rips through the resounding "Other One" chord progression. The rout is on. During this segment, Garcia's insane playing conjures up thoughts of a surfer gliding through massive pipeline waves. The Harding Theatre is dancing in the stars. Weir sings his final verse and the band comes to an abrupt pause due to a broken string. This was broadcast on FM radio, and the announcer just says, "Wow!" Enough said.

4-21-72 Beat Club, Bremen, West Germany: This is the last song of a studio performance filmed for a TV audience. Only a small portion of this show was aired for the West German audience, but Deadheads had an opportunity to enjoy this performance at a Grateful Dead meet-up at the movies gathering forty years later. One cool aspect of this "Other One" performance is that Jerry is standing behind the band as he jams like a demon. With his bushy beard, black leather jacket, and flashy, multi-colored guitar strap, he looked like the hippest star in the galaxy.

Following Truckin' > Drums, Phil ignites a brilliant, twenty-three-minute "Other One." Garcia's shrieking leads blaze a trail through a path of pounding bass detonations. The jam dissolves, reorganizes, and strengthens before Weir sings, "Spanish lady comes to me, she lays on me this rose." Between verses there's an aural inferno before the instrumental dissolves into a dreamlike state, drifting in and out of consciousness— time out of mind terrain. With a subtle shifting of tempo, the jamming becomes more furious than before—Garcia's searing leads spiral round and round in a tight blizzard of sound. "Escaping through the lily fields I came across an empty space," howls Weir. On this day, Apollo 16 landed on the lunar highlands of the moon. All this cosmic improv captures the flavor of the day.

Back in Bremen, the Grateful Dead's allotted studio time is almost done. Instead of an abrupt ending, the band noodles on as they resist the temptation of breaking into a new tune before improvising a climactic instrumental conclusion. The next two "Other Ones" in Frankfurt (4-26) and Paris (5-3) are monster versions worth checking out.

3-1-69 Fillmore West, San Francisco, CA: On the next-to-last night of this iconic Fillmore West run, Bill Graham opens the festivities with this intro: "The American version of the Japanese film *Magnificent Seven*, the Grateful Dead."

After "Cryptical," the drummers lead the band into an "Other One" bombardment. Weir strums vital chords that open a path for the primal scream of Jerry's guitar against the psychedelic swirl of T. C. and Pigpen's keyboards. Phil's bombing away.

As they approach the first verse, the "Magnificent Seven" are recreating the vibe of a Vietnam battlefield. The following instrumental is restless and fearless, and it captures the essence of Neal Cassady. This "Other One" is more than substantial, but the "Cryptical" reprise elevates this performance. The intertwining virtuosity of Lesh and Garcia strikes like a psychedelic sledgehammer. And then the trip gets stranger as they segue into "New Potato Caboose."

11-14-73 San Diego Sports Arena, CA: An amazing "Other One" loop kicks off set two: Truckin' > The Other One > Big River > The Other One > Eyes of the World > The Other One. Half of this one-hour presentation is filled by "The Other One." The initial Truckin' > Other One segue starts off as a hybrid jam between the tunes. When the band commits to "The Other One," the distinctive sound amazes the senses. If music can drip like paint, this is it.

In late '73, the Dead are in the masterpiece business. We're lucky to have all these different approaches while the band was on top of their game. The music effortlessly straddles jazz and rock for nine minutes, leading to "Spanish Lady." Several minutes of trippy playing winds into "Big River."

"The Other One" chord progression returns convincingly after "Big River." As the band cooks, the "Cowboy Neal" verse seems inevitable. Nothing's for certain with these guys. The jam detours into "Eyes of the World." As this engaging version winds down, they shorten the ending jam because there's unfinished business. Weir strikes up "The Other One" again. This must have blown minds in San Diego. At last Weir escapes through the lily fields and the music never stops as our heroes roll into "Wharf Rat." If you're a fan of "Other One" loops like this, check out 7-18-76 Orpheum Theatre.

7-31-83 Ventura County Fairgrounds, CA: I was on hand for this seventeen-minute gem, an outlier from the era it came from. This version emerges from Space. One of the pleasures of "The Other Ones" from the '80s was how they emerged from Space. The drawback of this development was that the noodling intro usually led to a short power jam after Phil laid his signature bass line down.

On this occasion, Garcia noodles on, eight minutes of endless anticipation before Lesh detonates the bombs. Garcia's en fuego as the band rocks behind the Bearded Maestro. As they approach the verse, Phil bombs away again as Weir smashes on the whammy bar. High-voltage jamming possesses both solos. Phil's thundering! These blasts will test the audio dynamics of the speakers you listen on. Without the opening noodling jam, this would have been a contender to make this list. With it, this three-tiered monster is a no-brainer.

2-5-78 Uni Dome, University of Northern Iowa, Cedar Falls, IA: If you're employed, you might want to make sure your disability and life insurance premiums are paid up, and you might want to review the provisions before listening to this. It's the shortest of the versions listed here, but Jerry and mates unpack a devilish jam. There's no pulling punches, there's no buildup or space, just pure knockout power. At the end of the second jam, Garcia goes off on a tirade where he unloads the highest and hottest notes you'll ever hear in an "Other One." Two other versions similar to this that you might enjoy are 4-6-82 Philly and 9-23-82 New Haven.

6-16-85 Greek Theatre, Berkeley, CA: When the Dead took the stage on 6-16-85, there was a giant banner behind them showing a skeleton with a guitar, dressed and posing like a Minuteman in front of an American flag. The banner read, "Grateful Dead Twenty Years So Far." This was the third and final show of the three-night Greek run celebrating the band's twentieth anniversary. There had been some exciting moments during this three-night celebration. The first show was solid all the way through, with a hot "Morning Dew" to open set two. However, Deadheads were still hoping for an enormous breakout tune like "Dark Star," "St. Stephen," or "Cosmic Charlie."

After an exciting Scarlet > Fire > Samson opener to set two of 6-16-85, the Greek Theatre went berserk when they heard Weir and Garcia strike the poignant opening chord progression of "Cryptical Envelopments." This had been last played thirteen years earlier, and it struck the perfect sentiment for this grand occasion. Garcia choked on some of the words early, but tears of joy began to flow when he crooned, "All the children learnin', from books that they were burnin'. Every leaf was turnin', to watch him die, you know he had to die."

Without a drum interlude, Phil's bass blasts launch "The Other One." If you close your eyes, it's 1969 in the Fillmore West and the Grateful Dead are unleashing a tornado of swirling, psychedelic sound. The band nails the jam with relentless intensity. After the "Spanish Lady" verse, Garcia and Lesh let it rip again. This was one of longest and fiercest versions in many years. Then the band finishes off the memorable journey with the last half of "Cryptical Envelopments," making this a complete "That's It for the Other One."

ENCORE

BIRD SONG

Oops! I was listening to "Bird Song" a few days before the publication of this book when a sickening thought entered my mind. Did I forget to include "Bird Song" in *Deadology Volume II*? I definitely selected it as one of the thirty-three jam anthems, and I wrote the entry for it. But I couldn't recall the process of editing it. I wrote each entry in a separate Word document file, but I failed to merge "Bird Song" into the master file. I would have been justly chastised by the Deadhead community if I failed to include this here.

That left me with two options. I had to replace one of the existing jam anthems, or encore with "Bird Song." Although the Grateful Dead played it 296 times, "Bird Song" never appeared as an encore. I'll honor "Bird Song" as the encore of this endeavor, and let's consider this selection 33A+.

The first "Bird Song" took flight on February 19, 1971, in Port Chester's Capitol Theatre. The night before, the Dead debuted "Bertha," "Loser," "Greatest Story Ever Told," "Playin' in the Band," and "Wharf Rat" in Port Chester. Hunter wrote "Bird Song" in memory of Janis Joplin. Over the course of listening to this gorgeous tune for many years, I never realized the Janis connection until I read about it in Hunter's *A Box of Rain*.

"Bird Song" first appeared on *Garcia* (1972). This evocative composition creates a dreamy aura of birds soaring through the skies as Garcia's voice and guitar licks sing a *tune so sweet.* And with space for a substantial instrumental, "Bird Song" swiftly became a hypnotic jam anthem.

The first thirteen performances of "Bird Song" in 1971 lack the presence of future versions as the Dead tried to find the right tempo and texture for the "Bird." It was taken out of the rotation after being performed on 8-24-71 in Chicago. "Bird Song" triumphantly returned to the lineup in the third spot of the opening set during the legendary 7-18-72 Roosevelt Stadium show. Garcia discovered the perfect guitar tone, and with Keith playing behind him on piano, the sweet melody had charisma. As the year rolled on, "Bird Song" became a force with a pair of powerful jams. There are several outstanding versions from the fall of '72. After thirteen performances in '73, "Bird Song" flew on. Mysteriously, it wasn't played for seven long years.

In addition to giving fans an intimate experience, the 1980 acoustic sets from San Francisco, New Orleans, and New York reunited the band with songs that had slipped out of the rotation. Acoustic gems from this tour, like, "To Lay Me Down," "Jack-a-Roe," "It Must Have Been the Roses," "Deep Elem Blues," "On the Road Again," and "Bird Song," were played in electric sets after Radio City. "Bird Song" was the opening number of the first acoustic show in the Warfield Theater on 9-25-80. Garcia sang the song with more passion than ever before. After the acoustic tour, "Bird Song" would, for the most part, remain a beloved electric staple in the rotation.

The electric versions of "Bird Song" after Radio City featured one long, flexible jam where Garcia and company wandered and drifted. This instrumental seemed to capture the unique flavor of Jerry's playing: hypnotic, moody, and subtle. The two jam "Bird Songs" from '72 and '73 were more consistent and focused. The post-Radio City versions better reflected Garcia's mood in the moment. And while we are considering the instrumental prowess of "Bird Song," the acoustic versions can't be overlooked. During Dead and Garcia acoustic performances, "Bird Song" was usually the standout acoustic jam.

I'm extremely fond of the introductory chord riff of "Bird Song." It sounds like an old TV commercial: "Doctor Pepper—drink Doctor Pepper; Doctor Pepper—drink Doctor Pepper." The pressure-free structure of the instrumental enabled "Bird Song" to maintain its value as Jerry's virtuosity declined during his final years. Branford Marsalis and Bruce Hornsby both seemed to cherish improvising during this jam. "Bird Song" is pure Jerry.

3-7-80 Cole Field House, University of Maryland, College Park: What possessed Señor Garcia during this performance? Jerry's voice was unusually subdued as he sang "Bird Song," but his guitar solo was as garrulous as could be. There's no delay as Garcia soars early on with piercing runs. Within a few minutes, you realize this is a classic. The feathery flow of Jerry's fretwork swirls and spins. The band is supporting Garcia as he goes one-on-one with the audience. He's toying and teasing and teasing and toying. Licks stream in multiple directions.

The audience and his bandmates are in awe. The Great Garcia is spooling away, endless flight. It's amazing, but there's little repetition as he orbits planet Earth. After a substantial soar through the clouds, Garcia lands softly in the chorus . . . *Dry your eyes on the wind*. Jerry's vocals are soft once again, but everybody in College Park witnessed an outlier eighteen-minute performance of "Bird Song" that will forever be cherished by Deadheads.

6-22-73 P.N.E. Coliseum, Vancouver: Keith Godchaux is the catalyst for this dazzling "Bird Song," which took flight in the sixth slot of a fifteen-song opening set. Keith's electric piano imbues this performance with a thick sound. As the jam ascends, Keith, Jerry, and Bobby carve out a beautiful instrumental—three little birds singing the same song—finishing each other's thoughts. Phil/Bill create a jet stream to guide the swirling lullaby. The Keith/Jerry improvisation meshes in a Chick Corea/Miles Davis style.

After the jam subsides into Billy's drums, the feathery flight leads back to the whisper of Jerry's lonely and somber voice. The instrumental farewell is astounding as the jam bounces around. The tension mounts as the birds chirp in unison and form an exciting groove that's very danceable. It's a stirring finale, powerful and focused, a fitting exclamation point for a memorable flight.

8-27-72 Old Renaissance Faire Grounds, Veneta, OR: This "Bird" takes flight in the fourth spot of set two between "Jack Straw" and "Greatest Story Ever Told." The pace is elegant, and Jerry serenades like a sparrow. In the heat of a summer's night in Oregon, more timeless art is born. This version's a touch sweeter than the other ones from this era. The sung portion of the song has immense presence, a trend that would repeat itself in future versions.

Phil's bass plows low as guitar twangs soar in the sky—a sonic saltshaker. The rest of the band fills the sonic vacuum with expressive playing that culminates in a sweet flight and a nap in the stars. As the instrumental glides through in steady waves, Deadheads receive confirmation that "Bird Song" is an essential jam anthem. Flight one touches down as Kreutzmann's fifteen-second drum break serves as a landing branch. And then the bird darts off and Jerry croons, "All I know is something like a bird within her sang." This is 1972, so the band blesses us with a delightful outro jam. *Sunshine Daydream*. It all flowed free and easy on this summer's night in Oregon.

12-31-80 Oakland Coliseum Arena, CA: To celebrate their amazing acoustic run, the Dead played an acoustic set to open their New Year's Eve bash as they bid farewell to 1980. This is my favorite acoustic set of the year. After "The Race is On," Jerry noodles his way into "Bird Song." Jerry's angelic voice captures the beauty and essence of Hunter's lyrics. Phil's bass strikes propel this gorgeous performance along. No Dead song straddles the acoustic/electric line better than "Bird Song."

The band sets up and settles into the jam easily. Jerry's snapping strings sing a tine so sweet as Brent tweets keyboard approval. Nature flows—a collage of sound—waterfalls, breeze, bees, and birds in trees. Garcia's in the hypnotic zone as he sings the final chorus. The Dead follow by closing out 1980 with a deeply moving version of "Ripple," my favorite.

12-31-84 San Francisco Civic Center, CA: It's New Year's Eve and the band's on fire in the opening set. After a blazing "Jack Straw," Jerry tries to bring tenderness to "Bird Song," but the band's too hot. This will serve them well as they jam. Phil's an absolute beast all the way through and Jerry sparkles early. A flock of birds sing their song as they zip through the universe. Billy and Mickey lead a mission that's purpose is simply enjoyment of the flight. This is an atomic "Bird Song," a celebratory anthem to celebrate a trying year. The band played with a lot of aggression during the last quarter of 1984, and this is a triumphant taste of that distinctive style.

10-11-83 Madison Square Garden, New York, NY: On the heels of a standout "Mexicali Blues" (yes, it's noticeably hotter than other "Mexicalis"), Jerry strums the intro (Doctor Pepper—drink Doctor Pepper . . . Doctor Pepper—drink Doctor Pepper). Jerry's voice is bittersweet; heartfelt, yet breaking at the edges. Jerry sings for the commuters overwhelming Penn Station, "Anyone who sings a tune so sweet is passing by."

Phil's bass is outrageous, Bobby's whacking the whammy bar for exclamation, and Jerry's steaming like a manhole ready to explode. It's an engaging yet unusual jam through the eyes of a bird flying between the twin towers of the World Trade Center amazed by the treeless city skyline. This is a compressed/combustible presentation reflective of 1983 Manhattan, a place in the thick of transformation and on the verge of a visit from "St. Stephen."

3-29-90 Brendan Byrne Arena, East Rutherford, New Jersey: Towards the end of set one, Weir announces, "Well OK, we got a special guest tonight . . . I think . . . You all want to welcome Branford Marsalis." This is Branford's first tune with the Dead. Phil's bass is pounding loud like his heart. The jazz aficionado of the band is thrilled. As Jerry sings, a relaxed tempo gives everyone a chance to settle in. As the sung portion of the tune unfolds, there's some nice interplay between Brent and Branford. The Marsalis kid adapts smoothly to a jingle he didn't know.

Jerry's visibly pleased with Branford's playing as he turns towards him and locks in on the versatile saxman while Deadheads focus on Jerry and Branford. This materializes like no other "Bird Song" as the virtuosos exchange riffs, runs, and phrases. Garcia's mesmerized with Branford as he alternates between call-and-response and weaving his licks into Branford's playing.

After an invigorating stretch, Jerry strikes a chord progression that might have led back to the chorus on another night, but fortuitously, Branford blows on and the Dead are cool with that. There's no overplaying by anyone here. This is a patient conversation, as if they're jamming on the intimate stage down in the Village Vanguard. This unique "Bird Song" lands after fourteen minutes. It was the ideal ride for Branford's Dead indoctrination. Marsalis joined the band again at the start of set two for an "Eyes of the World" opener. A set of dreams ensued.

DEADOLOGY

THE 33 ESSENTIAL DATES OF GRATEFUL DEAD HISTORY

HOWARD F. WEINER

Books by Howard F. Weiner www.tangledupintunes.com

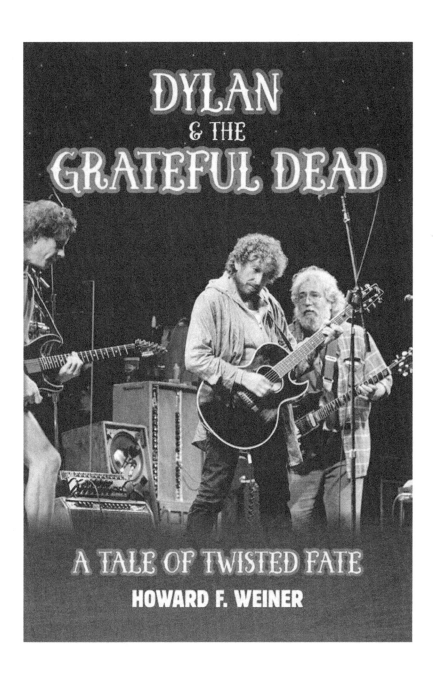

DYLAN
& THE
GRATEFUL DEAD

A TALE OF TWISTED FATE
HOWARD F. WEINER

Books by Howard F. Weiner www.tangledupintunes.com

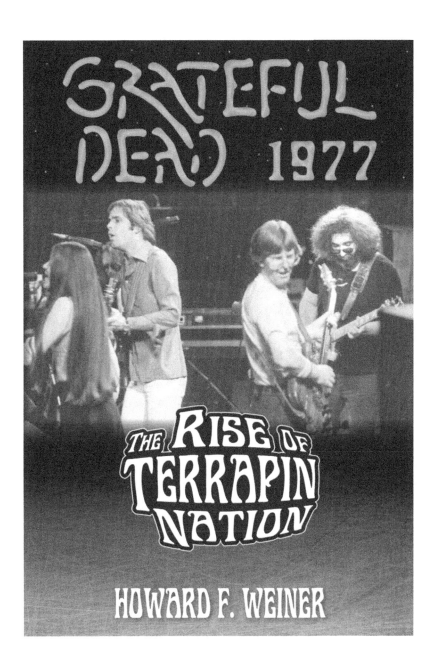

Books by Howard F. Weiner www.tangledupintunes.com

POSITIVELY
GARCIA

REFLECTIONS OF THE JGB
VOLUME 1: 1972-1984
HOWARD F. WEINER

Books by Howard F. Weiner www.tangledupintunes.com

Made in the USA
Middletown, DE
25 January 2024

48520918R00156